REBEL WITH A CAUSE

REBEL WITH A CAUSE

FRANKLIN GRAHAM

This Billy Graham Evangelistic Association
special edition is published with permission
from Thomas Nelson Publishers.

Thomas Nelson, Inc.
Nashville • Atlanta • London • Vancouver

Published in Nashville, Tennessee, by Thomas Nelson, Inc., and distributed in Canada by Word Communications, Ltd., Richmond, British Columbia, and in the United Kingdom by Word (UK), Ltd., Milton Keynes, England.

Unless otherwise noted, Scripture quotations are from the NEW KING JAMES VERSION of the Bible. Copyright © 1979, 1980, 1982, 1990, 1994, Thomas Nelson, Inc., Publishers.

Scripture quotations noted PHILLIPS are from J.B. PHILLIPS: THE NEW TESTAMENT IN MODERN ENGLISH, Revised Edition. Copyright © J.B. Phillips 1958, 1960, 1972. Used by permission of Macmillan Publishing Co., Inc.

Scripture quotations noted KJV are from The Holy Bible, KING JAMES VERSION.

Scripture quotations noted NIV are taken from the HOLY BIBLE, NEW INTERNATIONAL VERSION®. Copyright © 1973, 1978, 1984 by International Bible Society. Used by permission of Zondervan Bible Publishing House. All rights reserved.

The "NIV" and "New International Version" trademarks are registered in the United States Patent and Trademark Office by International Bible Society. Use of either trademark requires the permission of International Bible Society.

Library of Congress Cataloging-in-Publication Data

Graham, Franklin, 1952–
    Rebel with a cause / Franklin Graham.
      p.   cm.
    Includes bibliographical references.
    ISBN 0-913367-96-6
    1. Graham, Franklin, 1952–   2. Samaritan's Purse
(Organization)—Employees—Biography.   3. Church charities—
Biography   I. Title.

*This book is dedicated to my wife, Jane Austin,
who has lovingly stood by my side all of these
years, and to our four wonderful children
she brought into this world:
Cissie, Edward, Roy, and Will.
I love them all dearly.*

CONTENTS

A C K N O W L E D G M E N T S

I would like to express my sincere thanks to all those who helped in the various phases of this project:

To Rolf Zettersten, who helped get me started in the right direction.

To Cecil Murphey, who spent hours helping me outline and draft my life's story.

To Bruce Nygren, who edited the material and gave me valuable advice and when I got stuck, came up with the right concepts to get me going again.

How do I adequately thank my mother, who brought me into this world, raised me, and seemed to find time to keep a detailed diary while I was growing up? She also spent countless hours reading the manuscript and "correcting" me when needed.

To the scores of friends who double-checked facts and helped to jog my memory.

To my secretary of fifteen years, Donna Lee Toney, who worked graciously with all the above and much more—a special thanks.

INTRODUCTION

Anyone who would attempt to write his life story faces a task much more difficult than I ever would have imagined. The obvious question is of course "What do I put in?," because it's impossible to "tell it all." So, therefore, I have elected to let Mama and Daddy have the "last word." (See Afterword.)

I have attempted to tell the portions of my story that I believe illustrate most clearly how God has taken the raw material of my life and shaped it into something I pray is useful for His glory.

It's true that I was blessed to be born one of the children of Billy and Ruth Graham. Being their child has without question brought to me a unique set of opportunities and challenges. I consider my father a man whom God has used in a remarkable and unique way to advance the gospel. My relationship with him is special, and I welcome the opportunity to share some of my unique experiences and insights on my father—and my mother too.

But what is important about my story is important about every person's story: God has a plan for each of His children, and He will bring that plan to successful completion. That makes every person very special—whether or not you happened to be born into a famous family.

So, I will do my best in the pages that follow to tell not just my story but how God has been involved in every part of my journey, even when I wanted to keep Him as far away from me as possible.

The one thing I have chosen not to do in this book is tell the stories of other people, in particular the stories of my sisters and brother, as well as those of my own children. I think each person has the right to his or her privacy. My omission of incidents concerning these family members should not in any way imply that God hasn't used each one of them in important ways in my life. He has, and I love each one of them dearly.

Here I would like to briefly describe my sisters and brother (as I will my own children) so you will have at least a cursory understanding of how God put the Graham family together and how I fit into the mix.

The first child born to Ruth and Billy Graham was Virginia (we call her Gigi). She is seven years older than I. She married Stephen Tchividjian in 1963 and is a mom to seven children. Today she is a well-known writer and seminar speaker.

Next in the Graham clan was Anne, who came along five years before I did. She married Dr. Danny Lotz, a dentist and former college basketball player. Anne is a real theologian (like Mama) and has the gift of public speaking (like Daddy). She and Danny have three children.

Ruth (we call her Bunny) was the third child in our family. She is just two years older than I, and she and I have always been very close. Bunny is a capable writer and has worked as an editor for several publishers. She now works with me at Samaritan's Purse and is the mother of three children. Bunny and her husband, Richard McIntyre, live in Virginia.

I was the fourth child, then six years later came my kid brother Nelson (Ned) to complete the Graham family. Ned is president of East Gate Ministries, a missionary organization devoted to serving Christians in China. He and his wife, Carol, have two sons and have been very successful in placing Bibles in the hands of believers in that country.

When I was growing up, my sisters and brother were just there—the other people, in addition to Mama and Daddy, who were part of my life and hung out at our house. Since I was such an ornery kid, I thought they were there to be targets for my teasing and tormenting. Now I realize what great, gifted people they are, and I'm so glad they are not only sisters and brother, but friends.

My wife, Jane Austin, and I have been blessed with four children. Our oldest son is William Franklin Graham IV. He goes by Will. He was born on the birthday of his maternal grandfather and named after my father and me. We do that sort of thing in the South. Will is a college student and feels God is calling him to the ministry. He spent the summer of 1995 in Rwanda with Samaritan's Purse.

Our next son is Roy Austin Graham. He was named after my good friend, Roy Gustafson, and Jane Austin's mother's side of the family. Roy loves to work—much like my father and me and Jane Austin's daddy, Mr. Cunningham. I see a lot of myself in him. Roy is in high school.

Our third son is Edward Bell Graham. He's named after Jane Austin's father, Edward (Ned) P. Cunningham, and my mother's father, Nelson Bell. He is in high school and enjoys hunting and riding motorcycles. He's already six feet tall, and it looks like he'll be the tallest in the family.

Our fourth child is our only daughter, Jane Austin Graham. She's obviously named after her mother and grandmother—another southern tradition! The boys immediately nicknamed her Cissie. She's in grade school and enjoys soccer and horseback riding. She's a big tease, which frustrates her older brothers from time to time.

We live on a forty-acre farm with a variety of barnyard critters, including our pet pig, Alice "Petunia" Graham, so there has always been plenty to do and lots of room for recreation. That's what I wanted for my kids—lots of space and things to do at home. Our children have grown up much like Jane Austin and I did.

Our barn is filled with motorcycles, a tractor, and a fishing boat; I think the love of things that make noise and blow smoke will be inherited.

My schedule prevents our having extended family time together. Jane Austin is my strength on the home front. Much like my mother, she has had to keep the home fires stoked while I've been away. It would be impossible for me to express how important her patient efforts behind the scenes have been to my ministry.

We both dread the day when our children are on their own. We love having them at home and want them to be every bit a part of our lives.

One of the events we always anticipate as a family comes at Christmas. We go to Jane's parents' home in Smithfield, North Carolina. I am fortunate to have the greatest in-laws possible. Ned and Jane Cunningham are the best. I love them and treasure their support.

For years, Mr. Cunningham has taken his son, Phil, and sons-in-law, Steve Wilson and me, with our boys to the "Hunt Club" during the holidays. This is a remote area on the Roanoke River in eastern North Carolina. It's a wonderful time for all the guys to be together and do some things we all love—hunting and fellowshipping. These are treasured memories for my boys, who dearly love their grandparents.

I enjoy my life, even though there have been many moments of struggle and pain. I share my life, not because I think there is anything particularly special about it, but because I want you to understand how great and capable God is of using anyone's life to accomplish His goals. If there's anything special about my story, it's not because I'm the son of Billy and Ruth Graham—it's because I'm a son of the living God.

REBEL WITH A CAUSE

Big Footprints to Fill

If I had understood the messages people were sending me on the day I was born, I might just have crawled right back in where I'd come from and taken a rain check!

You think I'm kidding? Yeah, I am. But how would you have liked to kick off your arrival on this planet with sentiments like these:

"Welcome to this sin-sick world and the challenge you have to walk in your daddy's footsteps," read one Western Union telegram.

A card read, "May his great father's mantle fall on him."

"Dear Little Billy Frank, Jr.," a note read. "We heard . . . that your Daddy has new help for preaching God's truth. Praise the Lord! So grow up fast."

"Good luck and best wishes to the young preacher," said another.

"Countless thousands of us are rejoicing and thanking God for your birth," wrote one woman.

One Catholic admirer had a detailed scenario for my life: "I'll bet that your new boy will be a Catholic some day, maybe priest, bishop, or cardinal, possibly pope. He would then be infallible in matters of faith and morals."

I had no idea what I was getting into! People all over the world admired Billy Graham as a spiritual leader. I suppose it only seemed natural to them that his firstborn son would eventually plant his tiny feet in those large footprints.

Not one of those telegrams or cards ventured that I might grow up to enjoy career success as a cowboy, jet pilot, doctor, or motorcycle mechanic. No, I was destined to be a preacher—with a capital P!

All of those who applauded my birth meant well—not a one of them, I'm sure, would have knowingly put pressure on me to live up to unusual or unreachable expectations. But I wasn't too old before I sensed that being Billy Graham's son would be both a blessing and a burden.

I was born in the South, where it's a tradition to pass the family name to the oldest son.

Confusion often follows after several generations.

My daddy's father was named William Franklin Graham. He was called Frank.

My father was born on November 7, 1918, and named William Franklin Graham II. He was called Billy Frank by his family and close friends in his hometown of Charlotte, North Carolina.

When I arrived on the scene July 14, 1952, my parents appropriately named me William Franklin Graham III. To cut down on further confusion, Mama and Daddy decided to call me Franklin.

My parents lived in Montreat, North Carolina, a small community about fifteen miles east of Asheville. In my opinion, it's one of the most beautiful spots on earth—in the heart of the Blue Ridge Mountains. For as long as I can remember, these mountains and wooded hills of western Carolina have been the only place I ever wanted to call home.

As a young boy, I had no idea that my father was well-known. As with any kid, he was just "Daddy" to me. I'm told that by the time I was three, tourists were finding their way to Montreat and beginning to poke around our house, which sat on the main road. Every now and then, caravans of cars would pull up and stop in front of our house. People would climb out to gawk and snap pictures. Those who were brave would walk to the front door and try to peek in through the windows.

My older sisters, who apparently were quite the entrepreneurs, saw a business opportunity. They set up a lemonade stand and sold "Billy Graham's favorite lemonade" to the tourists for five cents a glass.

Since Daddy was often gone to crusades for many weeks at a time and Mama was alone with us kids, she had to deal with these intrusions into our private life by herself. She became increasingly frustrated and, like a mother hen, wanted to protect us children.

"That's enough," she said one day after another visit by tourists. "We need some privacy."

It wasn't too long before my folks bought 150 acres of heavily wooded mountain land outside of Montreat. The rear of the property bordered thousands of acres that were part of the Asheville reservoir's watershed, known as the North Fork, so it was an ideal location for a family needing some seclusion and space. Mama named it "Little Piney Cove." I call it "home."

When my folks acquired the property, there were some abandoned buildings on the land but no house. So Mother began planning her dream home. Mama is a free, independent spirit who is not afraid to cut her own path. Also, as a result of growing up in a missionary family in China, she is extremely practical and always eager to make do with what's available. So she decided to build a roomy, old-fashioned log home to house our large family.

Although log homes are popular again in certain areas of the country, in the 1950s most people who had a choice didn't live in a log cabin! But this is what Mama wanted, so she searched the Blue Ridge Mountains for old logs and ended up buying three abandoned cabins—at a very good price, I'm sure. These cabins (some were over two hundred years old) were dismantled and the logs brought to Little Piney Cove.

There, with her plans in hand and a team of mountain craftsmen, she built our home. Mama always found projects like this to work on while Daddy was away preaching. I'm sure this helped pass the time and eased the loneliness she felt.

When construction of our log home got underway, Mama drove up the rocky mountain road just about every day to supervise. I loved tagging along to watch. From as far back as I can remember, I have loved the outdoors, so the excitement of a construction site in a rugged setting like Little Piney Cove was about as good as it got for a boy like me.

I've been told that I was "quite a handful" when I was a kid. Most boys love to explore, learn how things work, and experiment—I certainly was no different. I was just being me. (When Mama was reviewing the manuscript for this book, she said I was just a normal boy, in her words "as good as I could be, and as bad as I could get by with.")

While Mama talked to the foreman and workers, I found creative ways to entertain myself. I stayed right on the heels of the carpenters, watching their every move. The thing they did that intrigued me most was smoking. I was fascinated by it. I caught on that if I ran quick enough when they pitched a cigarette, the butt would still be lit. I would grab one and puff away, thinking no one would notice.

Out of nowhere, of course, would come Mama. She'd grab the cigarette out of my mouth and fling it away. "No, Franklin!" She would lecture me on all the evils of smoking, but that didn't stop me. I just got more clever at not getting caught. The workmen thought it was funny and would purposely throw a half-smoked cigarette in my direction, hoping I would pick it up. Then they would watch to see if Mama would catch me.

I remember one day after lunch a carpenter lit up, took a big drag, and blew the smoke down a piece of pipe. I was on the other end and sucked it all in. About that time Mama came into the room. When she saw what was going on, she was madder than a hornet. She jerked that pipe out of his hand—I thought she was going to whip him with it. Needless to say, he never did that again.

This was the beginning of what later became a bad habit for me.

The entire family was relieved when we finally moved into our new yet old-looking log home. Although it was very comfortable and modern, because of the old logs and the antique furniture Mama had found, the home looked like it might have been built a hundred years earlier.

I especially loved playing outside in all the open space at Little Piney Cove, often pretending I was Matt Dillon from *Gunsmoke* or one of the Cartwright brothers from *Bonanza*. I had a complete set of cowboy gear—boots, jeans, shirt, hat, and most importantly, a holster and pistol. I would dress up in my cowboy duds and play in the woods for hours.

I was fascinated with toy guns—I guess because in my mind it was the closest I had to the real thing at age four. Mama recalls that shortly after we moved up to the log house, I persuaded her to let me camp out on the front porch. When she checked up on me the next morning, there I was on a camp cot, fully dressed in my jeans, denim jacket, and boots—with my toy gun propped against the side of the cot. As Mama tells the story:

> *"How did you sleep last night?" I asked him.*
> *"Fine," Franklin said.*
> *"And you weren't afraid of the skunk?" (One had visited us the night before.)*
> *"No, ma'am," he replied, "I had my gun with me."*
> *"But Franklin, it's just a toy gun."*
> *He looked at me with a twinkle in his eye and said, "Polecat didn't know it!"*

During my cowboy phase, Daddy was invited to appear on the TV show *This Is Your Life,* which was broadcast from California. After watching so many westerns on TV, I was afraid that Daddy would be harmed on his trip out West. I just assumed that anyone who traveled out there was likely to be shot in a stage holdup or scalped during an Indian raid.

"God will take care of him," Mama said to me, trying to calm my fears.

"Yeah?" I asked. "What if He don't?"

"I'm sure God will," she said.

I thought about that for a few seconds, then said, "Well, I don't know about that, but I guess Roy Rogers can take care of him."

But my days were not completely filled with fantasy—I got a dose of reality from time to time. Mama definitely believed in "spare the rod, spoil the child."

When I was about five or six I went through a spitting stage. Mama can't recall where I picked this habit up, but I do. I'd seen those heroes of mine doing it—the carpenters building our house. When they weren't smoking, they pinched tobacco and spit the juice in all directions. Let's face it—could there be a more disgusting and fun thing for a boy to copy than that? As my kids would say now, this was cool.

I never did understand then why spitting was such a crime. The carpenters didn't get scolded by Mama. But I got punished for doing it several times.

One day I decided to do some target practice spitting on my buddies, Johnny and Tommy Frist. They were older than I, but that didn't stop me. I spit on both of them. I thought this was pretty cute.

"Stop it, Franklin," Johnny said.

I spit some more.

"You spit one more time," Johnny said, "and you'll be sorry."

This was really getting to be fun. I spit again.

Johnny swept me off my feet and carried me to the large wood bin that had been built in the stone wall by the kitchen fireplace; I was kicking and struggling all the way. He stuffed me into the bin and latched the door from the outside.

I guess he thought that would teach me a lesson. But I didn't mind. It was fun in there, like having my own little cabin. I found a couple of spiders to play with and laughed as Johnny and Tommy stood outside, teasing.

"Ready to behave?" one of them asked.

"No way!"

After a while, I got bored and was feeling a little cramped. "You let me out of here!" I yelled.

Neither of them answered.

"Listen, Johnny, I'm going to count to ten, and you had better let me out."

No answer.

"One. Two. Three." I stopped counting.

After a lengthy silence, I finally heard Johnny's voice: "Franklin, what's wrong?"

"I don't know what comes after three!" I yelled.

Johnny started to laugh. I knew I had him. He opened the wood bin and set me free.

As you might expect, an active, rambunctious kid like me didn't have too much interest in church or "spiritual things." I was having a ball exploring the mountains around Little Piney Cove—that's what basically occupied my mind and time. Of course, being a member of Billy Graham's family meant you had to go to church. I knew it was something I had to live with.

Though my folks insisted we go to church every Sunday, as far back as I can remember, my parents never crammed religion down my throat. They did try to instill in all of us kids the importance of a personal relationship with God. Every evening our family had devotions before we went to bed. Mama or Daddy would read a short passage from the Bible and then we would each say a sentence prayer. In the morning, after breakfast, Mama or Daddy would lead us in prayer before we left the house for school. It didn't matter who was in the house at the time—our housekeeper, caretaker, or guests—it was just something everyone did in our home. I can't remember a day when this didn't happen.

My parents also encouraged us to memorize Scripture verses. One of the ways they did this was on Sunday after church and lunch, before we could go out and play, we had to memorize a verse and recite it to Mama, almost word perfect. She did make a few exceptions. When we complained that the verses were too difficult, she let us pick our own. She didn't care as long as it was the Word of God. This got us reading the Bible to find short verses—such as "Jesus wept." It didn't bother Mama. Mama and Daddy believed that the time would come when their children would need the strength of God that comes through His Word. They knew that one day we would be out on our own; yet God would always be with us. And they were right.

I didn't mind the devotions, especially at night, because Mama often told stories from the Bible and mixed them with her own experiences from growing up in China. But if she got long-winded, I fidgeted—I just couldn't sit still.

One night I got really bored and found a clever way to entertain myself. While Mama was still praying, I began mimicking a dog bark.

"Arp, arp," I said, then peeked through the corner of my eye at Mama.

She stopped praying and looked around the room. When she didn't see anything, she bowed her head again. I could barely contain a giggle. I sounded off again, "Arp, arp."

I interrupted her several times. Near the end of her prayer I detected a different tone in her voice. It sounded like she might be getting angry, so as soon as Mama said "Amen," I jumped over to the other side of the bed and looked under it.

"Mama, I heard something go 'Arp, arp' when you were praying. Did you hear it?"

Mama began to laugh.

I somehow escaped a spanking that time. I was lucky that Mama had a good sense of humor—sometimes it got me off the hook.

Mama was always fair. She was strict at times, but even then, she was a lot of fun.

My favorite dessert as a kid was watermelon, and in the summertime Mama often gave us a big, juicy piece after supper. One night at bedtime, I begged, "Can I have another piece?"

"No, Franklin," she said. "It's not a good idea at bedtime—"

"But I haven't had a piece since supper."

"Yes, you have. Only a few minutes ago I cleaned up some seeds, juice, and a rind on the front steps."

"That wasn't me."

"Franklin! You know it was."

"It had to be somebody else. Bunny? Maybe Anne."

"Bunny and Anne weren't around. Besides, you and Bea [our housekeeper] were sitting on the front steps together."

"It was somebody else, Mama."

"Okay. Who?"

"I forget."

"Then remember."

"I can't."

"You know what I've told you about lying, Franklin. If you dare to tell a lie—"

"I'm not lying, Mama. I, well, I forget."

"Think hard."

"I can't."

"Let's get down on our knees. You ask the Lord to help you remember."

"You ask Him. He listens to you."

"You ask Him, Franklin."

"No, you ask."

"You're the one who forgot!" Mama said, as she helped me to my knees.

"You pray first, Mama. Then I'll ask."

Mama started to pray, but it didn't sound as much like a prayer as it did a sermon about how the devil can get into your heart and take away your victory. Finally, she stopped. "Now you pray, Franklin."

"Dear Jesus," I began, "help a little boy remember . . ." I probably said more, but that's all I recall.

When I looked up, Mama stared at me. "Well?"

"He's not helping me very much."

"Oh yes, He is. He's already told you. You see, Franklin, He knows who ate the watermelon."

"Mama, God doesn't really know. He's just guessing."

"God never guesses. He knows everything. He sees everything."

"I'm beginning to remember now."

"What do you remember?"

"I was the one, Mama."

She put her arms around me. "If you had persisted in your lying, I would have had to take the belt to you," she said.

"I know, Mama, and I'm sorry."

Instead of spanking me, Mama brought me a small piece of watermelon, and it tasted a whole lot better than the piece I had sneaked out to the porch earlier that evening.

Of course Mama and Daddy insisted that I behave, but I had a very strong will. I suppose I wasn't a horrible child, but I definitely had a rebellious streak. When I wanted to do something, I did it—even if I knew I would be disobeying my parents and risking punishment. And I found real delight in avoiding getting caught or flaunting my rebellious ways. This would all catch up with me later.

My habit of finding cigarette butts and smoking them got so bad that when Floyd Roberts, our caretaker, came up to the house one evening to see how everything was, Mama asked to borrow the pack of cigarettes he was carrying in his pocket.

"I'm going to teach Franklin a lesson," she told Floyd.

She brought me into the kitchen and sat me down in front of the fireplace. *What is she up to?* I wondered.

She opened the pack, pulled out a cigarette, and handed it to me. "Now light it and smoke it—and be sure to inhale!" Mama wanted me to get sick, thinking that if I threw up I would never want to touch a cigarette again.

I couldn't believe Mama was actually giving me permission to smoke! I remembered Daddy telling me how his daddy whipped the taste right out of his mouth when he was a boy after Grand-daddy caught him smoking—and it had worked! So I was surprised that Mama was actually letting me smoke with her blessing. This was great.

"Sure," I said, and lit the first cigarette and inhaled deeply.

Mama watched as I puffed, her face expressionless. "Keep smoking," she said.

I did. When I finished the second one, my face turned as green as a cow's cud. I ran into the bathroom and threw up. I washed my face and headed back to the kitchen for more. I picked up the third cigarette, and with a cocky grin, struck the match and went at it again. Within minutes, I raced back to the bathroom to puke again. I wasn't easily deterred.

By the time I had finished all twenty, I must have vomited five or six times. I felt horrible. Every time I got sick, I'm sure Mama thought her approach was working, but it gave me great satisfaction not to give in. That wasn't the result Mama wanted.

I wasn't sure my stomach would ever stop churning. But if there had been another pack of cigarettes, I probably would have smoked them too!

Mama didn't give up trying to make me quit smoking, but she never used that tactic again.

In those days, we didn't know the health dangers involved with smoking. As a kid, I probably wouldn't have cared anyway. I can still see those carpenters with cigarettes dangling from their lips, the smoke rising in tiny clouds above them. To me it was cool.

Most of these guys were World War II veterans; they were my heroes. You couldn't help but look up to and admire them.

Like many boys living in a family populated with older girls, I chose to establish my place in the family by pestering my sisters to death. As I grew older, a good day for me was to have all three of them either crying or screaming at once, and me still laughing. But, of course, that got me in trouble.

A treat for us was to go into the "big town" of Asheville to eat. Mama occasionally took all four of us to a drive-in, one of those fad restaurants of the sixties where cars pulled up, parked, and the order was called in through a speaker.

Apparently on one of our rides to the drive-in, I wouldn't stop aggravating my sisters, no matter what Mama said. I was in the backseat, out of the range of her quick backhand. Sometimes she used a woman's shoe tree—a piece of spring metal with a wooden toe on one end and a wooden heel on the other—to extend her reach. When I got popped with that shoe tree, it got my attention real quick. But this time, even though she kept warning me to behave, I had no intention of leaving the girls alone.

"If you don't stop right now," Mama said, "I'm going to pull over and lock you up in the trunk." I could tell her patience was about gone.

But I was one of those hardheaded kids who didn't respond to such simple threats. The thrill of seeing the girls squeal and fight me off was too irresistible. Besides, where in the world would Mama pull over on a busy road? I started pinching them again.

"That's enough!" Mama pulled off to the side of the road and stopped the car. Before I knew what was happening, she opened the back door, grabbed me with both hands, jerked me around back, opened the trunk, put me inside, and slammed the lid shut.

"Can you breathe in there?" she asked.

"Yes, ma'am," I said. It was hard to keep from laughing. This wasn't punishment. It was a new adventure.

"Good," she said, and she got back in the car and drove onto the highway.

I wasn't expecting Mama to drive all the way to Asheville before letting me out, but she drove on and on. I really didn't mind because I occupied myself with the spare tire and the car jack. When we arrived at the drive-in, Mama came around to the back of the car and opened the trunk to get my order. "What do you want to eat?"

"Cheeseburger without the meat, french fries, and a Coke."

She slammed the trunk again and climbed back in the car and placed the order. It didn't take long before the waitress was back with our food. As she hooked the tray to the car window, the waitress was shocked when she saw Mama open the trunk and hand me my food.

I took it, expecting her to let me out. Not Mama. She was determined that I would learn my lesson. She let me eat right there in my own private dining car.

That was Mama. She always took the unorthodox approach to solving problems. And with me she gained plenty of experience.

Guns, Dogs, and Rock 'n' Roll

Growing up I was like any kid—I loved being with my daddy. I remember running into his arms and seeing his smile, then soaring in his grip high above his head. But Daddy was often gone on long trips. I missed him, but even as a child I knew he was away doing something very important.

Back in the fifties and even the early sixties, if you traveled to Britain or Europe or Asia, you usually went by ship. And the Billy Graham meetings often lasted for weeks and, in some cases, for months.

The crusades my father has held in recent years are often just a week or less—then he flies home. But years ago, when Daddy said "good-bye," from a child's perspective it often seemed that he vanished from the face of the earth. But I got used to it; I didn't know anything else.

When Daddy was home, he did as much with me as he could. He had grown up on a farm, so he shared my love for the outdoors. I'm like him—we're both country boys at heart, and Daddy was instrumental in developing my interest in guns. He gave me my first rifle when I was about ten—a .22 caliber rifle his daddy had given him as a boy. This was my first real gun, although I had owned a BB gun since I was six or seven.

Like most country boys, Daddy enjoyed walking through the

woods with his guns. He wasn't an avid hunter, but he and I liked to hike and find targets to shoot at.

During one fall we hiked to an area our family called The Bears' Den. When Little Piney Cove was first settled around the turn of the century, a man named Solomon Morris had discovered a family of black bears living under the rocks. After a while, the bears moved on, but their den remained.

Right below the old den was a large black walnut tree. Daddy and I started shooting walnuts out of the top. Then, from about two hundred yards above us at the crest of the ridge, we heard several rifle shots. The bullets slammed to the ground close to us. Daddy and I hunkered down, fearing that someone was using us as targets.

Daddy gave the benefit of the doubt to whoever was pulling the trigger—that they were not trying to ambush us. He yelled up through the holler to let them know we were on the mountain too.

Two more shots rang out, and the bullets ricocheted off the rocks approximately fifty yards away. Daddy stooped behind a tree, picked up his rifle, and shot three or four rounds into the trees above their heads. They stopped firing in our direction. We never knew who they were, but Daddy had gotten their attention. Considering my thirst for adventure, incidents like this always made it great to have Daddy home!

When Daddy was around, you could usually count on something peculiar happening. Quite often strange people would show up at our house. Some claimed to be prophets with a special word from the Lord that they wanted to be sure Billy Graham was aware of.

Daddy hadn't been home long from one trip before a real crazy showed up. Daddy answered the door, and I watched through the side window. I couldn't hear what was being said, but the man must have made some kind of threat because Daddy hauled off and slugged him. The guy fell to his knees as Daddy stood over him, his fists cocked like a hammer on a gun ready to let him have it again if need be.

When the man began to cry, Daddy knelt down beside him and talked for a while. Then Daddy prayed with him, helped him to his feet, and sent him on his way. He never bothered us again.

The incident didn't surprise me. I knew Daddy was strong and wasn't to be pushed around. He had come off the farm and was tough as an old ax handle. I knew that when anyone threatened his family and got him up against the wall, he wouldn't back down.

Although our family tried not to be paranoid about strangers, my father's notoriety made him a target of certain radical groups. Over the years he received a number of death threats, and in the sixties the FBI became so concerned for his safety that they suggested a security fence with electronic gates be built around the acres near our house. Mama and Daddy finally decided to do it, and that pretty well took care of the unwanted intruders.

Our family's attitude toward security was this: When Daddy or any member of the family was in a public place, we would not carry weapons and would depend on others like the police to protect us. But inside our own home, we would not allow anyone to threaten our well-being. For years I kept a loaded rifle on the wall above my bed—just in case. After all, when Daddy was gone, I was the man of the house. And Daddy kept a weapon handy, too, when he was home.

It was inevitable, and necessary, that with Daddy gone so much I would seek other men to be father models for me.

Of course I imitated the carpenters and other workers who came to Little Piney Cove. But a greater influence on me was my friend, Gizmo. His name was really John Rickman. I'd given him the nickname because of a cartoon character I'd seen on TV. I hung around John and looked up to him.

John became our caretaker after Floyd Roberts left and did odd jobs like cutting the grass, chopping firewood, and painting. He also provided security, which I thought was great because he carried a .38 special revolver and always had his shotgun handy.

He was extremely loyal to our family and would have died for us. We all loved him dearly.

John never seemed to mind my following him around the place. I learned from him many things fathers teach their sons, like how to work with my hands. He showed me how to use a shovel, an ax, a chainsaw to cut wood for fence posts, and how to string a barbed wire fence.

Gizmo was always patient with me. If I didn't catch on fast enough, he'd patiently take the tool from me and say, "Here, let me show you how it's done." I'd try again. "Yeah, you got the hang of it now," he'd say. That was high praise from John.

One bad habit of mine that upset John, however, was not returning his tools. He never minded my borrowing them, and sometimes I would use them to work on my bike or whatever. Like most kids, when I finished, I dropped the tools right where I had used them.

"If you take my tools," he said one day in that stern voice he adopted when necessary, "you put um back." He held up the forgotten wrench and screwdriver to remind me. "Got that? Right where they were when you took um."

"Yes, sir," I said. Somehow it never occurred to me to argue with or disobey John.

John hardly ever offered me advice. Maybe that was one of the reasons I liked him so much. He was fatherly, but more than that, he was a friend I could always count on. I could talk to John about anything that bothered me, and he listened and understood. I trusted him, and I never worried that he would tell my parents on me.

Mama didn't seem to mind the time I spent with John. I loved to hear him tell his World War II stories, about how he had served on a Navy landing ship known as an LST.

As he smoked one Lucky Strike after another, I remember him showing me the big letters printed on the bottom of the pack—LSMFT.

"You know what that means, Franklin?" he asked.

"No, sir."

"Landing Ships Make Fine Targets," he said and laughed as he pointed to each letter. It wasn't until years later that I learned that those letters actually stood for Lucky Strikes Mean Fine Tobacco.

Because John was around when I needed someone, it was not as hard having Daddy gone so much. If I hadn't had people like John Rickman in my life, Daddy's absences probably would have bothered me a lot more.

Gizmo retired from working for us at Little Piney Cove in the early seventies, while I was in college. He died from lung cancer in 1975.

Not long ago, while reminiscing with my mother, she showed me a book filled with memories of us kids she's kept all these years. She had written when I was six years old that while sitting with her under an apple tree on a Sunday afternoon I had asked, "Mama, when is the world going to end?"

"I don't know. I hope tonight," she said, "then we can all go to be with Jesus."

"I hope not that soon," I said.

"Why?"

"'Cause I'd like to spend one more day with Mr. Rickman."

That says it all.

Mama was always a great example to us children in every way. One was by having a good attitude about Daddy's long trips. She longed for her husband when he was away, and she knew that we missed him too. But she was determined to make the best of it.

When it came time for Daddy to leave again, it was Mama's lightheartedness that held us together as a family. She didn't complain. "He'll be back in a month," she would say matter-of-factly.

If the washing machine broke down or there were other problems while he was away—and often there were—Mama handled them herself. And that would be the end of it.

But perhaps the most wonderful gift she gave us related to Daddy's trips was that she never threatened us with "Wait till your father comes home. I'll let him handle this." She was wise and knew that if she resorted to that tactic, we would always live in dread of his return.

It may sound trite, but it's true: Without my mother's faithful, dependable, strong presence on the home front, my father's world-wide preaching of the gospel of Jesus Christ to millions might never have been possible.

When Daddy was home he tried to find ways to make up for his absence. He wasn't much of a camper, but he knew how I loved the woods. So the first time Daddy mentioned that the two of us should go camping, I couldn't wait to get my gear packed.

We climbed the ridge behind the house that overlooked Black Mountain and discovered a good campsite. We built a big campfire and settled in for the night. As we roasted marshmallows above the hot coals, Daddy told me stories about Granddaddy Graham and about his own boyhood days on the farm. I hung on every word. Daddy could be a very dramatic storyteller, especially as it got dark, and he would begin to make up ghost stories. He could make the hair stand up on the back of your neck.

When the sun went down, we laid our bedrolls close to the glowing coals of the fire. Daddy threw his down on unleveled ground, and I wondered why he didn't pick a smoother spot. I crawled into my bedroll and before I knew it, the morning sun was shining in my eyes.

When I sat up and looked for Daddy, he was gone! I jumped up and looked around, my heart pounding. Where was he? Then I saw his sleeping bag about twenty-five yards away next to a fallen log. I ran to the bag and bent over. He was in it. To my amazement, he was still fast asleep—completely unaware that he had been on quite a journey during the night. If it hadn't been for that log, he may have rolled all the way to the bottom of the mountain.

It was always an adventure to camp with Daddy. Another time he took me up to Clingman's Peak near Mount Mitchell, the highest mountain in the Blue Ridge (six thousand-plus feet). We weren't quite prepared for the bitter chill and shivered in our sleeping bags all night.

I think Daddy was glad when day broke. He got up and decided he was going to fix a true country breakfast. I rounded up the wood, and Daddy got a roaring fire started. Soon the skillet was red hot. He cracked a couple of eggs into the dry pan—no grease or butter. Needless to say, breakfast was "cooked" in an instant; the eggs burned to a crisp and stuck to the bottom of the skillet. Daddy grabbed a spatula and tried to scramble them, but the eggs were already scorched.

I sat there quietly as he scraped them out of the blackened pan and onto my plate. "Here, give that a try."

I gave it my best shot, reluctantly taking a little bite. The charred eggs tasted terrible and burned my mouth. I spit them out. "Them ain't eggs," I said.

Daddy, not totally convinced, tasted them cautiously, but with the first swallow he gagged too.

Neither of us said much as we quickly packed up our stuff. We loaded the car and headed for lower ground. I smiled when Daddy pulled into the parking lot of a little restaurant at the foot of the mountain. We ended up having our "country breakfast" all right, but not by the campfire!

During my childhood, next to Daddy and John Rickman, one of the most influential men in my life was Calvin Thielman. He became the pastor of the Montreat Presbyterian Church when I was just a boy. Mama's parents, the L. Nelson Bells, former missionaries to China, were members of that church.

On many occasions, Calvin would take me hiking. One time we decided to go to Lookout Mountain, just outside of Montreat. Lookout had two approaches: One was an easy trail that followed the ridge; the other was a granite cliff known as "Suicide." I asked Calvin if we could climb Suicide.

Calvin was scared to death! I guess I was too young to realize the danger we were in, hanging off the side of the rock. All I remember saying was, "Hey, Calvin, isn't this fun?"

Calvin was also the ultimate Texan. He had that strong Texas drawl and just looked the part. Best of all (to me), he could really shoot a pistol. Many times he impressed me by flinging a coin into the air, pulling his .22 caliber revolver, and blasting the coin while it was still somersaulting through the air.

Although Daddy had given me my first rifle, it was Calvin who really ignited my interest in guns.

When I was about eight or so, Grady Wilson, one of Daddy's close friends and the first one to join his evangelistic team, gave Daddy a .22 caliber Ruger Blackhawk pistol. I wasn't the only one who wanted to wrap his finger around that trigger. Calvin wanted to try it out so bad he could taste it.

One afternoon Calvin called and invited me to go target shooting with him. "Franklin," he said, "bring your daddy's new gun, and we'll try it out."

As we often did, Calvin and I hiked up the backside of Little Piney Cove and soon found ourselves down in a deep hollow.

"How about that?" Calvin said as he pointed to an ugly old knot on a big oak tree. "Looks like a great target, huh?"

"Sure," I said with a grin. "I guess it's big enough for you to hit."

Calvin didn't seem to take offense. He knew he was a good shot. I knew it too.

"Now, Franklin, I'm gonna draw my gun, aim, fire, and try to hit that knot." I guess he figured he needed to practice his Texas quick-draw technique.

He hesitated a moment and then said, "Hey, let me try out your daddy's new pistol," as he pointed to the .22.

I handed him the gun and stood back. "Go ahead, Calvin!"

He drew, fired, and to my surprise, missed the knot. Calvin frowned and examined the pistol. Everything seemed in order.

Calvin returned the pistol to his holster. He wasn't about to let that .22 get the best of him. He nodded at me.

When I said go, he drew, fired, and missed the second time. With obvious disgust, he repositioned himself and waited for me to call out again.

"Go!" I hollered.

He yanked the gun from his holster. But before he'd raised the barrel to the target, he prematurely pulled the trigger, sending the bullet ripping into the back of his leg instead of into the side of the tree. I was watching the knot and heard the shot but didn't see the bullet hit the tree. I couldn't believe it! He'd missed again.

I turned and looked at Calvin for an explanation. He staggered back a few steps, his hand at his side—then slumped backward, the pistol still in his right hand.

I forgot that we were supposed to be having fun. I rushed over to him. "Calvin, you okay?"

Calvin, a little puzzled, said calmly, "I just shot myself!"

I was too shocked to speak. I wasn't sure what to do. Was he going to die? Should I run for help?

Calvin stared at his leg. He pulled his pant leg up but there was no blood. Then we both saw it, a lead mark on his skin. I began to shake. The bullet had apparently lodged in his leg, and the skin had closed up the wound.

By now it was late afternoon, and the sun was setting. "Let's get out of here," Calvin said. "I think I can still walk."

I didn't say much as we started back. I was too scared. Calvin's leg began to bleed. He insisted we keep on going, and we walked the two miles home.

Just before we reached Little Piney Cove, Calvin lectured me, "Now, Franklin, don't tell your mama what happened. Don't you dare say a word."

"I won't," I promised, as Calvin got in his car and headed for home.

Supper was on the table when I walked into the kitchen. Mama called out, "You all have fun today?"

I said nothing. I remembered Calvin's warning.

Mama came around the corner. "You okay, Franklin?" she asked. I didn't respond. "Did you and Calvin have an argument or something?"

"No, ma'am."

Mama just stared.

I didn't say a word during supper. Mama tried to get me to talk. "Are you feeling all right?"

"Yes, Mama."

She studied my face. It was hard, but I was determined not to break my promise. Calvin's secret was secure with me.

The evening dragged. When bedtime came, Mama sat down with us kids to read, as she did most every night.

Just after she opened the book, the phone rang. Mama answered, "Hello, Calvin." Then she listened.

"No, he hasn't," I heard her say in a puzzled tone. "As a matter of fact, he's been unusually quiet tonight."

"What happened, Calvin?" Mama asked.

I sat frozen as she listened. She started to laugh, and every muscle in my body relaxed. I knew that Calvin had told her the truth. Calvin would be okay.

What became so funny about the incident was that Calvin prided himself on his gun safety. Mama thought it was hilarious that he had shot himself while showing me how to handle a gun. Calvin didn't think it was too funny—at least at the time. That next Sunday morning, as he limped to the pulpit, the congregation burst out laughing.

For me it was a valuable lesson. I learned early that it only takes a split second to make a careless mistake, one that could affect the rest of your life.

I didn't look up to Calvin only for what he taught me about guns out in the woods. I also learned from him as he preached from the pulpit. When he stood in his black robe behind the pulpit on Sunday mornings, he filled his sermons with stories—many of them about his days growing up in East Texas. He always found effective ways of communicating that right is right, and wrong is wrong, regardless of the consequences. I really liked that.

He was a consistent example of a true follower of Christ. A few years down the road, when I began to drink and smoke, Calvin knew what I was doing but never lectured me. Once in a while, when Mama put him up to it, he would take me aside and talk to me, but only as a friend, not as a pastor. Maybe that sounds a little odd, but even as a kid, Calvin treated me more like a buddy, which meant he could say things to me that others couldn't.

Unfortunately, he wasn't quite powerful enough to make me change. God would have to take care of that later.

In the summer of 1960, when I turned eight years old, Daddy took our family on an extended trip to Europe. We had been invited by Ara Tchividjian, a wealthy Swiss Armenian, who had become a Christian after reading Daddy's first book, *Peace with God*.

I wasn't overjoyed at the thought of missing the whole summer in Montreat, where I always found fun things to do. When we left I wondered if the summer would ever come to an end so I could be back home. Mama kept saying, "It's just three months." But to me that seemed like nearly a lifetime.

We went by ship from New York to Le Havre, France. On our way across the ocean Mama assured me that the mountains in Switzerland were bigger than ours in North Carolina. She was right—as usual. The mountains were bigger, but when Daddy started talking about moving to Europe, I got worried.

Move to Europe and leave North Carolina? I couldn't believe what I was hearing. Who would ever want to live anywhere other than Little Piney Cove?

When he first mentioned it, I had no idea how serious he was. Daddy sometimes just thought out loud, but he really was considering this.

Thank goodness, my mother's heart remained in Little Piney Cove too, and she made that clear to my father. Once that was settled, I relaxed and began to roam the countryside.

The Tchividjians had rented a quaint house in Vevey, a little town outside Montreux on Lake Geneva. After a few weeks I didn't long for Little Piney Cove as much, because I was doing all sorts of things that would have been impossible in North Carolina. The Swiss Army had built forts and tunnels all through the mountains that were used only in times of war. Since they had been vacated, I was able to explore them, one after another.

It was always a highlight to go on special family outings with the Tchividjians. We did it often and got to see places like Saint Bernard Pass and Zermatt. We were constantly busy, sightseeing and learning about life in Europe. It was a real education. Looking back now, I realize that the trip gave me a valuable experience that would help me later in the work of Samaritan's Purse.

The family's visit proved to be a life-changing event for my older sister, Gigi. Three years later, she married Ara Tchividjian's oldest son, Stephan, whom she met on that trip.

During our stay, Mr. Tchividjian gave us a shorthaired St. Bernard, whom we named Heidi. We brought Heidi home to Little Piney Cove, and she became our faithful watchdog.

We were probably the only family in western North Carolina at that time who owned a St. Bernard. Heidi was huge, and her size caused fear in everyone outside the family. The fact that her "hobby" was biting strangers may have had something to do with it! Before long the word got around concerning Heidi!

Only a few months had passed after our return from Europe when Daddy began to talk about spending the winter of 1960–61 in Vero Beach, Florida. I knew Daddy was thinking seriously about moving to Florida. He loved the warm, sunny weather.

"Do I have to go?" I asked. The look on Daddy's face answered my question. Bea and Mama packed us up and we headed south for the coast.

I really didn't want to go. I'd seen other places, but I just knew that I belonged in those western Carolina mountains.

After we arrived in Vero Beach, Daddy spoke enthusiastically about moving us there permanently. Once again, though, Mama stepped in and settled the topic for good. "Bill, if you're going to travel, I'm going to live near my parents. I'm going to need their help in raising this family."

Once that decision was out of the way, I learned to enjoy some of the outdoor activities Florida has to offer. Playing on the beach was okay. But I really missed hunting after school. Fishing became a substitute. I also missed the rest of our "family"—John Rickman and Beatrice Long. John and Bea could just as well had the last name Graham—they were family. Bea even lived in our home and was like a mother to me when Mama wasn't there. Mama later said that Bea was actually the mother—she was just the "assistant mother."

Bea's room was near mine, and I would call out to her in the middle of the night when I was sick and Mama was away. She was awfully good to me, but she did make me mind—even if it meant giving me a swat now and then with the end of her broom or the back of the spatula.

We packed up and left Florida for home the next spring. I was very excited, to say the least, when we entered the gate of Little Piney Cove. I flung the car door open and ran into the house and hugged Bea.

"Sure missed you," Bea said, when she returned my hug.

Next I had to see John Rickman. I found him walking near the woodshed. "Hey, Gizmo, I'm home," I hollered as I barrelled toward him.

"Hey, Budrow," he said (his nickname for me). He smiled. There was no hug, but I could tell from the look on his face that he was glad I was back.

"Tomorrow I plan to start clearing the apple orchard. I expect your help," he said and walked away.

I couldn't wait. He knew I'd be there.

I think Mama was just as happy as the rest of us, maybe more so. That mountain home was her nest. Back in her bedroom, she had her own study desk—a big, wide, flatboard table that she had gotten out of an old mountain cabin and restored. She had it pushed up against the wall, and stacked on top were her study Bibles, commentaries, and concordance. I can remember as a boy getting up early and going into her room. She would be sipping her coffee while quietly studying.

We were all glad to be home.

Going to school just never was "my thing." Most indoor activities didn't appeal much to me, so having to sit at a desk all day and look at books was a problem.

I knew my parents were bothered about my poor performance in school, and it's probably good that I didn't know just how concerned they were and the step they were considering.

Since the academic subjects didn't interest me much, I found other ways to break up my boredom, and many of them got me into hot water—fighting, for example.

I could always count on Bunny to give a full report after school to Mama on what kind of trouble I'd gotten into on any given day. One afternoon when we climbed off the bus, Bunny headed right for Mama. "Franklin got in a fight again today," I remember hearing her tattle on me. "He hit a boy in the mouth."

Mama knew the other boy had a reputation of being a bully.

"He's the meanest, nastiest boy in Montreat," I said in my own defense.

"But I thought he had improved," Mama said.

"If so, he improved worser!" I said.

I didn't fight just to fight. It was a justice issue with me. I didn't like seeing big kids pick on little ones. So I appointed myself to fight for them when I thought they needed help. I came home bloody more than once.

Many years later I would find myself still involved in scuffles, because I didn't like seeing people getting hurt when they couldn't do much to help themselves.

School was a trial, but my joy always returned when I went into the hills and mountains. I would go every chance I got. Since Mama wouldn't let me camp out on school nights, I lived for the weekends. I didn't care if it was raining or snowing. When Friday night came, I would grab my gun, holler for the dogs, and head out. Sometimes I took a friend along, but most of the time I went alone—just my dogs and me.

As soon as the sun had set, I'd build a campfire, fumble through my knapsack for my transistor radio, and tune it to WBMS in Black Mountain, North Carolina. I'd lean up against a tree stump and stare at the stars as I listened to Elvis, Johnny Cash, Jerry Lee Lewis, Chuck Berry, Little Richard, and all the others. It helped me forget about school and anything else that was troubling me. There was nothing better than spending a night in the woods. That was real living—true freedom.

As my grade-school years neared an end, sitting in a classroom may have been a painful bore to me, but I could always daydream about my outdoor adventures. I had no idea how soon those happy, carefree escapades would come to an end.

The Rebel Goes North

"Franklin, I need to talk with you." My father's distinctive voice echoed through the log and frame house. He sounded serious. *What now?* I wondered.

We met at the dining room table where the whole family enjoyed Bea's country cooking. That June afternoon was hot, the kind of day I loved to spend messing around in the woods, down near the creek where it was cool under the canopy of leaves.

"Yes, sir?" I said.

Daddy looked straight at me, his blue eyes steady. "You're going to Stony Brook!" he said, in that forceful, emphatic way he made his points while preaching. Just the way he said it, I knew it would be pointless to argue. His mind was made up.

It was 1966. I was thirteen years old.

I felt dull ache in my chest. This was my worst nightmare coming true. My parents had enrolled me at Stony Brook School for Boys, an elite Christian boarding school on Long Island in New York.

New York? If he's going to send me away, why not a school in the South? I thought. My ancestors had shed their blood fighting the North. New York, in my young mind, was enemy territory.

They weren't punishing me by sending me away, but it felt like it. I knew they meant well. My grades in school were average at best, and my parents were concerned. The truth was I didn't study. Or as my teachers often said diplomatically, "Franklin just doesn't apply himself."

No doubt Mama and Daddy expected the strict discipline at Stony Brook would help shape me up, and I knew they wanted me to get a first-class education. I'm sure they thought their oldest son would profit from a more sophisticated environment.

But I couldn't have cared less. I was a born and bred southern boy. I loved the mountains, my dogs, my guns, and my friends.

Sending a thirteen-year-old boy away from home for months at a time was not a big deal to my folks, especially my mother. After all, she had been raised by missionary parents in China and gone to boarding school at thirteen, in what is now Pyongyang, North Korea.

But I was devastated. Although I spent the remaining weeks of that summer wandering through the hills and hollers near our home, I could not shake the feeling that unhappy days were just ahead. Even at thirteen I knew I wouldn't be happy living anywhere other than Little Piney Cove.

Daddy drove me to Asheville for some last-minute shopping at the Man's Store on Patton Avenue. He picked out a new wardrobe for me that included two Hart Schaffner & Marx suits, two wool sports coats, a navy blue blazer, shoes, socks, ties, overcoat, raincoat, and even rubbers for the shoes. These fancy clothes seemed ridiculous to me. As long as I could remember, blue jeans and cowboy boots were my attire.

"Daddy, I'm going to have to dress like some Wall Street person!" I protested miserably.

My father just smiled. "That's right, son. You'll be expected to wear either a suit or a blazer every day—and always a tie."

This was not good news. My spirits sank even further. I felt like I was being exiled to a foreign country.

The dreaded day in August arrived. I tearfully hugged Mama and Bea good-bye. The dogs got hugs too. I just shook hands with John Rickman. Our eyes met, but I quickly turned away—I didn't want him to see my tears.

Daddy took me to New York, and we drove out to the school on Long Island. The campus was impressive. It definitely had the boarding school look, with large, red brick buildings fronted by white columns. A long, maple-lined driveway led into the main buildings, which were surrounded by neatly manicured shrubs and lush, green grass. But it would not have mattered to me if it were a tropical paradise. I wanted to be back in the South, preferably Little Piney Cove.

Daddy went with me to my room and helped me unpack. The president took us on a tour of the school facilities. Then that moment I had dreaded for so long came—when Daddy had to say good-bye and leave me there alone. I wanted to be tough. I didn't want him to see me crying. I can still remember hugging and kissing him and watching the car disappear down the drive past the maples. As the car crept away, Daddy waved. I don't think I had ever had a more lonely feeling than I did at that moment. I ached. I wanted to run after him. Instead, I just stood and watched him disappear.

Dormitory life was a shock. I was used to having my own room, which looked out into the tall pines. I missed the fresh mountain breezes blowing through my window. Here I was crammed in a stuffy dorm that smelled like an old locker room.

We were placed two to a cell—I mean room. My first roommate was Jonathan Olford, son of noted preacher Dr. Stephen Olford. He was about my age, and we got along fine. But for a loner like me, it was uncomfortable having to share life in a dorm full of boys.

Each day our room was inspected. Beds had to be made, clothes stored away, and everything put in its proper place. I was shaken by all of the dramatic and rapid change in my life. It gave new meaning to the word *homesick*.

I missed everything—my parents, Gizmo, Bea, my gun, the dogs, my time in the woods—even my sisters and brother!

On top of all that, I had to adjust to a much tougher academic environment. And I resented it when they made me repeat the eighth grade because Stony Brook was more advanced than my school in North Carolina.

Another irritation was the requirement at Stony Brook that every student participate in some kind of sports activity during free time. I had grown up in a small community that didn't have organized team sports. I knew how to use a rifle and hunt, but I didn't know how to play ball. My awkwardness was humiliating, and I found every way I could to escape.

Some relief came when I met a junior named Jim Oliver. When some of the kids picked on me because of my southern roots, Jim stood up for me.

"Leave him alone," Jim said more than once, "he's my friend." They listened to him because he was on the school football team and bigger than most of the other guys. Jim was from "southern" New Jersey and under the circumstances, that was good enough for me. Jim's friendship made life a little more tolerable.

The rules at Stony Brook, like wearing a tie, keeping your room clean, and playing sports, were annoying, but I could tolerate them. I was bothered, though, by the rules they didn't seem to keep.

Having been raised in the South, I'd been taught that the important things in life were telling the truth, helping others in times of trouble, and respecting your elders. Almost as soon as I could speak I had been taught to say "Yes, sir" and "No, ma'am." I knew I would be disciplined if I displayed any disrespect. No matter how rebellious I became later, it never crossed my mind to intentionally "sass" an older person.

But showing respect didn't seem that important at Stony Brook. I was confused because they put so much emphasis on how you dressed, but didn't seem to care that much if you mouthed off to an adult.

I couldn't believe what I saw in my Latin class. My teacher was Pierson Curtis, popularly known as "PC." He had been on the faculty since the late 1920s and was in his seventies when I arrived on campus. He wore a hearing aid, and when he turned to write on the chalkboard, kids would joke about him and throw spitballs. He would whirl around and try to catch the culprits, but usually he didn't. "Who threw that?" he would demand. But no one ever confessed, nor got into trouble.

Such blatant disrespect for authority was an eye-opener to me. Back home that was unacceptable behavior no matter how you cut it. Whether I was right or not, I concluded that my classmates were mainly a bunch of rich, snotty brats whom the school administrators feared to discipline because if they did, and ultimately sent them home, Stony Brook would lose the tuition money.

In the school back in North Carolina, if I had showed that kind of disrespect or disobeyed an elder, I would have been whipped—I knew, because I'd gotten my share. Once I was sent to the principal's office because I'd refused to spit out my chewing gum.

"Okay, Franklin," the principal said, "you know what to do." I did. I bent forward and grabbed my ankles. Out came the wooden paddle. He gave me three or four heavy swats. When he finished, I didn't show any tears, but my backside sure throbbed for awhile.

At Stony Brook, no one ever got paddled. Instead, students were punished with demerits. After a certain number accumulated, the guilty boy had to sit in study hall. Big deal! But I don't recall anyone getting demerits for talking disrespectfully. It was a student's right, I guess, or his civil liberty—or something!

It didn't take long for me to learn that I just didn't fit in. I was a southerner—born and bred, accent and all—surrounded by a bunch of Yankees. (I've since gotten a bumper sticker that says, "American by birth, Southerner by the grace of God!") As I look back, I guess this was a great lesson for me. At an early age, I was forced into a setting where I had to learn to get along with people from different walks of life, races, and religions. I had to learn to respect their views and ways even if I didn't fully understand them, which has helped me all of my life as I work and serve in so many countries.

Letters from home became one of the few bright spots. Mama wrote faithfully, usually sending two or three letters a week. With my first glance at the envelope I could always detect Mama's letters from the others. Her distinctive, backslanted handwriting was unmistakable, and she always used a broad-tipped pen. Here's a sample:

Mama's letters always seemed to arrive when I needed them most. It was like a ten-minute visit to Little Piney Cove. When she shared news, I could picture the log house and almost smell the chicken frying in Bea's pan. But more than anything else, Mama's letters were spiritually encouraging—like those penned by the apostle Paul writing the early church. Mama's letters always had a verse, a word of comfort, from the Lord. A spiritual lesson. She always concluded with her love and how proud she was of me. I treasured those letters and read them over and over.

Still, there were times I was miserable. It was unlike me to show my feelings, but for at least the first two months, each night when the lights went out, I lay in my bed, covered my head with a blanket so my roommate wouldn't hear, and cried myself to sleep.

Daddy called me one day in the middle of the semester to say he was going to be in Washington that weekend at the invitation of President Lyndon Johnson. Daddy had asked if it would be okay to bring me with him, and the president had said yes.

I wanted to spend time with Daddy, but this was not my idea of weekend fun—the only time we could wear blue jeans. Now I would have to stay dressed up in a suit and tie and listen to grown-ups talk about things that didn't interest me in the least. But since Daddy wanted me to go, I said yes.

President Johnson was in a grumpy mood that weekend. He had the weight of the world on his shoulders. The Vietnam War was not going well, and I think he was burdened for the families of the young men and women who had lost their lives, and others who would. He seemed to snap at everybody. But Lady Bird covered for him in her sweet and gracious way.

Back at school, time seemed almost to have stopped. As the days and weeks dragged on, whatever dim hope I had concerning my future attached itself to the upcoming Thanksgiving holiday. In early November I began to count the days until I could go home, like a prisoner awaiting the end of his sentence.

Finally the grand day came. I boarded the Long Island Railroad to Penn Central Station in New York City, where I connected to the Southern Express. Just seeing the name "Southern Express" made me smile. The train pulled out at 5 P.M.

My parents had arranged for a small compartment with a fold-down bed. Before turning in, I asked the conductor, "When will we be crossing into Virginia?" I knew that this border was the old Mason-Dixon Line.

"Some time around midnight," he answered.

After crawling into bed, I peeked through the window blind, realizing that with each click of the wheels I was a little closer to home. Several times during the night, I pulled back the curtain and peered into the darkness, eager to catch the first glimpses of something that looked like home.

By seven o'clock the next morning the train had slowed. I could tell by the terrain we were somewhere in the foothills of western North Carolina. "Almost home," I whispered. "Almost home!"

When the train rolled into Black Mountain about 9 A.M., I saw Mama and Daddy standing on the platform. John Rickman was there too. I jumped down the steps and into the arms of my mother and felt Daddy's arms come around and hug me.

Within fifteen minutes we were at Little Piney Cove. I walked into the house and smelled the aromas of wood burning in the fireplaces and one of Bea's spectacular breakfasts cooking in the kitchen. I sniffed. Hot coffee, biscuits, and bacon. I had about ten choices of things I wanted to do all at the same time. I needed to hug and kiss Bea, eat the good breakfast she was preparing, pet my dogs, see what Gizmo was doing, run into the woods, grab my guns and go hunting. But in the end it really was no contest: I sat down and enjoyed every bite of Bea's breakfast.

I treasured every moment of those few days, but the time flew by. Before I knew it, I was back in the dormitory at Stony Brook.

The next fall, when I entered ninth grade, my roommate, Jonathan, who was a tremendous athlete, moved in with another football player. I had several other roommates after Jonathan, and most were rebels like I was becoming.

In my sophomore year I managed to get a room by myself on the third floor of Hegeman Hall, directly above the school's kitchen. It was so small that there was room for only one bed. Most students didn't want to be cramped like that, but for me it was great. At last I had some space that was mine alone.

The room had an added benefit that fit my needs perfectly. I discovered I could climb through my window onto a narrow side roof. There, behind a large chimney, I could smoke all I wanted without anyone seeing me.

It wasn't long before some of my fellow smokers discovered my hideaway. They sneaked up to my room one at a time and crawled through the window. I wondered if someone would observe this unusual stream of guests and snitch to the faculty, but I wasn't too bothered. I got a kick out of staying one step ahead of the "law."

Without realizing it, I was slowly becoming more and more rebellious. Deep down I really resented having to go to school away from home. Breaking rules like "No smoking" was a way to show some of my feelings.

Being the son of a preacher and from the South meant that I was the focus of constant teasing and, sometimes, unusual practical jokes.

One afternoon after picking up my mail, I headed to the dining hall, where I had been assigned to eat at the dean of student's (Karl Soderstrom) table along with six other guys. It was typical of students to open their mail during lunch. I slit into an envelope that had no return address and pulled a handful of dried, ground-up leaves from the wrapper.

"What's this?" I asked innocently.

"Let me see it," Mr. Soderstrom said as he held out his hand.

After he examined the contents carefully, he said, "I think I should keep this."

I shrugged. "What is it?"

"I think I should keep this," he repeated.

A couple of boys near me snickered. After the meal ended, they told me what I had pulled from the envelope and laughed at my ignorance.

How was I supposed to know? I had never seen marijuana before. I could have ended up in trouble, but apparently my honest, innocent reaction was convincing, because Mr. Soderstrom never did question me.

Don't get me wrong—I certainly wasn't a candidate for any "model student" award. Although I was ignorant about marijuana, I knew plenty about tobacco. I sneaked cigarettes every chance I got and would get a beer whenever I could manage it. But other drugs never interested me.

I had discovered a delicatessen near the school and got to know some of the guys who worked there. They would let me smoke in the back room and also let me sneak beer out the rear door of the deli.

By my sophomore year I was smoking habitually. In some unexplainable way, my cigarettes were a friend. When I smoked, it reminded me of home, of the mountains, and especially of John Rickman.

I thought I was fooling everyone and that somehow my actions were justified by my circumstances. But now I believe that is when my spiritual rebellion sprouted.

In January of 1969, Daddy called and invited me again to join Mama and him in Washington. They were going for the inauguration of President Nixon and a special dinner at the White House. After my last experience with Lyndon Johnson, I wasn't overly anxious to return, but I went. I met them in Washington and asked if I could stay at the hotel while they went to the White House for dinner that night. To my relief, they said yes. I had a lot more fun ordering room service, watching TV, and enjoying a cheeseburger and french fries.

The next day I joined Mama and Daddy at the White House for lunch with the Nixon family. Mrs. Nixon was as gracious as Lady Bird had been, and the girls, Julie and Tricia, were every inch ladies—not stuffy, and even a lot of fun. To my surprise, President Nixon talked to me and asked me about school and what I wanted to do when I grew up. I was impressed that he would find time to talk to me on his first day as president.

No matter how good it was to leave school for a weekend, the fact I had to go back hung over my head the whole time. I hated Stony Brook with a passion because of the structure and confinement. Every minute of every day was organized and scrutinized. No matter how wonderful everything may really have been at the school, I still would have hated it because I felt the experience was being forced upon me.

I couldn't confront my parents directly and tell them, "I'm not going back to Stony Brook." That just wasn't done—I hadn't been raised that way. So I endured the best I could.

There were quite a few rebels at Stony Brook, and as always seems to be the case with such kids, these were the guys who became my buddies. They didn't like being at school any more than I did, and we found some comfort in our mutual misery.

I developed almost a "prisoner of war" mentality. What kept me energized was a mindset that I would not be broken or brainwashed to conform to the school's rules or way of thinking. To my youthful mind, this was enemy territory. And I wasn't going to surrender.

Whatever was expected of the student body, I wanted to do the opposite. I took pride in my individuality and tried to see how far I could stretch rules before getting reprimanded. Many of these infractions were minor, but everything added to my rebellion. Instead of getting my esteem from achieving within the system, I got my thrills and identity from challenging the system. I was following the classic pattern of every rebel.

I'm not sure my parents really knew the extent of my frustration. In addition to their letters, I received frequent phone calls, and they visited Stony Brook whenever they could.

Sometimes I would tell them how much I missed being at home. They comforted me but did not change their minds. I think my pleading was especially hard on Mama, even though she believed they were doing what was right for me.

They kept telling me, "It'll get better. You'll make a lot of friends. You'll adjust."

When their visits to the campus would end and I'd watch them drive away, I ached inside. I was now "too old to cry," but I never got too old to hate being away from home.

At the beginning of my junior year in 1970, in reviewing my courses, the dean of students brought up the dreaded topic of team sports. All students were still required to participate in some form of athletics, whether it was trying out for one of the organized teams or playing intramurals.

"Well, Franklin, what do you want to do this fall?" Mr. Soderstrom asked.

I had an idea, but knew it would be a challenge to get him to agree.

"Could I cut trees for the senior logs?" I asked.

Each year it was a Stony Brook tradition that the seniors carve their names on logs and then shellac them. The logs were used to line the driveways of the campus.

"That involves a lot of work," Mr. Soderstrom answered.

"I can do it, and I really want to."

After we discussed it for several minutes and I assured him I knew how to fell large trees, he agreed to let me try. "If the job gets too big, come in and we'll talk," he said.

I was so relieved. This would be a lot harder work than playing games, but I didn't mind as long as I could work on my own. I had worked with John Rickman, side by side, on many occasions cutting trees on our property. This was something I knew how to do, and I loved it.

The school owned a large tract of land behind my dormitory. I soon had a new ax and all the privacy I wanted. The trees were probably sixty feet tall, but that didn't bother me. I did all the cutting myself. The only time I needed help was when I got ready to drop a tree. Two men who worked in the kitchen would come out and hold the ropes.

Otherwise I was left alone, and I couldn't have asked for a better workout. New York was not North Carolina, but at least now I could get closer to the land. Hearing the birds sing and the sound of my ax echoing through the woods, I almost could imagine for awhile that I was back chopping trees at Little Piney Cove.

The staff at Stony Brook knew that I was smoking, because my breath, hair, and clothes often reeked of tobacco. But they never could catch me.

I was questioned frequently: "Franklin, have you been smoking?"

I always had some excuse to hide the truth: "I just came from the kitchen—one of the cooks back there was smoking, and he blew on me," I might say without batting an eye.

I'm sure they knew the truth, but without evidence I couldn't be proven guilty.

I felt it was only a matter of time before I got nailed for smoking or something else—and they would kick me out.

I really didn't care and maybe even wanted to be expelled. But my feelings were mixed. Although I would have welcomed almost any event that got me out of Stony Brook, I didn't want to disappoint my parents or be a bad reflection on my father's name. So I lived each day on a tight rope—flirting with disaster, but unable to change my rebellious ways.

By Thanksgiving of my junior year, I knew that the handwriting was on the wall. The noose was tightening around my neck at Stony Brook. I felt it would be better if Mama and Daddy would let me come home at Christmas and finish school at Owen High, just outside of Montreat. I was desperate. I had to try something.

Back in North Carolina I finally worked my courage up and found my father alone in his office. "Daddy, I'd like to finish school here in Black Mountain," I said with a catch in my voice.

"Stick it out, Franklin. Next year you will graduate," he said, trying to encourage me.

"Daddy, if you don't let me come home by Christmas, they will probably kick me out sometime this year! Don't you think it would be better for me to bring it to an end gracefully?"

Deep down in his heart, I think Daddy knew that I was breaking most of the rules. My attitude at Stony Brook had become hard and calloused. I was a cynic. I rebelled against authority at every level.

I didn't have nearly as hard a time convincing Daddy as I thought. His blue eyes stared into mine, and I could sense his disappointment. He shook his head and said, "I'll have to talk to your mother and pray about it."

The next day Daddy surprised me—I really never thought he would let me come home: "Stay at Stony Brook until Christmas and then you can come home."

"Yes, sir," I said. I could hardly conceal my excitement.

Returning to Stony Brook after Thanksgiving wasn't nearly as traumatic this time. I managed to stay out of trouble for the next month. Now I had hope and felt a real sense of accomplishment.

Packing before the Christmas break was great. I smirked as I threw the neckties into the suitcase. I wouldn't be wearing those anymore. I was going home—to blue jeans and boots. This rebel was headed south.

Telling the guys I was leaving was fun. When I left I just said, "So long, fellas. I'm out of here for good."

On the train ride home I was totally elated. I had escaped. I was free at last. What I didn't realize was that I hadn't left my rebellious attitudes and bad habits at Stony Brook. They came home with me, just like the blazers and gray slacks I had rolled up and stuffed into my suitcase. It would be years before I admitted that I was responsible for the failures in my own life. I couldn't blame my problems on Stony Brook or anything else. I had to take responsibility for my own actions.

Looking back, as miserable as I was, good things did come out of the Stony Brook experience. At an early age I cut the cord that bound me to home. While at boarding school I learned to be independent and to make decisions for myself—challenges I still must face on almost a daily basis.

If my parents had to do it over again, I'm not sure they would send me to boarding school at thirteen. But I survived, and I guess Mama and Daddy knew I would. I grew up a little faster and it made me tougher.

I've thought about this experience as it relates to my own kids. I decided I never wanted them to grow up quite as fast as I did. I'll keep them at home as long as I can. And I dread the day they will pack up and leave for good. "Home" just means an awful lot to me.

Fights, Rednecks, and Cops

Just being home would have been more than enough to make me happy. But then I received more good news.

After my parents enrolled me at Owen High School, which was the public high school nearest to Montreat, the school checked my records and determined that because of the advanced curriculum at Stony Brook, I qualified as a senior! If I worked hard and didn't fail anything, I could graduate the following June. I was stunned. Life was definitely on the upswing.

But not all was euphoria. School and Franklin Graham didn't mix that well, and trouble seemed to follow me. One thing I never had been able to tolerate was watching a bully take advantage of someone. That always pushed all of my buttons.

My button-pusher at Owen High was a big, tall guy named Kal (not his real name) who just happened to be black. His buttons were being pushed by a few white students who, unknown to Kal, wanted race trouble.

Kal was big—so big that he thought no one would mess with him. But I wasn't afraid of him. To me he was just a bully.

The problem started in biology, where Kal and I sat across from each other. I told myself it really was none of my business, but it really bugged me when Kal started talking dirty to a nice girl who sat in front of me. His words shocked me, and I just stared at him in disbelief. It was beyond my comprehension that a guy would talk to a girl that way.

My blood boiled. I wanted to kick his teeth out right then, but I kept my composure. I didn't forget what had happened, though.

One day in class, Kal was shining his shoes with a Kleenex. When he finished, he wadded the tissue up, but instead of throwing it in the trash, he tossed it over onto my desk. It ticked me off. Who did he think he was? I wasn't going to let anyone throw his trash on me. I threw the Kleenex back. The teacher was busy at the front of the room, and she didn't see what was going on.

Kal threw the dirty tissue at me again.

I threw it back.

"What you gonna do?" Kal said as he threw it in my face.

"I don't want to mess with you today, Kal," I said. "Leave me alone." I threw it back.

"Stand up!"

I stood. I think he was surprised. In the back of my mind I still remembered how he had insulted that sweet girl a few weeks earlier.

Kal slowly got up.

John Rickman had taught me that if I was going to fight, it was best to hit first and hit hard. Before he got completely up on his feet, I slugged Kal with all my might. I doubt that I hurt him much, but the surprise on his face showed he hadn't expected me to fight. He seemed a little confused. I threw a few more punches as fast as I could—I now had the advantage. He swung at me. I got hit, but I didn't feel it. By now my adrenaline was pumping, and I grabbed him around the waist and threw him against the chalkboard. When he came down, he hit the chalk tray and ripped the board off the wall. It crashed to the floor behind him.

"Fight! A fight!" the teacher screamed as she raced from the room like the building was on fire or something.

In almost no time she returned with two male teachers. By then Kal and I were in a full-blown brawl.

"That's enough! Break it up!" as the teachers separated us.

The whole fight probably lasted less than a minute, but it seemed much longer.

Kal was screaming like a stuck pig. He was humiliated. I had gotten the best of him; he was calling me every four-letter word he could think of.

The teachers were trying to find out who started the fight. Naturally, I said Kal had started it. And of course Kal blamed it on me. If it hadn't been for the teachers holding us back, we would have gotten into it again, right then and there.

"That's enough," the teacher yelled again. "Both of you shut up." The two male teachers marched us down to the principal's office.

The principal, Charles Lytle, had been my tutor several years before I left for Stony Brook. He looked like a marine: He had a flat-top haircut, and he stood over six feet tall, had arms the size of telephone poles, and a neck as big around as a watermelon. He probably weighed 260 pounds and could have licked his weight in wildcats.

When we walked into his office, Kal and I were no longer worried about each other, we were scared to death of Mr. Lytle. He didn't care if we were rich, poor, black, or white, he wasn't going to take any nonsense from anybody. He sat us down and gave us an extended lecture, then sent us both home to cool off.

Before I could get home to tell my side of the story, Mr. Lytle had been on the phone to my folks, telling them what had happened and that he had suspended me. As I left, the school rednecks were yelling, "Way to go, Franklin! Don't back down. You did the right thing, you sure showed him. That guy deserved it; next time knock his head off."

By the time I got home, I was grinning like a possum—totally pleased with my performance that day. I had challenged the bully and walked away victorious.

Mama and Daddy were not so pleased, but I knew they were proud that I had tried to make things right for the girl Kal had talked dirty to.

A week later I returned to school, but before I could go to class I had to talk to Principal Lytle.

"I'm not going to take any of this from you," he said as he leaned forward in his chair and pointed his finger at my face. "I can't afford to have problems here, especially between blacks and whites." I was scared. Just looking at him made most of us high-school boys back off. He had the strength and will to throw some-one's head through the wall if he got riled.

"You've only been back in Carolina a short time," he contin-ued, "but I'll tell you this much, Franklin, you're not going to mess this school up. Do you understand what I'm saying to you?"

"Yes, sir."

After they let me come home from Stony Brook, I'm sure my parents wondered a few times if they had made a mistake. I had been gone for over three years. Although I had bent the rules at Stony Brook to the breaking point, the school had still been a tightly structured environment that kept me under control. I was ready to let loose!

Now that I'm a parent with teenagers of my own, I realize how I must have driven Mama and Daddy half-crazy.

I had not lost my enjoyment of teasing others—just like I had done with my sisters when I was small. Since the girls were married and no longer at home, I had to find other targets, and sometimes Mama and Daddy were the only ones available besides my little brother Ned.

Like most teenagers, I found a type of music that I just knew my parents would never appreciate—loud rock and roll.

Back in the sixties the music at my father's crusades was of the traditional church variety—the great old hymns and mild-tempo melodies sung by a choir or a great soloist like George Beverly Shea. In this vast difference in musical tastes that existed between my parents and me, I fiendishly saw an opportunity to have a little fun at their expense.

I recall Mama telling me that if I had to listen to what she called "stuff," I had to keep it turned down with the door to my room closed. She returned to the house one afternoon with a group of church ladies for a meeting. I was nowhere in sight. I had my door open at the top of the front stairs and when Mama came in, I cranked the record player way up—the music blared all over the house. Mama came up the steps two at a time! In one swift sweep, she cut the stereo off and confiscated my records for a whole week.

Our home had an intercom system. One night I placed a speaker from my stereo in front of the intercom box and turned it on full blast. I roared with laughter as Johnny Cash's "Ring of Fire" boomed through every room of the house.

Daddy appeared rather quickly.

"Turn it down!" he said, having to shout to be heard above the music. His look and voice meant "Do it now, and don't do it again."

I did things like that just to get a reaction. And it worked! (Never did I dream at that time that a few years later Daddy and Johnny Cash would become good friends.)

Although I probably deserved tougher rules, as I look back, my parents really did give me a lot of freedom. When I took to wearing my hair long, which had become the style by the end of the 1960s, neither of them made any ruckus over it. I was lucky because most of my friends were hassled by their folks about their hair. I bragged to my friends about how "cool" my folks were.

My parents were also really pretty good about giving me liberty to come and go as I pleased. I didn't have a curfew like my friends. I came home at night when I was good and ready—as long as it was sometime before midnight.

But my mother, like most mothers, had her own way of getting her point across. She always sat up and waited until I got home—no matter what time it was. It really bugged me, because it made me feel guilty.

I don't know how many times I tried to slip in late. There she would be, dressed in her robe, sitting in her rocker with a book or a Bible on her lap. "Thank God, you're all right," she'd say. That was it! She never lectured me or made threats.

"You don't need to wait up for me," I'd say sheepishly.

Mama would just smile, say goodnight, and go to her room. No matter how I begged her to not wait up for me, she was always there with the light on when I arrived.

As intent as I was on showing my independence and partying late if I wanted to, after awhile Mama's night watchman routine got to me. I began to feel ashamed that Mama was losing sleep waiting up for me.

I knew my mother well enough to know that she was not going to change her ways, so I had to change mine. I finally just gave up and started coming home earlier. I ended up with a curfew—of my own making!

One morning Mama called me to get up for school. I had been out late the night before, and I didn't feel like budging.

My mother is a very unpredictable woman, and I'm sure I get plenty of my spunk from her. I was half-asleep, thinking she had given up on waking me. She quietly walked in my room, grabbed the overflowing ashtray by my bed, and dumped the cigarette butts and ashes all over my head.

"Now get up!" she said.

I jumped up, madder than a hornet. I could hear her laughing as she walked down the hall.

The next night I locked my door. The following morning Mama found a little firecracker of mine in her tool box, lit the fuse, and slid it under the door. To say the least, I sprang up thinking a terrorist car bomb had gone off.

Mama wasn't about to give up—neither was I. The next morning not only did I have the door locked, but I had wedged a wet bath towel into the crack under my door. I thought for sure I was safe from a firecracker blowing me out of bed. About that time, I heard Mama coming down the hall. I was in bed laughing to myself as I heard her jiggle the door handle and try to push something under the door. I had outfoxed her this time.

But Mama, being the resourceful women she is, persisted. All of a sudden I heard the window in my brother's room next door squeak open. I slid out of bed and peeked out the window. Here came Mama crawling on all fours across the roof! This time she was carrying a cup of water, which she had gripped in her teeth. I stifled a laugh. She was planning to douse me. Just as she got to my window, I grinned at her and said "Sorry!" and slammed and locked the window. I stood there laughing and making faces at her as she peered into the window. There she was wondering what to do next. She reminded me of our cat with a dead mouse in its mouth, standing at the window wanting to come in.

She couldn't help herself—she grinned, too, in spite of the cup. Because the roof had a fairly steep pitch, now she had to back up on all fours. It was a sight to behold! Suddenly, though, this wasn't so funny. I worried a little about her sliding off the roof, but it was obvious she was quite surefooted and would be okay. I made it to school on time that day too.

These confrontations with Mama weren't mean or bitter. On the one hand, my parents made it clear what they would accept or reject in my values and behavior. But on the other hand, they never squashed my individuality or demeaned me as a person. They knew much more clearly than I did the pressures I faced being a "preacher's kid" as well as the oldest son of a "Christian legend." I'm sure God gave them wisdom to know that if they pushed me too hard to conform, I might take off running and never come back—not just away from them, but perhaps from God too.

By throwing in good doses of humor and fun, our relationship was full of grace and had some space for the tensions to ease. I didn't always agree with my parents and certainly at the time didn't appreciate much their lifestyle and values. But I respected them and never doubted that they loved me.

At school I was doing my best to hang on academically and stay out of trouble. Graduation was only weeks away. My fight with Kal had not been forgotten by a few of the redneck boys, who were looking for some way to liven things up. They kept egging me on to fight Kal again. One or two of them would stop me in the hall and ask, "Have you heard what Kal's been saying about you?"

"I don't know, and I don't care," I would answer. All I could think about was not messing up and getting out of school for good. But the boys persisted.

"Come on, Franklin. Kal goes around bragging that he can whip you any time and any place. You're not going to let him get away with that, are you?"

One day at lunch a boy told me, "Kal is out there at the incinerator. He says he's waiting for you, if you're not too chicken."

"Let him wait," I said and started to walk away.

"Don't you worry, we'll go with you," another said. "We won't let anybody else jump you. We'll back you." That sounded kind of nice.

"You're not afraid of him, are you?" asked one of them.

Instead of just laughing it off, I took the bait. I thought I was trapped. They had convinced me that I had to fight or be considered a coward.

I went out to the incinerator. When Kal saw me he began to strut like a big rooster, then he tried to stare me down. I knew he was a big guy, but for some reason, he suddenly looked much bigger than I had remembered. He had to be at least 6'3" and weighed 220 pounds. I was 6'1", but only weighed about 180 pounds. I knew my size was a drawback, so I could only hope that being smaller meant I could move faster. But as he got closer, I began to have my doubts. It looked like I was going to get pounded.

My mind flashed back to Stony Brook. One of the sports I had endured there was wrestling. I remembered that my best bet would be to try and pin him to the ground as quick as I could. I made my move, but before we really even got started a teacher appeared and broke it up.

Back to the principal's office I went with a sense of doom. *How could I have been so stupid?* I thought.

Facing Kal hadn't scared me much, but I got weak in the knees waiting to see Mr. Lytle, especially after promising him I'd stay out of trouble.

"I'm not going to let you start a race riot in my school," he told me. "This happens one more time, and I'm going to have to expel you for good."

"I won't get into any more fights, sir," I promised. I was pretty sure that both Kal and I had been set up by those rednecks. All I had to do was stay clear of them. Mr. Lytle stared right through me for several seconds before he said, "Okay, Franklin. Your last chance."

When I got home, Mr. Lytle had been on the phone with my parents again. I could see the concern on their faces. He had made it clear that if I got into trouble one more time, I was out of high school for good. That meant I would miss college that fall.

Daddy told me, "Franklin, I back Mr. Lytle 100 percent." Mama agreed. I got no sympathy from them. I had gotten suckered in by the wrong crowd trying to prove something when I didn't need to prove a thing.

I stayed away from Kal, and we both finished the remainder of the year without another incident. It was probably a valuable lesson to learn—don't let other people set your agenda and don't allow yourself to be used in life for the wrong purpose.

I guess it was inevitable that I would eventually have a run-in with authority outside of school or home. But it never crossed my mind that I might end up being interrogated by a police officer.

Everyone in Montreat knew one another, and we were like one big happy family. It was kind of like Mayberry on the old *Andy Griffith Show.* I was so familiar with everyone in our little community that I felt I could get away with just about anything. I had ridden my motorcycles and driven cars on the streets of Montreat long before I had a license. No one complained. And as I got older, each year I had gone faster and become more reckless.

Since Montreat was really just a village, the community could only afford hand-me-down police cars from nearby cities. When I got my driver's license I started driving my own used clunkers. I'd buy a car for two hundred bucks, the engine burning and dripping oil. Each week I'd spend my entire Saturday under the hood working on it so that I could get through the rest of the next week. When it would finally break down for good, I'd put it up on cinder blocks and get another one.

I always got a riot out of purposely speeding by our Montreat policeman, Pete Post. He ignored me and never even gave me a warning—until I did it one time too many.

Pete was such a good guy, and his police car was such a junker, I just never felt threatened by him. So I was very surprised when I saw the red flashing bubble in my rearview mirror, after I had roared past him in my old, beat-up, green Triumph Spitfire.

Pete closed in and signaled me to pull over, but I just kept going and raced toward home. This wasn't smart, but it seemed like great fun at the time.

As I approached our driveway, I pushed the button on the remote opener for the gate and sped up our mountain road, closing the gate behind me.

I laughed as I imagined the look on Pete's face as he sat in front of the locked gate at the bottom of the hill.

I screeched to a halt, slammed the car door, ran up to my room, and locked the door. My heart was pounding with excitement. I had seen this kind of thing on TV, but this was a new thrill for me.

My exhilaration didn't last long. Within minutes my father's voice rang out, "Franklin, come down here!" I met him in his study.

"Pete Post just called," he said, as he stared a hole right through me.

I tried to look indifferent; I wasn't going to volunteer any information or incriminate myself.

"What happened?" Daddy asked.

I told him. I was still thinking how funny it must have been when Pete saw those closed gates.

Daddy didn't laugh. He didn't even smile.

"Pete Post is on his way up," he said. "I've opened the gate for him. You and I are going to have a meeting with him. If he wants to arrest you, I'm going to support him." Daddy had a way of cocking his head and looking at me when he was serious or angry.

A holy fear crept over me. I was sorry—not for what I'd done, but for getting caught.

Daddy walked away and left me to suffer alone.

Within ten minutes, Officer Post arrived. He came into the kitchen and the three of us sat around the table. He didn't look quite so foolish now. In fact he looked like a mighty fine officer of the law. Daddy said little, and I said nothing. Pete did most of the talking.

He gave me a lecture about careless driving, not respecting authority, and trying to hide behind my parents. "If I ever—even once—catch you doing anything like this again, I'll not only take your license, I'll haul you off to jail," he said, and turned to my father for confirmation.

Daddy nodded.

"Franklin, this isn't a game," Pete went on. "You could have killed someone or yourself. Do you understand that?"

"Yes, sir."

The lecture seemed to last for hours. It was humiliating. I don't remember ever feeling as genuinely sorry for my actions as I did that day. Pete had given me a serious wake-up call. After that I did drive more carefully and tried to watch the speed limit.

I also learned something that I had not known before: If I got into trouble and was wrong, I couldn't count on my daddy to fix it or defend me. I never forgot his promise to stand with Pete Post, even if it meant seeing me dragged off in handcuffs.

I knew that being the son of Billy Graham had given me advantages. Up to this point, I had gotten by with things other kids wouldn't have. Now I began to realize this was a two-edged sword. It was a plus to be Billy's son, but it had its down side as well. If I screwed up, the book would be thrown at me a little harder. I was catching on to the fact that people expected me to be some kind of example and would hold me to a higher standard.

I thought this was unfair, and to some extent I still do. But it was reality, and I needed to start getting used to it. One thing never changes: With privilege comes responsibility.

Alaska, Motorcycle Mama, and Wings

The school year was nearly over when a bomb dropped. I found out that somehow I lacked one credit to graduate. I could not believe it!

Daddy knew how important it was for me to get out of school before something else happened. So he called Richard LeTourneau, the president of LeTourneau College in Longview, Texas, and explained my situation. Mr. LeTourneau said that he would allow me to enter the college and make up the necessary credit during my freshman year if the high school principal would agree. Now all Daddy had to do was to convince Charles Lytle.

Daddy wasn't surprised when Principal Lytle said, "No problem, Dr. Graham."

What a relief! Not only for me, but I'm sure for Mr. Lytle too.

"You want to go where?" my father asked, surprised.

"I'd like to go to Alaska this summer and work before starting college at LeTourneau," I said.

He shook his head. Daddy had just straightened out my academic problems at high school and now I could graduate. He probably thought that after begging to come home from Stony Brook, I wouldn't even think about leaving Little Piney Cove and my beloved mountains at least until fall when I would go to college. I've always had that spirit of adventure. Alaska was the last frontier, and I wanted to see it before it was gone.

Daddy didn't give me an answer about Alaska right away. I think he wanted to wait a few days to see just how serious I was. He knew me well. For most of my life I've been involved in one adventure after another.

Why this is so, I'm not really sure. I don't think I'm just a thrill seeker or have a death wish. But somehow one event leads to another, and I find myself doing something that leaves me hanging out over the edge.

Combined with this talent for finding excitement, I have always had a great curiosity about mechanical things. If there's a machine or device that makes noise, goes fast, and blows smoke, I want to have one and take it apart to see what makes it work—and put it back together again! *That's* my idea of fun.

One machine that has all the necessary elements—noise, speed, and smoke—is the motorcycle. When I was eleven, my parents finally relented and let me earn money doing odd jobs so I could buy a Rupp minibike. It had a very noisy two-and-a-half horsepower Clinton four-cycle engine. I rode it everywhere and wore out the tires faster than I could earn money to buy new ones. I've had a motorcycle of one kind or another ever since.

I'm confident that some of this inclination toward machines, danger, and adventure is inherited. My mother has always been curious and willing to swim against the tide to try new things—and she encouraged that quality in all of us kids.

After watching me ride motorcycles for years—my hair flying in the wind and a crazy grin on my face—I think Mama just had to find out what was so exciting about it. Even though she constantly warned me to be careful, she knew there was something particularly thrilling about roaring down the road with the wind in your face. Finally, her curiosity got the best of her, and she asked our old family friend, Johnny Frist, if she could ride his Harley-Davidson motorcycle.

He laughed at her and said, "Women don't ride Harleys!"

"I'm serious about this. Let me try," she said. She had wanted to try it ever since her father had ridden a Harley-Davidson motorcycle in China fifty years earlier.

Somehow Mama talked Johnny into it. They set the date for her first ride.

Johnny pulled into Little Piney Cove one afternoon. The sound of that big V-twin Harley engine roaring up the valley was sweet music to my ears. Since Mama didn't want anyone to recognize her, she disguised herself in black jeans, dark sunglasses, and a scarf tied tightly around her long brown hair. She hopped on behind Johnny, and they roared off to a deserted section of a two-lane road near Black Mountain. Johnny showed her a spot where she could make a trial run, turn around, and come back.

Johnny explained how the gas and brake on the Harley worked. Then he cranked up the engine, and Mama climbed back on by herself. Johnny pointed her in the right direction, gave her a push, and away she went.

When Mama got near the turnaround, she slowed down just the way Johnny had told her. She put her foot down on the pavement while cornering to steady the motorcycle, but she wasn't prepared for its weight. She leaned too far, and right in the middle of the road, she fell off and the bike toppled to the ground beside her.

Just as it happened, a big eighteen-wheel tractor trailer pulled up. The driver slammed on the air breaks, hopped out, and ran over to Mama. "Can I help you, lady?" he asked.

With a laugh, Mama scrambled up, brushed herself off, and said, "If you could turn this motorcycle around and crank it up, that would be just fine. I've got a friend at the other end." She pointed down the road. "He'll stop me when I get there."

The driver, who was a hulk of a man with tattoos and muscles bulging out of a sweaty T-shirt, just shook his head and gave a grunt as he lifted the bike. He kicked the starter and held the bike upright while Mama climbed back in the saddle. She gave him a big smile, thanked him, and roared back down the road.

She made it safely back to Johnny.

She continued to try to ride the motorcycle, but for all her desire, Mama just didn't seem to have the coordination and strength to maneuver a big "hog" bike like that.

Later she arranged with a local Montreat College student who attended her college Sunday school class, Jim Ernest, to let her ride his Honda. The Honda was smaller and lighter than a Harley and easier to handle.

One day she took off on Jim's black motorcycle headed for Camp Rockmont, where she could practice without interfering with traffic. Following close behind her was Bruce Douglas, another motorcycling friend, hollering out instructions. Mama was getting pretty good; however, just as she got to the lake at Rockmont, Mama twisted the gas throttle instead of breaking. She and the bike roared right into the pond.

Mama wasn't hurt, just wet. Jim got a wrecker to pull the Honda out of the water, and Mama apologized profusely for the damage. "Whatever I've messed up, Jim, I'll pay for," she said.

"I'll find out what it's going to cost and call you," he said.

That night Jim called Mama.

"Mrs. Graham," he asked, "do you plan to keep riding my motorcycle?"

"Why do you ask, Jim?" she said.

"Well, I thought I'd wait until after you're through with it before getting the bike fixed up."

Mama laughed as she hung up the phone. I don't think she ever rode Jim's motorcycle again. And she never got a bill.

When Daddy was sure I was serious about working for a summer in Alaska, he called his friend, Wally Hickel, who at the time was Secretary of the Interior under President Nixon. Daddy mentioned my interest in a job and asked if he knew of any summer job openings.

Alaska was much in the news because of the proposed pipeline. There was a lot of excitement, and thousands of people were applying for jobs. It sounded like a blast, and since I would turn eighteen in July, I figured what better place to spend the summer than the Alaskan wilderness. Within a few weeks, Secretary Hickel put Daddy in touch with one of the construction companies in Anchorage that was hiring men for the summer, and I finally got something lined up.

Not only did I have the promise of a job, so did my buddy from Stony Brook days, Jim Oliver. As we were making plans he suggested that we start the trip by stopping through Long Island for the graduation exercises at Stony Brook to say good-bye to some of his friends who were graduating. That was hardly the way I wanted to begin my summer vacation, but I could tell Jim really wanted to go. It sounded like more fun when I realized I could tell all my former classmates, who were juniors, that I was heading to college that fall instead of being a senior in high school like them.

I said good-bye to everyone in Montreat and met up with Jim. When we arrived at Stony Brook, the guys were dumbfounded that I was headed to LeTourneau College that fall. They kept asking, "How in the world did you pull this off?"

I just grinned and wondered why they didn't just assume it was my fantastic grade-point average!

After twenty-four hours on Long Island—plenty enough time for me—Jim and I flew out. When we arrived in Anchorage, some bad news was waiting. Our jobs had evaporated. Protests from environmentalists and a court case had caused a temporary halt in construction of the pipeline.

I wasn't too worried. I figured there had to be more than one summer job in Alaska, and I was right—the company we had planned to work for had other opportunities, but Jim and I would have to split up. They sent me to Nome to help build low-income housing, and Jim stayed in Anchorage to wash company helicopters. Disgruntled, he went home after a few weeks.

I flew with the company owner's son, who was about my age, and a few other guys, on an Alaskan Airlines 737, which landed on Nome's gravel runway. I didn't know you could land a jet on a gravel runway—that was something I had never seen before. The project foreman met us at the shack they called the terminal. We rode in the back of his green Chevy pickup truck about two miles to a boarding house, which was just the basement of an empty building. Each of us was given a tiny cubicle framed out of plywood. Inside were a bunk and a chair, about all there was room for.

I had never seen such barren landscape. Nome was an old mining town that looked like it was frozen in a time warp. It resembled a Hollywood movie set. There were no paved streets, and the small town was surrounded by thousands of square miles of treeless tundra. It was not a glamorous spot, and the few warm weeks of the summer were nearly spoiled by a horde of large, vicious mosquitoes.

We worked hard, usually twelve hours a day, six days a week, rain or shine.

Because Nome was so close to the Arctic, the summer sun shone about twenty-three hours a day. Each morning we woke at five o'clock, ate breakfast at five-thirty, and were on the job by six o'clock.

This rigid routine was fun because I had chosen to be there. When you're doing construction, every day is different from the day before. While building things, you can see progress being made. Besides, I was getting paid for it. Since I wasn't old enough to join the union, I was the lowest-paid man on the crew. Still, I got three meals a day, a bed to sleep in, and almost a hundred bucks a day by working twelve-hour shifts—plus overtime.

I'd never had so much money and freedom in my life. I even managed to save a few bucks because there was little to spend my money on—except in the bars. That's where we headed as soon as we got off work each day. It became part of the cycle. We would stay in the bars playing cards and listening to the jukebox until eleven or twelve o'clock. Then we would stumble home, with the sun still shining.

The next morning, we roused ourselves at 5 A.M.—sun shining—and started all over again.

The routine was invigorating for a few weeks, but then the boredom and loneliness set in. The other men seemed to experience the same thing. Maybe it had something to do with the vast wilderness that surrounded us.

Letters from home were a welcome sight. My parents wrote regularly, and I really appreciated notes from my grandparents. I would have been wise to follow my grandmother's advice, but I wasn't much into wisdom at the time. Mother Graham, as she liked to be called, was seventy-eight years old, but she still had her sense of humor and burning love for the Lord. She wrote:

> *Just wanted to say "greetings," with much love to you "away up" in Alaska. And by the way, when you come home in August I may want to borrow a little money, as I understand that you have a terrific job—money-wise . . .*
>
> *Franklin—I am writing you just as I often wrote John Graham, as I wrote your dad, Aunt Catherine, and Aunt Jean while they were away in college—should there ever be a time of discontent, or a bit of homesickness, just fall to your knees and thank the Lord for your blessings; for parents who love the Lord; for a good upbringing in a Christian home; plus all we have been privileged to have in Christ Jesus—how could we ask for more?*
>
> *This is not intended as a sermon to you, my dear Franklin, but with a heart full to overflowing with real love for you and all your interests. It is so wonderful to me—to have One who never leaves or forsakes me, but who is by my side day by day, so of course my one longing and desire is that each of my children and grandchildren may know and love the Lord, even as I have.*

Instead of dwelling on those tender words, at night I would sit around with the guys and listen to them talk about their girlfriends or wives. There was a lot of crying in the beer. Up to this point I hadn't been that serious about a girl, but listening to the other guys describe their sweethearts, I began to pine some myself. After a week or so of this, I became kind of lovesick and even began to contemplate marriage.

Back home I had casually dated a girl. She was a free spirit like me. About the time we met, she had had some kind of religious experience and joined the church. But she was still definitely uninhibited. She said what she thought and felt and hardly ever turned down a dare. Like me, she loved the outdoors. She was just a lot of fun to be with, and I was attracted to her. But when I had left for Alaska, she had simply been a friend and someone I enjoyed dating.

Now, listening to all of my working buddies longing for their women, I began to imagine that I missed her terribly—and the feeling always intensified after two or three beers. I finally got the bright idea of proposing to her. I wrote a long letter telling her how much I loved her and missed her. Then I asked her to marry me.

She shot a letter right back: "Yes!"

This was big news, so I wasted no time alerting my parents—who were spending the summer in Europe working on a book—to my wedding plans. I didn't find out until much later, but shortly after my letter arrived, Mama decided it was time for her to return home, and she headed immediately for North Carolina.

I stayed in Alaska for a few more weeks until I couldn't stand it any longer. I had to see my wife-to-be. I turned in my notice, said my good-byes, and flew home.

A buddy of mine, Robert Jones, picked me up at the Asheville airport. On the drive home, I thought I saw Mama's car right in front of us. Sure enough, there she was! *What's she doing here?* I wondered. She was supposed to be in Europe.

I hadn't shaved for two months, my hair had grown down to my shoulders, and I looked like I had just crawled out from under a bush.

We beat Mama back to Little Piney Cove, and I was standing in the drive waiting when she pulled in. I ran to the car to meet her and give her a big hug. "Mama, I thought you weren't coming back for another month."

"Oh, just wanted to check on things here at home," she said nonchalantly.

Sure, I thought. *You would make some kind of great poker player.* She never let on what she was really thinking, but I guessed my letter about getting married had worried her and Daddy to death. She knew how young and immature I was, and I'm sure she just didn't want me to marry the wrong person. She never said a word against the girl I thought I wanted to marry or the wedding. In fact, she said very little. But her silence always got my attention.

After I had been home a few weeks and my girlfriend and I had time to think about getting married, we both agreed it wouldn't work and decided to stop dating. Maybe Mama's prayers had something to do with that. Mama seemed relieved, and to be honest, so was I.

The love bug had ended my Alaska adventure as well as Mama's and Daddy's summer in Europe. I thought I was through with romance for awhile. Not so—I was in for a surprise.

I was driving my mother's Jeep as usual—too fast—with Robert Jones one afternoon near the horse stables in Montreat. We came flying sideways around a curve and almost ran over a girl riding a horse beside the road. The horse reared, but the girl didn't fall off and kept the animal under control. I was impressed, and when I got a closer look, I realized the rider was Jane Austin Cunningham.

I had known Jane Austin since I was eight years old. She'd earned my admiration then because she was a fantastic minibike rider. In fact, I'd come to think she was a very *cute,* fantastic minibike rider.

I would think about Jane Austin from time to time but never imagined I could get a date with her. She was a little older than I was and always seemed to go out with older guys.

I turned the engine off to keep from scaring the horse further and apologized to Jane Austin.

After exchanging a few friendly words, I got back in the Jeep and took off. I was distracted, though. In the back of my mind I kept thinking, *Man, does she look good.* I had taken a careful inventory of her pretty hazel eyes and tanned complexion.

A few days later, another friend, Ronnie Currie, and I were cruising Montreat's main street. A heavy thunderstorm suddenly hit the mountain, and through the fast-moving wipers, we saw a girl walking in the rain alone down the street.

"Hey! That's Jane Austin!" Ronnie hollered. He pulled over and stopped right in front of her. "Hey, Jane Austin. Looks like you're getting wet. Do you want a ride?" he said.

"Sure do!"

I swung the door open and she slid in beside me.

She was drenched and laughing. We made small talk about the weather and other things that didn't matter. But only one thought was ricocheting through my head: *Do I dare ask her where her boyfriend is?* I thought I'd heard they were engaged. Finally I blurted out the question.

"Oh, we broke up a while back," she said. "We're not dating anymore."

I couldn't contain a smile. *Now ain't that interesting?* I thought. *Could this be the opportunity of a lifetime?*

"Hey, Jane Austin," I said, "a bunch of us are going over to Robert Jones' place tonight for pizza—you want to go?" I figured the invitation was general enough that if she turned me down, I wouldn't feel completely rejected.

"Sure," she said. My heart began to beat a little quicker.

And that's how it all started with Jane Austin and me. The relationship was very casual at first, but we spent a lot of time together before we both started school that fall. Jane Austin was a lot of fun and easy to be around. I could be myself with her.

In September I left for LeTourneau College. I'd been looking forward to living in Texas, a state that had always fascinated me—

probably because of all the stories I had heard from my Texan pastor, Calvin Thielman.

LeTourneau College did not exactly have that Ivy League look. The "campus" was outside of town and housed in stark, white-framed buildings that once had been a Veteran's hospital, so it looked like a military compound.

The school was named after R. G. LeTourneau, a prominent Christian businessman, who had been an early supporter of my father's crusade ministry. Mr. LeTourneau was quite a visionary. He was one of the first businessmen in America to have a corporate airplane. After World War II he had purchased a B-24 bomber and retrofitted the interior for passengers. After working during the week at his heavy equipment factory, R. G. would fly on weekends to various places throughout the United States to preach and attend missions conferences.

R. G. had a tremendous desire to spread the gospel world-wide, and he realized early on that the airplane could be a strategic tool for missionaries. So he had started a technical school where aviation would be a major course of study. R. G. wanted to prepare pilots and engineers for missionary service.

LeTourneau College was also designed to provide other tradesmen, such as welders and machinists, for R. G.'s factories, which were nearby. While I attended the school, some of those factories were manufacturing bomb casings for use in the Vietnam War.

No, this wasn't Harvard or Yale, but I didn't want to go to a school like that anyway. One of the most exciting things to me about LeTourneau was the aviation program. I really wanted to learn how to fly.

A few years before, our family had vacationed in southern California at a place called Pauma Valley, just outside of Escondido. Here we got to know the Lyles family. Mr. Lyles had a V-tailed Bonanza airplane, which he used to commute to his ranches. He often took his son, Warren Jr., and me with him. While Mr. Lyles worked, Warren and I took our rifles and shot coyotes, jackrabbits, and anything else that moved.

But the highlight was always climbing aboard that little airplane. I was fascinated by the many switches, dials, levers, and other gadgets. I had found another machine that had all the right qualities: speed, noise, and smoke! From those days on the Lyles' ranch, I knew I wanted to fly. So when I got to LeTourneau, the first thing I did was sign up for aviation courses.

About the first person I met in Longview was my assigned roommate, Bill Cristobal, a solid guy with an infectious smile and laid-back personality. He was older than I, in his mid-twenties, and had just finished three combat tours in the Army as a helicopter pilot in Vietnam. It's funny what you remember about a guy, but I particularly recall that all his underwear were a drab, Army olive green. I'd never seen boxer shorts like that before, and I teased him about them a lot. He didn't care.

Nothing ever seemed to bother Bill. The Vietnam War had matured and toughened him, and I don't recall ever seeing him unnerved. Most of the time he had a toothpick in the corner of his mouth. When things got tense, he sucked harder on the toothpick and just smiled. Inwardly, he may have been a nervous wreck, but you never would have known it by looking at him. He was as cool as the proverbial cucumber.

Bill was focused; I wasn't. He knew where he wanted to go in life; I didn't. Most important, Bill had a strong relationship with Jesus Christ, and though I didn't, I admired Bill for that. We shared many common interests—the love of the outdoors, hunting, flying, and camping—which we did almost every weekend.

Bill had his own airplane, a real clunker that was an ongoing project. Something was always breaking down. It was a two-seater 1938 Aeronca Chief with a sixty-five-horsepower engine. The plane had fabric wings, no radio, and minimum instruments. But it was a plane and it flew—sort of. On many occasions, we would go flying and Bill would let me take the controls. To me it was as good as a Lear jet.

Bill and I spent many nights camping in East Texas. Often we'd throw camping equipment into Bill's plane, land at some remote airstrip, and camp under the wing of the airplane. What a life! I had probably never been happier.

Sitting by the fire, with a gleam in his eye, Bill would tell me stories of the battles he'd flown through in Vietnam. I sensed that in some respects he missed Army life and his combat buddies. I could tell he loved the art of flying.

"What are you doing here?" I once asked him. "Why didn't you stay in the Army?"

"I want to be a missionary pilot," Bill said. He explained that in order to become a missionary pilot, he had to qualify as a mechanic. LeTourneau College offered excellent courses to prepare for the Airframe and Powerplant Mechanics' rating.

The thing that probably impressed me the most about Bill was that even though he was an avid, born-again Christian who lived the kind of life that reflected his beliefs and convictions, he wasn't stuffy or uptight, and he really knew how to have fun. He was willing to get into any kind of mischief as long as it came under the label of "clean fun."

Bill was one of the big reasons I was happy at LeTourneau, but also for the first time, I was enjoying most of my classes. Finally, I was taking courses that contained information that I felt I could use later in life.

I dated a few girls at LeTourneau, but I couldn't get Jane Austin off my mind. She had enrolled at Stratford College in Danville, Virginia, and wrote often. We talked occasionally on the phone, and she became the standard by which I measured all others.

By February of 1971, I had my pilot's license. A few days later, I rented a Cessna 182 Skylane and flew cross-country to North Carolina. I was anxious to show my piloting skills to my parents and friends, but most of all, to Jane Austin.

Taking everyone on a sightseeing tour around the Smoky Mountains seemed like a great idea, so off I flew with Jane Austin, Robert Jones, and a friend from LeTourneau, Lee Dorn. After an hour or so, we decided to stop for a Coke in Sevierville, Tennessee. I wasn't as familiar with the plane as I should have been. As I approached for landing, I was too high and too fast. When I flared, instead of the plane settling down on the runway, it floated, and floated, and floated. I was over halfway down the runway and the plane still hadn't settled on its landing gear. I was simply going too fast.

I thought about applying power to the engine and going up and around for another try, but because of inexperience I waited too long. About two-thirds of the way down the runway, I finally touched down. The end of the runway was approaching quickly. I panicked. I stepped on the brakes as hard as I could, which locked the wheels. The plane started to skid. Within seconds, both main tires blew out.

I could see what looked like a grassy field at the end of the runway. *Whew, no problem!* I thought. I would roll out onto the field, stop, turn around, and taxi back. The plane was still bumping along at a pretty good clip when we left the end of the runway. To my surprise I saw a twenty-foot drop-off—before the start of the field. Now it was too late: The go-around was no longer an option. I could only chop the power and hope for the best.

We sailed over the drop-off, but then crashed in the middle of the field. The front nose wheel collapsed, the prop bent as it ripped into the ground, the left wing ended up with a huge dent, and my ego was totally crushed.

My immediate concern was the safety of the others. No one said a word. They just stared in total disbelief, but everyone was okay.

We had to find a ride back home, and then I had to take a commercial flight back to Texas. It would take weeks to repair the plane. The owner, Barney Barnwell, a former employee of Mr. LeTourneau's who flew the B-24 bomber for him, sent a pilot later to get the plane back to Texas. I was totally humiliated. Within hours after my return, the word had spread across the campus about what had happened.

When Bill heard, he didn't say much. He just sucked on his toothpick and grinned.

For about a month, I didn't eat any meals on campus to avoid facing ridicule from other students. Most of the time I went straight from classes to my room.

I wasn't sure I would ever fly again. The experience had not only embarrassed me, but it had shattered my confidence in my piloting abilities.

However, my good friend Bill gently coaxed and encouraged me, and soon I was back in the air again—no doubt a more careful pilot than I had been before.

A few months later, my parents invited me to spend a weekend with them in Vero Beach, Florida, where they were vacationing.

I told them I'd come, but I'm sure they were not thrilled to hear I was renting a turbo-powered Cherokee Comanche to make the trip. The memory of my last trip back east was quite fresh in their minds. More to reassure Mama and Daddy than anything, I took along Calvin Booth, my flight instructor, his wife Dorothy, and Lee Dorn.

Friday afternoon we flew from Longview's Gregg County Airport and navigated across Louisiana and the southern portions of Mississippi and Alabama to Florida's panhandle, then across the state to Vero Beach. Mama and Daddy were waiting for us when we landed. The flight was smooth, and I landed the plane perfectly.

Sunday, after church, we headed back to Longview so we could be there for classes the next day. The weather wasn't good, so we skirted the Gulf of Mexico and landed at Mobile, Alabama, to refuel at dusk. We called Flight Service for a weather update. They told us the conditions between Mobile and Longview were "deteriorating rapidly." A spring squall line of thunderstorms had developed. The weather briefer advised, "If you go north toward Jackson, Mississippi, and cut to the west, you should get around the northern edge of the thunderstorms and bad weather." Every pilot knows you never mess with a thunderstorm.

I thanked them for the information, and we took off from Mobile a few minutes after 7 P.M. Once airborne, we headed for Jackson.

Only minutes after we'd taken off, the lights on the instrument panel flickered then dimmed. I turned the rheostat up to make them brighter. As we climbed through the clouds, I noticed the instrument lights growing dimmer. Again I cranked up the rheostat. This happened once or twice more. About an hour into the flight, the light became so dim on the instrument panel that I could scarcely read the dials. Just then the flags on the navigational instruments flipped to the off position. These flags warn the pilot that the instruments cannot be used for navigating.

Suddenly I had no navigational instruments and the radio was dead. I knew something was wrong, but I didn't know what.

Because of the storms, Calvin had been occupied reading the charts. He hadn't noticed the problem. "I've just lost my navigation instruments," I said to him. "The lights have been getting dimmer, and now they're off."

He started checking, and about that time the cabin lights went out. We were in total darkness.

Calvin and I grabbed our flashlights. He kept his trained on the charts, and I aimed mine at the instrument panel. I figured that we might have forty-five minutes or maybe an hour before the flashlights gave out from continuous use. We had to do something soon.

I wasn't particularly scared. I knew Calvin could take over the controls if things got dicey. His presence made me feel secure.

Calvin read the emergency checklist. We checked, double-checked, and reset the circuit breakers. Nothing happened.

We were definitely in trouble. I knew it; Calvin knew it. Calvin was scared—he told me later—but he outwardly didn't show his fear. Instead he grinned. "Looks like we'll have to figure out what to do, or we'll be in big trouble. Right?" he said calmly.

The last time we talked to the controller who had vectored us by radar around the squall line, we had been forty miles south of Jackson and flying at about eleven or twelve thousand feet. All pilots are taught that in an emergency, you are to fly a triangular pattern. By doing this, radar controllers can see you on their screens and know that you are lost or in trouble. We flew one pattern.

"This is nuts," Calvin said in a calm voice. "Even if they see us on the radar, what are they going to do? Send somebody up for us?"

"What do we do now?" I asked. I still wasn't overly worried because I had Calvin with me.

"We need to go down," he said.

I knew the elevation of the Jackson area meant it would be safe for us to descend to around fifteen hundred feet at Measured Sea Level (MSL). Down, down, down we went in the dark through heavy clouds. Finally, we broke out between layers and could see a light glow through the thin layer of clouds below us. Calvin pointed. "That's got to be a city underneath. It's probably Jackson."

Calvin pulled out the chart to see where the airport was located. I decided to descend over the city lights. We weren't sure what the cloud base was. This was important. If the clouds were very low to the ground, we would run out of altitude and crash. We needed about fifteen hundred feet.

With everything inside and outside of the plane so black, the glow from the city beneath renewed our hope and eased our fears. Lee and Dorothy were praying in the back seat. I'm sure by now Lee was wondering why he had been so stupid to fly in another airplane with me at the controls.

I gripped the flashlight in my teeth as we started a slow descent. We broke out of the clouds at two thousand feet MSL. At least now we could see the city lights clearly. Calvin pointed to what he thought was the airport.

Following the proper procedure, we entered five hundred feet above the airport traffic pattern. The Federal Aviation Administration (FAA) uses light signals from the tower to communicate with an airplane that has lost its radio. We circled for about three minutes, waiting for someone to see us and give us the proper light signal. To me it seemed like an hour.

"Look!" I pointed. "A green light."

The beam came from the tower, which indicated that we could go ahead and land.

"The tower has seen us!" I yelled to the others. "We've been cleared to land!"

Lee and Dorothy, who had been praying feverishly, cheered.

We had one slight problem. Without electrical power, how would we lower the landing gear? Calvin got out the emergency checklist and said, "There should be a handle between the seats under the floorboard. See if you can find it."

I unbuckled, and using my dimming flashlight, lifted the floorboard. Sure enough, there it was—a handle! I pulled and pumped it several times to get the gear locked into position.

Calvin took over the controls for the landing. As we made the final approach, all the runway lights came on high. Obviously, the FAA authorities wanted us to see the runway. It was a wonderful sight!

Calvin made a precise, smooth landing. But before we could finish our ground roll and exit the runway, oddly, all the runway lights went out.

"That's a little strange," Calvin said. "They could at least have waited until we got off the runway before they shut off their lights." I was so relieved to be down that I didn't mind.

When we taxied to the end of the ramp, nobody came out to meet us, pat us on the back, and tell us what a good job we had just done.

By the time we had climbed out of the Comanche, a man appeared. He scowled at me and then yelled, "Did you just land?"

"Yes," I said, "we sure did." I started to tell him our problem, but he cut me off.

"Who authorized you to land?"

"We got a green light from the tower."

"You got a green light?"

I nodded my head.

Calvin started to explain what had happened, and again the man interrupted us, "Could you come in here, please?" He ushered us into the building and we spoke with two other officials.

We went through the whole scenario as they listened intently.

"And you got a green light?" the man asked again.

"Definitely," I said. So did the other three with me.

"Something wrong?" Calvin asked.

He shook his head.

Not much else was said, but it was obvious they had not expected us. All three of them acted a bit strange and never did clarify what had happened with the green light or the lighting of the runway.

We spent the night at a nearby hotel. The next day a mechanic found a wire burned out in the alternator. He made the repair, and we left by mid-afternoon.

What really happened that night? It would be years before I finally found out. Someone saw an article in a newspaper and sent it to my mother.

Baptist Record—Thursday, April 15, 1971
Jackson, Mississippi

Under His Wings
By Wilbur M. Irwin, Pastor
Forest Hill, Jackson

There was nothing unusual about Sunday afternoon, March 21, when a small single-engine plane took off from a Florida airport with [four] people aboard. It was just a routine flight from Florida to Texas by way of Jackson, Mississippi. The sun eased out of sight behind the distant horizon and the light of day turned into a shadowless night. The darkness of night received help from a cloud coverage to make visibility almost impossible. The small plane continued its flight pattern according to its navigated course.

The control tower at Thompson Airport was carrying out its routine duty, that of directing air traffic. Sydney McCall was on duty and had picked up the pilot of the Texas-bound plane on radar and radio. He gave instructions, and the plane continued above Jackson and on toward Vicksburg and the Louisiana state line. Sydney was satisfied with conditions and instructed the pilot to contact the Memphis Center for further directions.

In the meantime, Gary Cornett, minister of music at Forest Hill Baptist Church, and his wife, Pat, had arrived at the airport at Sydney's invitation to see the various operations. They were allowed to go up into the tower, and Sydney began demonstrating the various equipment. He had received a call from Memphis concerning the small plane but assumed that they had made contact with each other and passed on to other matters. Sydney demonstrated a light-gun which has tri-colored lights. He turned on the red light and a white light while the gun remained inside the tower, but for an unexplained reason he held the gun out the window when he demonstrated the green light and said, "If I were going to give a pilot clearance to land, I would point this light directly at him and turn the green light on." A fellow worker asked Sydney if he would demonstrate the run-way lights. Sydney started to turn them on, and gradually they got brighter and brighter until they reached the state of high-intensity. The latter degree of lighting is for emergency, and the lights are designed to pierce fog and clouds to give pilots in emergency situations a view of the runways.

Sydney had scarcely completed these demonstrations when his coworker said in excitement, "There is an unlighted plane coming in." Sydney responded, "There isn't a plane within fifty miles of us in the air." Upon closer examination it was quickly learned that an unlighted single-engine plane was coming in for a landing.

When the plane had landed the security officers brought the pilot into the control tower for an explanation. According to the pilot, the small plane's generator had quit working soon after Sydney McCall turned the flight instructions over to the Memphis Center. It had not been possible for radio contact to be made with Memphis or anyone else. In fact, the radio and lights and everything else about the plane's electrical system was helpless. In that distressing moment the pilot remembered that he had just passed Jackson so he dropped below the cloud coverage and using the lights of Jackson for direction, returned to the city in hopes of getting help.

He located Hawkins field but could not receive clearance for landing. Remembering the location of Thompson field, he made his way in that direction. It was at this point that precise timing came into prominence. When Sydney demonstrated the green light from the control tower, a pilot would have to be directly in front to see it. The pilot of the troubled plane saw the green light. Furthermore, after receiving the light signal to land, it would have been very dangerous to attempt a landing without lights. Within moments after the green light signal was given the runway lights were turned on. The landing was completed without harm to the aircraft or passengers.

In one sense Sydney McCall was demonstrating the lighting and signal system to Gary Cornett, but the pilot of that plane is positive that God's providential hand was in it all. Calvin Booth, one of the pilots, commented, "God's hand was in it. You see, we just left Billy Graham there in Florida, and he prayed for our safety before we departed."

It is a wonderful feeling to realize the power and grace of being "under His sheltering wings."[1]

Calvin never did tell them that I was Billy Graham's son and the pilot of that plane.

Whiskey, Women, and Four-Wheeling

G rowing up, my concept of a missionary was an older person with gray hair. Montreat had a small community of retired missionaries from different parts of the world who ate Chinese food with chopsticks and had garlic breath. I was not really exposed to the younger generation of missionaries. I didn't know they existed.

My grandfather had been a missionary doctor in China, where, of course, my mother had grown up. Mama had almost not married Daddy because she wanted so much to be a missionary herself to the people of Tibet.

My problem was that I had never seen missionaries in their natural element—on the field. Most of the missionaries I met were those who showed up in Montreat for a visit with my parents; however, some of my grandfather's retired friends were pretty cool, like "Uncle" Ed Currie and Ken Gieser.

In the summer of 1971—I had no clue what was about to happen—God gave me a whole new perspective on missionaries.

I had survived my first year at LeTourneau without any more plane crashes or near-death experiences. It was time to head out for my summer job. It looked like another adventure, right up my alley.

Roy Gustafson, an associate with the Billy Graham Evangelistic Association (BGEA), led tours to the Middle East. Roy was a tremendous Bible teacher whom my father had asked to teach the Bible in the land of the Bible. To do this, Roy led tours to Israel and the surrounding countries. Roy had helped me get a job with the travel agency that arranged the trips.

My job was to handle all of the logistics, making sure the luggage was transferred into and out of the hotels and onto the buses. I paid porters and took care of a multitude of other details. I wasn't by myself. David Schultz, a Wheaton College student, had done this before, and we worked together. He showed me the ropes.

We did four such tours that summer, back-to-back. Some started in Egypt, went to Athens, and then on to Israel. On others we went only to Israel and Jordan.

My first trip was a real eye-opener. I had no idea all that was involved in international travel, but I was a quick study. I hadn't turned nineteen, yet I carried a couple of thousand dollars in petty cash and was responsible for over a hundred people at a time.

Roy, even though he was thirty-seven years older, soon became one of my best friends. During the tours, Roy and I became so close that sometimes it seemed I was the son he'd never had.

I could talk to Roy about anything—and did. He was colorful, to say the least. He had a quick wit and was constantly joking and seldom took himself seriously. Just as my roommate Bill had at LeTourneau, Roy's easygoing manner made a strong impression on me that people could have fun living the Christian life.

Roy had the incredible ability to bring some of the most difficult passages of Scripture alive. The highlight for everyone on the tour was to gather each night for a Bible study when Roy would intriguingly set the stage for what we would see the next day. I found myself clinging to each word. The Bible was becoming a more interesting book to me.

Besides his deep love for God's Word, Roy had a great burden for missions, especially in the Middle East. He didn't want his tours to the Holy Land to just be little vacations. He wanted to expose the tourists to what God was doing in the lives of the people in the Middle East today.

One ministry that was special to Roy was the Annoor Sanatorium for Chest Disease in Mafraq, Jordan. This little hospital had been started by Dr. Eleanor Soltau, the daughter of American missionaries in Korea, and Aileen Coleman, a nurse from Australia. Eleanor had gone to the same high school in North Korea one year ahead of my mother when they were young girls, so I was eager to meet her and learn what her work was all about.

Roy had told me that the hospital was situated at a very strategic location. People from many lands and different walks of life passed by this little out-of-the-way place known as "the crossroads." At this point, the road from Damascus to Amman crossed with the road from Jerusalem to Baghdad. Of all the tour stops, the visit to Mafraq always seemed to be a highlight for everyone.

What was so intriguing about the work of the hospital was that it specialized in the treatment of tuberculosis (TB) among the nomadic tribal people, known as the Bedouin. They refer to themselves as the "true Arabs," living in tents in the desert much like Abraham did in Bible days.

Because of the harsh conditions of the desert, approximately forty thousand in Jordan were afflicted with TB in the 1970s, with less than a hundred hospital beds in the whole country to treat them.

The Annoor Hospital stood out not only for its unique medical care, but also because it was run by two women. The Middle East is a man's world, especially in the Arab countries. Women do not have basic human rights and are often treated as a man's property. Yet there, in the midst of such a male-dominated world, two women, both six-feet tall, were God's ambassadors to the world of Islam.

I was impressed. These two didn't match my old stereotype of missionaries. They were gutsy and tough as nails, much like my grandparents. Yet they were warm, gracious, and every inch Christian ladies.

I heard the women talk about how they needed to expand their work so that they could care for more Bedouin people. Incidentally, they were in the process of building a new hospital when I first met them.

The more I heard these two dedicated women share their stories with the tour groups, the more I felt the urge to help them in some way.

I began to think about how much fun it would be to drop out of school for a while and help them build that new hospital. But I doubted my parents would ever go for it.

I was impressed that in spite of overwhelming needs, the women didn't beg. In fact, it was like pulling teeth to get them to tell you their needs. One, however, was obvious. The hospital had only one beat-up car because, a couple of years earlier, the PLO guerrilla soldiers had stolen and later destroyed two of the hospital's vehicles during a bloody uprising against Jordan's King Hussein.

This need for a better vehicle sparked an idea in my brain. Maybe I could convince my folks that I was needed in Jordan for some missionary work after all.

When I got back home, I said to Daddy, "I've been praying about the mission field." Of course this was a bunch of hogwash—I didn't pray much, and certainly never about becoming a missionary. But this really got Daddy's attention.

I told him about Eleanor and Aileen and how they were struggling to build a new hospital—and how they really needed a new vehicle, a Land Rover fully equipped for the desert.

"If the BGEA [Billy Graham Evangelistic Association] would buy this for them," I said to my father, "I would sacrifice my education for several months to pick it up in England and personally deliver it to them. To make the time worthwhile, I could stay on to help them with the construction of the hospital."

My father was more than a little skeptical and had a puzzled look on his face. I had never laid a whopper on him quite like this before, but he smiled and said, "Let me talk to your mother, and we'll pray about it." I was stunned!

My deception didn't trouble me much. *After all,* I told myself, *I'm only doing this to help those two missionaries in Jordan.*

A few days later Daddy and I talked again. "You can go, Franklin. The association will pay for a Land Rover and the gas for you to drive it to Jordan. But you'll have to come up with your own spending money."

"That's fine, sir," I said, trying to hide the thrill of knowing I had pulled the wool over Daddy's eyes. I walked away in amazement. It wasn't long, though, before reality set in: How in the world would I ever get enough money to pay my way across Europe and the Middle East? I didn't know if Daddy was testing my sincerity or what, but I knew I couldn't go off on this expedition if I didn't come up with some cash. I wrestled with whether the trip was really important to me after all.

One option would be to sell my brand-new Triumph TR-6. That sports car meant everything to me. Fred Dienert, a close associate of my parents, had helped me buy it.

Fred had known that I smoked, and he hadn't liked it much. So he had offered me a deal I couldn't pass up: "I will personally give you a thousand dollars," he told me, "if you will quit smoking."

The money made his challenge quite appealing. I put down the cigarettes and picked up the TR-6. I fully intended to live up to my promise. And I did stop smoking—for one whole week. But when the fun began to wear off with my new wheels, temptation came knocking, and I gave in.

As I lit up and propped my foot on the fender, deep down inside I knew I was not only breaking a promise, but I knew "Uncle" Fred would ultimately find out and there would be a day of reckoning.

As the last few smokes smoldered on the ground, I couldn't stomp out the thought, *My car or the missionaries?*

As I weighed the pros and cons—driving a Land Rover across a foreign continent and working in the Middle East versus school—well, it was an adventure I just couldn't pass up. I finally traded my car for the ride of my life.

The Triumph sold quickly and all the plans were put into motion. The final glitch came when Mama expressed concern about my traveling across Europe and the Middle East alone. I cleverly convinced her that I could persuade Bill Cristobal to go with me.

That seemed to set well with both Mama and Daddy. They knew that Bill was older and more mature. He would know his way around and hopefully keep me out of trouble.

I phoned Bill. He loved adventure, too, so I wasn't surprised when he quickly agreed.

We both notified LeTourneau College of our plans, promising we would be back to start the second semester in January.

Then things began to happen quickly. Daddy contacted the BGEA office in London and spoke to Jean Wilson, the office manager, about our plans. He asked Jean for her assistance in purchasing a Land Rover. As Jean always did, she responded enthusiastically. Daddy told her that Bill and I would be in London in a few days.

She headed for the nearest Land Rover dealership. "I want to buy a Land Rover," she announced with great excitement when the salesman met her at the door, "fully equipped for the desert."

"Madam, one does not buy a Land Rover—one orders a Land Rover and waits. After several months, when it is ready, one is notified and comes to collect it. But one simply cannot walk into a showroom and make such a purchase."

"Really? Oh, I am terribly sorry, I didn't know. However, I do need one by Monday."

"We're sorry, madam, you don't seem to understand—that is quite impossible. If you wish to place an order—I'll be glad to help."

"But we need one now," she insisted. "This is really quite important." She explained everything to him.

The salesman was intrigued by her determination and seemed sincere in wanting to help, but as politely as an Englishman could be, he repeated that there was no way to arrange for an immediate delivery. He did assure her he would look into the alternatives and stay in touch with her.

"Perhaps if you just go and look, you might find a Land Rover lying around somewhere." And once more, just to be sure he understood, she added, "fully equipped for the desert." He walked away dismayed, knowing that if he didn't go look, she would not be satisfied.

Jean isn't sure just how long he was gone; she only recalls the look on his face when he returned.

"Madam," he began with some bewilderment, "I don't under-stand it at all, but we do have a Land Rover in stock—fully equipped for the desert—you may pick it up on Monday if you'd like."

"Of course, we'll take it!" Jean said, never really doubting that she would leave the showroom without having taken care of the business at hand.

Apparently a customer in the Middle East had ordered it months before and even put down a deposit. However, he never came back to take delivery.

Jean met Bill and me at Heathrow Airport in London and took us straight to the Land Rover dealer. Within the hour, I was behind the wheel of a brand-new, two-door, series III-109, four-wheel drive Land Rover. We thanked Jean for her help and headed to Dover, where we could catch the ferry across the English Channel to France.

Driving on the "wrong" side of the narrow, congested roads caused a few close calls, but I got the hang of it quickly. At last the adventure was under way!

Before boarding the ferry, Bill and I stopped for supplies. Our plan was to pack the Rover with enough gear so that we could camp out the entire trip. The proceeds from selling the Triumph had not provided us with enough money for hotels. We bought plywood and foam rubber and built a crude bed in the back of the Rover. After buying some food and other necessities, we were ready to roll.

After crossing the English Channel, we took several days to cruise through France and into Switzerland, where we spent a few days with my sister's family, the Tchividjians. Next we drove leisurely through Austria, Yugoslavia, and Greece.

We encountered few problems until we were told we needed visas for Syria. We had applied for Syrian visas in Athens, but the Syrian embassy refused our requests. We had no choice but to turn to the American embassy in Athens, but much to our dismay, we received little help or encouragement at the embassy.

I called home and told Daddy about our predicament. He phoned Washington and did everything possible to exert pressure, but nothing helped. The Syrians just would not give us permission to drive the vehicle through Syria and into Jordan. As we waited on further word from Daddy, an embassy worker said, "Why don't you take a chance?"

"What do you mean?" I asked with great interest.

"Why not drive through Turkey and show up at the Syrian border and see if you can get in that way?"

The challenge appealed to me, and Bill just shrugged his shoulders. We had both seen enough of Athens and were ready to move on. We gave up waiting on the Syrians and headed out.

Bill and I were amazed by the beauty of Turkey. Some of the mountain ranges reminded me of western North Carolina—but not enough to make me homesick. I was having a ball. At night we would pull off the road and camp beside a small stream. I would drag out my bottle of Scotch, smoke a cigarette, and plug in a cassette tape. Bill would sit enjoying the scenery and listening with me to the country music.

In the morning, I'd start the day with a cigarette, and Bill would reach for his Bible. I got my high on nicotine; he got his high on Christ. Bill never said anything to me about my smoking or drinking. I guess he had seen it all in the Army and was content to just be my friend. I'm sure he prayed, though, that God would bring some changes in my life.

Bill and I had no idea of the danger we were in while traveling through Turkey, a country notorious for roaming bandits who prey on tourists and travelers. We drove through the country like two fools, sleeping outdoors as though we were in Yellowstone National Park.

When we came in sight of the Syrian border, we both were scared, but neither of us showed it. I puffed on a cigarette, and Bill sucked on his limp toothpick.

We stopped at the checkpoint and the officer asked for our "papers." I shook my head and threw up my hands. We both stared at each other for a moment. Then, in somewhat broken English, the man explained that we could buy visas—right there, for a reasonable price!

I was speechless. After all we'd been through in Athens we now were going to get visas and cross the border for just a few dollars?

This was one of my first experiences dealing with bureaucracy in foreign countries. You never can predict what obstacles you will run into, but if you're persistent, there's usually a way to overcome them.

Within minutes Bill and I had the magic pieces of paper and crossed into Syria.

Driving down the Syrian coastline toward Lebanon, I remembered that Roy Gustafson had told me to look up a Lebanese friend of his who worked at the Phoenicia Hotel in Beirut.

That would mean going out of our way, but it was a good excuse to see Beirut, which was known then as the Paris of the Middle East. I liked the thought of the detour; it would give Bill and me a chance to check out the Lebanese beaches and bikinis.

We drove to Beirut and registered at the Phoenicia Hotel, one of the nicest in the city. Bill and I had been camping out for a week since leaving Athens, so a hot shower and a real bed sounded good.

While checking into the hotel I asked the desk clerk about Roy's friend—his name was Sami Dagher.

"I am so sorry, but he is not here. He has gone snorkeling at the Gulf of Aqaba [down on the Jordanian coastline] and won't be back for a few days. Is he a friend of yours?" the man asked.

"Yes, sir, kind of." I only knew of him because of Roy, but it seemed like a good idea to drop his name.

"If you're a friend of Sami's, then I shall give you a discount on your room," the clerk said with a smile.

I thanked him and headed for the bar. Since I had gotten a discount on the room by dropping Sami's name, I climbed up on the bar stool and said to the bartender, "I've been looking for a good friend of mine, Sami Dagher. Have you seen him?"

"He is out of town, but if you're a friend of Sami's," he insisted, "I'll give you a discount." Although I'd never met Sami, I was beginning to think he had to be one of my closest friends! Sami must be some kind of person, I concluded. I hoped I'd meet him someday.

Bill and I stayed several days in Beirut, especially enjoying the nightlife of the brightly lit city. We took long walks, seeing all the sights and hitting the most popular clubs. Bill would go anywhere with me, but he never participated in anything that went against his grain. It didn't bother me that he wouldn't smoke and drink—he was still a lot of fun.

By the time we got our second wind, we were anxious to get back on the road to Jordan. We wondered what would happen when we had to cross into Syria again. Sure enough, we were detained when we arrived. For no apparent reason—and no explanation was offered—we sat for hours waiting for authorization to cross the border.

When we were to the point of exasperation, the officials motioned us to come on through. We looked straight ahead as we passed into Syria. We headed cautiously toward the city of Damascus, then south toward the Jordanian frontier.

The experience was staggering. To the east were the famous Golan Heights, and the Syrian Army was deployed along our route. This was at the height of the Cold War, and Syria was under heavy Russian influence.

It made me a bit nervous, and I kept an eye on the rearview mirror. I kept thinking how bizarre it seemed for a southern boy like me and a former U.S. Army veteran who had been killing Communists two years earlier in the jungles of southeast Asia to be on this side of the fence. To us, the Israelis were the good guys and the country that America supported. But here we found ourselves on the Syrian side, which the Russians and East Germans were backing. We were in enemy territory.

We faced trouble once again when we came to the border between Syria and Jordan. We were told we couldn't cross into Jordan without something they called a *carnet de passage* (a type of international passport for cars). I had never heard of such a document.

"That's fine, but where do I get one of these?" I asked.

"Beirut."

Bill and I looked at each other. Now we began to feel very weary. We had been on the road for six weeks, but we knew what we had to do and didn't waste any time.

Back to Beirut we went. Getting a *carnet de passage* was no ordinary process. Nothing was routine in the Middle East. First, I had to join the Auto Club of Lebanon and then call the BGEA, requesting they transfer $10,000 to the Chase Manhattan Bank to be held as a bond. Once that was in place, the Auto Club issued the *carnet de passage*. This whole process took about a week. With the precious document in hand, Bill and I finally were able to cross into Jordan.

We were determined we wouldn't call it a day until we got ourselves to Mafraq. With only forty miles to go, I pressed the accelerator on the diesel Land Rover a little harder. I didn't think we would have a problem finding the town, but getting to the hospital after dark might be a challenge.

It was late as we entered Mafraq, a dirty town of sun-dried, mud-brick buildings. We stopped at a small shop lit by a single kerosene lamp. It must have been nearly midnight, but I could see the shop owner sitting in the glow of the gas lantern.

"Where is the hospital?" I asked. "How can I find the doctor?" He obviously didn't understand English. I kept repeating "doctor" and making motions of tying bandages and giving injections.

"Ah!" he smiled and nodded. He began talking, but I had no earthly idea what he was saying. He motioned with his arm, indicating we should follow him. He got into his Toyota pickup and started down a dark alley.

"Where do you suppose he's leading us?" I asked Bill.

He didn't respond, just chewed hard on his toothpick.

Finally the pickup stopped, and the merchant put his arm out the window and pointed to a house.

We climbed out of the Rover and cautiously approached the front door. I knocked timidly.

I was prepared for just about anything—what a relief when Aileen opened the door with a squeal of delight. "Oh, we've been expecting you!"

The mission was accomplished. Bill and I had driven thousands of miles through nine countries, including extremely volatile Syria. Now, here we were, sitting in Mafraq, Jordan, way past midnight, enjoying the cool desert breeze and talking to these wonderful women.

I had not the slightest inkling that delivering aid to needy people all over the globe would some day become a passion—a big piece of my lifetime's work.

Mohammed and the Desert Prayers

After fighting through the final obstacles to get the Land Rover into Jordan, Bill and I were exhausted. Aileen noticed how tired we were and insisted we turn in for the night. There was a room we could use at the new hospital construction site. It was located a few miles out of town in the desert. She gave us directions and we said goodnight.

When we arrived at the compound, the gate was locked. The guard had either wandered away or fallen asleep. All Bill and I wanted to do was turn in for the night, so we parked outside the gate, climbed into the back of the Land Rover, and slept until daybreak.

We were still dead to the world when a heavy tapping on the window startled us awake. A man was peering through the window with a very serious look on his face.

He wanted to know what we were doing there. He spoke some English, and after several attempts I was able to communicate that Aileen and Eleanor would be coming for us soon.

When he heard their names, he relaxed and his face lit up. We learned that his name was Victor, and he helped the women with various tasks at the hospital. It was good that we hadn't upset Victor. We found out later that he had been a PLO commando who had been captured during a raid into Israel and imprisoned for a number of years by the Israelis. He was eventually set free through a Red Cross prisoner exchange. After his release he became a Christian and ended up at the hospital helping Eleanor and Aileen.

Bill and I talked to Victor in the early morning sun. As we were getting our clothes on, I noticed that Victor kept eyeballing a pack of Marlboros I had on the front seat. I suspected that he wanted a pack for himself, and when I asked if he wanted a smoke, he smiled and said, "Yes, but not in front of Aileen—she doesn't like tobacco." When I gave him the pack of Marlboros a big grin crossed his face. We became close friends in the days that followed.

Bill and I didn't waste any time getting to work. It didn't take us long to figure out that there was more work than we could do during our planned stay. We mixed concrete, made cement blocks, and even dug ditches. I was thankful for all the handyman skills John Rickman had taught me, and the work in Alaska had given me valuable experience as well. Whatever needed to be done, we found a way.

Mafraq was not a glamorous spot. It was just a collection of mainly mud-brick homes in the middle of a blistering desert that looked amazingly like parts of Arizona. Every afternoon, when the temperature topped out, the wind would come up and tornado-like dust devils would boil through the village, driving sand into your face, choking your lungs, and coating everything in its path. Sand got into everything eventually. You just had to learn to live with it.

Our living conditions were rugged. While most of the guys chose to sleep inside, I claimed the flat roof that covered the workshop. After a hard day's work, I could climb up there by myself to smoke, sip on my Scotch, and listen to "Voice of America" by shortwave radio, which played country music during the night. Unlike Alaska, there were no bars in Mafraq to hang out in after work, so I would go to my roof, sprawl on the sleeping bag, and stare at the stars.

I often thought about the missionaries I was working with. Their dedication impressed me. Lester Gates was one of them. He was a retired farmer from the United States who had come to oversee the construction of the hospital. He had first caught the vision for mission work on one of Roy Gustafson's tours to the Holy Land. While visiting Mafraq, Lester had seen all the repairs and building that needed to be done and knew he had the necessary skills. After Lester's wife died, he was looking for a new purpose in life. Farming was no longer satisfying, and he had a keener spiritual focus. He saw an opportunity to use his skills to serve God there in the desert. He had gone home, packed his personal belongings, and moved lock, stock, and barrel to Jordan.

Lester was full of faith in God. He wanted to be a missionary. The fact that he had no theological training didn't hinder him. He thought he could communicate to the local farmers in his own way. I couldn't believe it when he planted forty acres of barley about a month earlier than everybody else. As he sowed the seed he told me, "I'll need rain within ten days for the seeds to germinate."

"But, Lester, it hasn't rained here for months," I told him. "What do you need to plant barley for anyway?"

Lester explained that if his crop came up earlier and thicker than the other farmers around him, they might come and ask how he did it, and then Lester could share his techniques with them and—more important—share his faith. But he needed rain.

Down on his knees he went and prayed: "Lord, if this crop can come up thicker and earlier, maybe the local farmers will see it and believe that You are the only One responsible. Please send the rain." This wasn't a religious "gig" with Lester—he desperately wanted his life to be a living testimony to those watching.

Lester got up, looked me in the eye, and nodded. "It will rain. God showed me in a vision. I was to plant the seed, and He would make the barley grow. Don't worry, Franklin, the rain will come." I thought to myself, *Sure, where are the clouds?*

Day after day, all we ever saw was the blazing sun.

Lester smiled. The calmness in his eyes showed his confidence.

I had been around sincere Christians all my life, but I'd not witnessed anything quite like this. I thought to myself, *It's Septem-*

ber, hotter than a firecracker and drier than a bone. This is the dumbest thing I've ever heard of!

I walked away shaking my head. I wondered if he was just naive or what. *It will really shake his faith when it doesn't rain. Then what will he do?* I thought.

I worried about Lester because it didn't rain—that night or the next two nights. By the fourth night, I had forgotten about Lester's prayer. I went up on the roof as usual, turned my radio on, and didn't realize I had fallen asleep until something struck my face. I brushed it aside and went back to sleep. Then I got hit again. I slowly opened my eyes. That "something" hitting my cheeks was *wet*.

I sat up and shook my head. It was raining.

I grabbed my homemade bed and belongings and scurried down the rickety wooden ladder and inside the garage. A man named Mohammed Makki, who was Lester's Arab interpreter and right-hand man, slept there to guard the woodworking equipment. He was an older Muslim who had been teaching me a few words of Arabic.

"Mr. Frank, what is now wrong?" he said as I started to clear a spot to lay my sleeping bag.

"It's raining, Mohammed!"

He broke into his trademark laugh, a rapid and gleeful hee, hee, hee, hee. "Oh yes—Mr. Gates prayed—Mr. Gates prayed and it is raining. This God of his does these things, you know," Mohammed said, continuing to giggle as he rolled over on his mat. Mohammed was not a Christian, yet he had shown more faith than I that Lester's prayer would be answered.

I climbed into my bag, thought about Lester, and listened to the soft rain falling on the roof.

I might have easily dismissed the answer to Lester's rain prayer, but I soon found out that this kind of miracle happened frequently in Mafraq.

I began to pay close attention to how Aileen and Eleanor took care of the financial needs of the hospital. To be honest, it freaked me out! The ladies never wrote newsletters or sent out appeals. "God knows our needs," Eleanor said more than once. "If God knows, that's all that counts, isn't it?" Who could argue with that?

Every Friday afternoon, which was the Muslim holy day, the two women asked all of us to meet inside the hospital for prayer. These meetings were unforgettable. Someone would read from the Bible and elaborate on what the passage meant. After this study of God's Word, a list of prayer requests was made. That's when the missionaries simply asked God to provide whatever was needed.

Sometimes the need was as basic as food. At other times it involved large sums of money for a phase of the construction or for hospital equipment.

Eleanor, Aileen, and Lester would all drop to their knees for a time of earnest prayer. Not once did I see them violate this approach of asking God, in faith, to provide. It must not have been easy for them, yet they never seemed to be in turmoil or to wring their hands in despair. I could not fathom how they lived in such peace in the midst of great need.

There were times we had nothing to eat but bread, cheese, olives, and maybe an egg or two. But I never heard a complaint from Aileen or Eleanor. Always they paused before a meal and thanked God for His "bountiful provision."

One time I remember Aileen feeling so bad that they didn't have better food to provide us younger guys. She saved up some of her own money and bought a couple kilos of beef. What a treat! She ground it up to make hamburgers, Arabic style. In the grinding process, though, she cut the tip of her finger off. She didn't want to waste the meat by throwing it away, so she kept grinding and didn't say anything about her "contribution" to the burgers until a few days later.

When she finally did tell us, I hollered, "What? You let us eat that?" She came right back with, "Well it didn't hurt you, did it? That's why I waited to tell you—besides, those burgers tasted pretty good!"

When I realized how short the funds were, I started going into town and buying food with my own TR-6 sports car money. Occasionally, I'd buy steaks—not hamburger meat—a real luxury. If we were out of butter, I'd canvass the stores for canned butter from England. Bill chipped in his funds as well.

One Friday, Eleanor asked that we pray for the Lord to provide funds to pay a medicine bill from a Swedish company. I recall the gist of her plea:

> *Lord, You know we don't have $1,355, but this is Your hospital. Your name is on the line, not ours. If this bill doesn't get paid, it's Your Name that gets discredited. If it pleases You, Lord, and if it be Your will, provide for this need. Amen.*

I tried hard not to be cynical, but I couldn't believe that the money would come in if no one on the "outside" knew about the need. I thought, *If they would just let their needs be known, maybe someone would care enough to help.* I had grown to love these women, and I didn't want to see them hurt. But I had completely missed the point; they had already told Someone.

The next Monday an envelope arrived containing a handwritten note, which read: "I have heard about the wonderful work you are doing there, and you have been in my thoughts. I had some extra money and wanted to send it to you. Enclosed is a check. Use it any way you see fit."

The check was for $1,355.

When Eleanor showed it to me, I don't know what was more obvious—my gulp or my eyes bulging out of my head. My cynical, immature view of how life worked was taking some major hits. I could not deny the reality of what I was seeing. This kind of thing happened week after week.

"The point is," Aileen said to me once, "the money comes in at the very time we need it. It doesn't come a week earlier, because we don't need it then, do we?"

"Guess not," I said, shrugging my shoulders. What else could I say?

Another Friday they prayed about a bill that exceeded $3,000, the largest amount mentioned during my time there.

They knelt in prayer. As I often did, I carried on my own internal monologue during the prayers: *God isn't going to give them their request every time they pray. These two poor women—I hate to see them disappointed.*

Wrong again. Within a week they had the money.

Until this point I'd only been a spectator. I got pretty hot under the collar the day Eleanor mentioned the mission needed $500 within a week and asked, "Franklin, will you pray for this need?"

Although I considered myself a Christian, I was backsliding in high gear. Sure, I knew how to say a prayer—I had the lingo down pat. But I didn't have the heartfelt conviction—the faith—to back it up. So I felt unworthy to pray on their behalf. I figured if anyone could mess up their record on answers to prayer, I could. But I prayed anyway.

The next week I was mixing concrete one afternoon when I saw Eleanor running up to me, waving a slip of paper in the air. "See, Franklin. Look! God answered your prayer," she said excitedly as she showed me the check. "Oh, thank You, Lord!" she kept saying.

I stared at the check. "But, Eleanor, it's only for $480. You better tell God that He's twenty dollars short." I definitely had an attitude.

We both laughed, but after she walked away, I was bewildered. I thought, *It's a coincidence. If she wants to believe that God answered my prayer, let her believe it.*

Construction came to a halt on Sundays, and occasionally Bill and I would take a long weekend in Beirut, which was the closest city where I could buy American beer and cigarettes.

On one of those weekend trips, I was determined to meet this Sami Dagher guy Roy Gustafson thought so much of. After all, I had used his name to get discounts at the hotel. I figured I should at least stop by and introduce myself.

When we checked into the Phoenicia Hotel on the next trip to Beirut, Bill turned in early. Not me. The night was still young, and I wanted to find Sami.

I wandered into the coffee shop and found an empty table. The tourist season was almost over, and there weren't many people in the hotel. When I sat down, I noticed a dark-skinned man across the room. He smiled as he seated the customers. His gracious behavior made me think that this must be the Sami that Roy had described in such glowing terms.

I smoked a cigarette and waited.

"Does everything please you?" a voice gently asked me. The maitre d' now stood by my table.

"Yes, sir," I said, "You're Sami Dagher, aren't you?"

"Yes, I am," he said, shyly. "Who are you? I believe we haven't met—"

"I'm a friend of Roy Gustafson."

"Roy! How is my dear brother Roy?" The big smile on his face said it all about Sami's feelings for Roy.

"Roy is fine," I said.

Sami sat down—he wanted to hear about Roy and learn what I was doing in the Middle East. It wasn't long before it seemed we had known each other for a long time. I never visited Beirut again without planning to see Sami. I didn't have to lie any more when I went to the Phoenicia Hotel and sat at the bar using Sami's name to get a discount. Sami Dagher really was my friend.

I was smoking and drinking quite a bit, and Eleanor and Aileen knew my habits. Never once did they give me a hard time about what I was doing. I really expected that these "godly missionaries" would lay the Bible on me or something, but it never happened. I was enough of a rebel that I might have bolted right out of Mafraq if they had done that. They probably knew it.

I went to Beirut often. Although war would virtually destroy it later, then it was a great city—a true oasis in the middle of the Arab world, where everyone could find freedom from the strict Islamic laws.

On one of the weekend trips I brought a gas hot water heater for the hospital. We had been taking cold showers, but late fall had arrived in the desert and I couldn't stand the thought of just cold water. When I presented the heater to Aileen and Eleanor, it was if I had given them a million dollars. I felt a little guilty for how they made over my gift; my motives weren't totally noble—after all I really wanted those hot showers myself.

Several months passed. I realized I was having the time of my life—learning Middle Eastern culture and the ins and outs of international travel. But more important, I was feeling the satisfaction that comes from helping others. It was a mighty good feeling.

I had come to Jordan for selfish reasons—adventure, excitement, the chance to get out of school—but God had other things in mind.

Kicked Out, Boots and All

Shortly before Christmas, 1971, Bill and I packed up and left Jordan. The hospital building wasn't finished, but we had promised to be back at LeTourneau to start the next semester. As I said good-bye to Eleanor, Aileen, Lester, Mohammed, Victor, and others, I had very mixed feelings. What I had seen in Mafraq certainly ranked as one of the highlights of my young life. But I missed home and family too. And thoughts of Jane Austin filled my mind.

She was everything I wanted in a girl. On the plane trip home I realized she had become more to me than just the girl next door: She was my friend and confidant. Besides her physical beauty, her sweet, carefree spirit attracted me. She was the kind of person who never met a stranger. And I liked the way she treated my friends. But more than anything else, she accepted me just as I was.

Bill and I landed in New York and then parted ways for the holidays. I went to Montreat, caught up on all the news, and had one huge meal after another. (I had lost over thirty pounds!) I enjoyed being back where there were plenty of trees and no sand.

Everyone was quite interested in learning about the trip with the Land Rover and my first experience in mission work. As always, I presented the "edited version," conveniently leaving out details that I knew would trouble my parents.

And I spent a lot of time with Jane Austin. With her I could be more candid. She loved adventure, too, and she laughed as I told her one tale after another. I felt close to her. No doubt about it; I was getting bitten by the love bug.

In January I was back at LeTourneau. School was school, but it was nice to enjoy the comforts of a real bed and a hot shower whenever you wanted one. I missed the people at Mafraq, but I didn't miss the rigors of desert life.

When I got back into the swing of my classes, I decided I could manage a part-time job in Longview. I worked for a roofer, hauling ninety-pound bales of shingles up a ladder. The hard labor didn't bother me, and the pay was good.

I began to feel settled in Longview. I liked the little town, and I enjoyed the independence the money from my job provided. I was flying every chance I could, and life was good.

Even though the rules at LeTourneau weren't as strict as they'd been at Stony Brook, I still resented being told what I could and couldn't do—like with my hair.

Most men, including my father, were letting their hair grow longer. But at LeTourneau hair couldn't touch the top of the ear or your collar.

When my hair got a little too long, one of the instructors stopped me: "Graham, go get a hair cut. It's too long."

I felt like a kid again and hated it.

With this same instructor one time I pulled out a dollar and showed him the picture of George Washington on the bill. "His hair came over his collar," I said. "Why can't mine?"

"Not at this school," he answered.

I shook my head. What I labeled "the hypocrisy of Christian schools" really got to me. If we wore our hair short, went to chapel, and didn't break the rules, in the eyes of the administrators we were saved and going to heaven. Yet many of the kids, including me, were lost and floundering.

My trip abroad, and the nearly boundless freedom it had provided, had only heightened my rebellious attitudes. I just refused to accept the idea that someone else had the right to police my personal life.

"Just whose business is it anyway, but my own?" was my rallying cry. I was repeating the pattern I'd started at Stony Brook: Push all rules to the very edge, secretly break some—like no smoking or drinking—and make the faculty squirm because they know I'm violating the school's standards but they can't catch me.

I knew that if I got caught, I could be expelled. But at the time I really didn't care.

By May of 1972 I had spring fever and was restless. The semester was about over, and I craved some excitement. I rented a little plane and talked one of the girls I had dated a few times into going with me to Atlanta.

On our way back to Longview on a Sunday afternoon, we encountered stormy weather. It was too dangerous to go on, and getting back to school on time wasn't worth the risk of flying through something that could tear the airplane apart in midair. For our safety, I landed in Monroe, Lousianna, where the weather socked us in. I called LeTourneau and told them I could not get back until the next day. As far as I knew, I had done my duty and satisfied the college's rules.

The next morning we were able to fly out early. When we landed at Longview and I returned the rental plane, the desk clerk handed me a message. It was from the dean of students. Before leaving the airport, I called him. "I want to see you in my office right away," he shouted. I could tell he was upset.

Why was he worked up into such a lather? I wondered on my way back to campus. I thought I had followed the rules and was actually proud of myself—we had only missed the first class. I figured there must be a logical reason for his call; maybe he was just having a bad Monday morning and was irritated about something else. I was dead wrong.

I walked into the dean's office and saw a deep scowl on his face. "We cannot allow this kind of behavior, Franklin," he said after I sat down. "This is a Christian school. We live by Christian principles, and we want the lives of our faculty and students to be above reproach. You were away overnight from the school with a co-ed. You've gone over the brink—living on the edge has finally caught up with you. It doesn't matter who you are. There are no more warnings."

What is he talking about? I thought. The school had never issued me a warning! I apparently had done the unpardonable. I set my jaw and tried not to react. I knew what was coming.

"You'll have to leave school, Franklin."

"Yes, sir," I said. This was something I had always expected to hear at Stony Brook, but not at LeTourneau.

"I have already notified your parents," he said somberly.

What gave him that right? Shouldn't I have the prerogative to tell my parents? But I held my tongue. I didn't think anything I would say would get me out of this mess. Maybe I felt guilty for all the things I had done and not been caught. Was I finally getting what I deserved? Probably so.

I was crushed. Since my return from Mafraq, I had tried harder to walk the straight and narrow. For the first time I had been more serious about my studies, and my life had more focus. Worst of all, I knew how disappointed my parents would be. Daddy had gone out of his way to get me into LeTourneau when I didn't even have my high school diploma. For the first time in my life I felt a deep, shameful pain.

I accepted my disgrace and packed up. Yet as I prepared to leave LeTourneau, anger swelled up inside. I felt betrayed that the dean had talked to my parents behind my back. In just two more weeks I would have finished the semester; now all my hard work was down the drain. Was there no mercy, no second chance? And

I hadn't even been given an opportunity to explain what had happened!

I was convinced that being Billy Graham's son had helped me get into LeTourneau, and I was grateful for that. But I also thought that being Billy's boy had, at least in part, helped usher me out. I imagined that it would be impossible in their eyes to be lenient with me because everybody knew who I was. I would make a good example of what would happen if anyone else broke the rules.

Almost every child who has a famous parent struggles with finding his own way and wondering if he is being viewed as an individual, not just an extension of his father or mother. It is the downside of belonging to a noted family. But even if I was held to a higher standard by LeTourneau College because my name was Graham, I didn't help matters by flaunting my rebellion. But my proud heart was not quite ready to deal with that thought.

The drive home from Texas was dreary. I was so paranoid and afraid I might get in more trouble that I drove *under* the speed limit. Maybe by driving slow I was just prolonging the inevitable: I would have to face my parents. I knew they had to be disappointed in me—I was. They had invested a lot of money in my education, and now I'd messed everything up.

I took my time driving back to North Carolina.

When the highway signs began to mention Asheville, my mind started to imagine the lecture my parents would give me.

I drove through the gate and started up the road to Little Piney Cove. So many times when I had come home I could hardly wait to say hello to everyone, find the dogs, and rush into the hills. No joy this time. I felt bad enough when I reached the house. Then I saw Mama standing on the front porch, and I wanted to run and hide in the nearest hole I could find. It was one of the few times I can remember not wanting to look her in the eye.

When I walked up to her, my body felt limp. I barely had the nerve to lift my head or extend my arms for a hug. I didn't need to. Mama wrapped her arms around me and, with a smile, kissed me like always, welcoming me back home.

The lecture never came, and I don't recall my parents ever bringing up my dismissal from LeTourneau. They knew I had learned a hard lesson and didn't pile on extra guilt. I sure didn't need somebody else to tell me how stupid I had been. I knew that all too well.

It was a lifesaver to turn my attention to another summer working with Roy on his tours to the Middle East. The travel—including stops in Mafraq and Beirut to see my friends—gave me a chance to rebound and consider my options. I tried to block out of my mind the fact that fall was approaching. I had no sense of direction and wondered what I should do.

One thing I was sure of: I'd had my fill of being away from home. In the past I'd had absolutely no interest in attending the small Presbyterian college in Montreat, Montreat-Anderson College (M-AC). Going away from home to college had appealed to my restless spirit, but now living at home for awhile seemed like a good idea.

I didn't know what I would major in, but I bit the bullet and enrolled at M-AC, which was a junior college at the time. My decision received an overwhelming blessing from my parents.

Essentially I had to start college all over again—no more than two or three credits from LeTourneau transferred. Even a junior college wouldn't accept Machine Tool 101 or Welding.

When I reviewed the course requirements at M-AC, I learned I would have to take several Bible classes. To my surprise, I soaked in all I could in those sessions—my mind had been opened to the Bible through Roy's tours.

Most of the students were from nearby. I didn't have to be a model or prove myself. I was just Franklin Graham, local boy, and that was good enough.

It had always irritated me at Stony Brook and LeTourneau when I was constantly introduced as Billy Graham's son. Some people even forgot to mention *my* name. I'm sure people didn't intentionally try to hurt my feelings, but when I was always linked to my father, it made me feel I wasn't worthwhile myself. I never could be sure I was liked for just being me.

This had nothing to do with my love or respect for my father. I was always very proud to be his son. I just wanted to have my own identity.

The best thing about M-AC was that when class was over, I was just a short distance away from the refuge of my beloved Little Piney Cove. I splurged and bought a Yamaha DT 250 dirt bike, basically a mule with wheels, and explored all the abandoned logging roads at breakneck speed.

My mother had never minded my obsession with motorcycles—until I started skipping church to enter races on Sundays. This was a definite "no-no" with her.

As usual, Mama didn't lecture me. She just said one day, "Franklin, I'm praying that the Lord will do something to get your attention—break your leg or put you in the hospital. I have prayed, 'Lord, don't kill him, but do whatever it takes to get his attention.'" Gee, thanks, Mom!

I should have parked the bike right then, put on my suit, and headed for church. But I wasn't quite that perceptive. A few weeks later I was riding on an easy trail—not even going very fast—when the root of a tree caught the toe of my boot and pulled it backwards under the foot peg of the motorcycle. I went about another fifty yards and the pain became so intense that I pulled over. When I put my foot on the ground to stand up, I fell over—I couldn't believe it! I had broken my foot.

Mama was right again. The injury got my attention. The motorcycle had to sit idle for a while—so did I—while my foot healed. I decided not to race on Sundays anymore.

Being at home under the watchful eyes of my parents caused me to take my studies more seriously. My pride had taken a beating when I got booted out of LeTourneau; I was determined not to fail in my own backyard. I didn't skip classes, and I did my homework faithfully. But no matter how hard I worked, reaching the top of my class just wasn't going to happen. I learned to be satisfied with Bs and Cs.

Part of the reason I tried hard to apply myself more in school was Jane Austin. She was smart and well on her way to finishing college. If I had any hope of making a lasting impression on her, I needed to get my act together.

There was only one possible "problem" that could come between Jane Austin and me: Did she, could she, love me? We had a lot of fun together, but I really didn't know if she felt about me the way I felt about her. And I was too scared to find out for sure—yet.

With school going well and the debacle at LeTourneau finally behind me, I began to think again about my friends at Mafraq. The lapse of time had not dulled my interest in the work they were doing in Jordan, and I wanted to help them if I could. I knew those ladies would never ask for themselves. But that didn't mean I couldn't ask for them.

One day I asked my father, "Do you have any ideas about how I can raise money for the ladies in Jordan?"

This topic wasn't new to Daddy since I had come to him once before on their behalf. But this time, I was really sincere and not just looking for an excuse to get out of school. Somehow I think Daddy sensed my motives had changed.

He thought for a few moments before speaking: "Franklin, why don't you start coming to some of the crusades, and I'll introduce you to some people who may have an interest in missions."

I've wondered if he did this so that I would come and be exposed to more of the gospel. I had lived under the same roof as the man who did all that preaching around the world, but the crusade setting always draws unavoidable attention to the message itself.

Regardless of his motive, I eagerly accepted Daddy's invitation. I called David Schultz who had already started raising money for Mafraq. We decided to combine our efforts. We started attending the crusade meetings. For the first time I really began to grasp what my father had been doing all the years I was growing up.

Daddy introduced us to all kinds of people. Some of them were successful businessmen, others were pastors, and one was the great entertainer Johnny Cash. Johnny listened carefully when I told him about the hospital at Mafraq, and he gave a sizeable donation. This really pumped me up! I couldn't wait to hear from Eleanor and Aileen after they had received Johnny's gift. Although I still didn't have a deeply spiritual reason for what I was doing, I sure did like the good feelings I had inside when I was able to help others.

The one person Daddy introduced me to who stood out from all the rest was Dr. Bob Pierce.

Bob had come out of the Youth For Christ movement of the late 1940s and had gone on to found World Vision, which later became one of the largest Christian relief agencies in the world. Despite all his success, Bob had struggled through overwhelming tragedies in his personal life and, ultimately, after a falling out with the board of directors, he had been forced to leave World Vision.

Although he was still reeling from the trials in his own life, in 1970 Bob had begun a new ministry called Samaritan's Purse.

At my father's crusade in Atlanta, Fred Dienert arranged for me to meet Bob in a ballroom at the Hilton Hotel. There I noticed a man sitting alone at a small round table in the middle of the room. Fred had described Bob; this must be him—he was the only one there.

The man was strikingly distinguished—impeccably dressed with a head of wavy, silver hair. He flashed an enormous smile and greeted me in a soft voice. It was easy to see that he really cared about people.

He was also businesslike. After exchanging only a pleasantry or two, he got right to the point: "So, Buddy," he said, "what do you want to talk about?" (I learned later that if Bob called you "Buddy," it meant he liked you.)

He listened while I told him about the missionaries and hospital at Mafraq. The more wound up I got, the more intense my presentation became. Bob remained expressionless. I told him about how Aileen and Eleanor got on their knees every Friday and petitioned the Lord for their needs. I even got choked up at one point.

"Those women need help," I finally concluded. "Daddy suggested I talk to you because he felt you might be willing to do something for them."

Without offering any comment, Bob stood up, shook my hand, and hugged me. "Thank you, Buddy!" I could tell our meeting was over.

He walked briskly out of the room and left me standing there speechless. I didn't know what to think. Obviously he hadn't been moved by anything I had told him. Had I said something wrong? I wasn't sure if I should feel disappointed, embarrassed, or both.

A month passed. I received a phone call one day at home. Bea hollered, "Franklin, somebody by the name of Mr. Pierce wants to talk to you."

My adrenaline kicked in as I ran to the phone.

"Hey, Buddy, I've been thinking about what you told me in Atlanta, you know, about the two women in Jordan. Before I can do anything, I want to go out there and see the situation for myself. I don't raise funds for anybody until I verify the need firsthand."

"That's fine. You'll love them," I said.

"Yeah, maybe so, Buddy, but I want you to go with me. How about it?"

My heart plummeted. "Dr. Pierce, I can't. School starts in a few days. I'd give anything to go with you, believe me, but I just can't."

"Well, all right then, Buddy. If you can't go with me, I'll go out there by myself."

True to his word, Bob went to Jordan and stayed at the hospital for ten days. As I knew they would, Aileen and Eleanor won Bob's heart. He was so impressed and moved by what he saw that he donated tens of thousands of dollars to their ministry.

Once more God had answered the prayers of the faith-filled missionaries in Mafraq. The irony was that unknown to me, I was slowly being prepared to be something of a missionary myself.

God's Hit Man

G od finally sent a hit man after me. His name was David
Hill. He came to get me in 1972.

I was living a sinful life and still wasn't ready to change, but
deep down in my gut, I knew I was wrong. David was sent to
help apply some heat to my conscience.

"Kid," David would say to me (he was eight years older) with
his Texas drawl, "you're running from the Lord." He spoke with
authority since he was an expert in this field. He had run from
God himself for years.

The story of his life and family background would have made
a good TV miniseries. His father was a famous World War II flying
ace and had flown for the acclaimed Flying Tigers during the war.

David's grandfather, Dr. P. B. Hill, was a missionary to Korea,
an illustrious Texas ranger, and eventually a pastor of the First
Presbyterian Church of San Antonio, Texas, which had been a
strong supporter of my grandfather, Nelson Bell, when he was a
missionary doctor in China. That was my link to this remarkable family.

I probably liked David initially because I related to his rebellion, although my experiences were far more tame than his.
While only a teenager he had left home for Paris where he lived
with a madam and made a small fortune playing cards. He drifted
into the drug scene, which eventually entangled him in the under-

world. He had ended up living with the Joe Bonannos—the noted New York mafia crime family—for a period of time in Tucson, Arizona.

While Daddy was holding a crusade in Phoenix in 1974, David actually took me down to Tucson to meet Joe Bonanno at his home. He was of the old school Sicilian family. He could have been anyone's grandfather. He was an extremely charming man and was a devout Catholic. He lived in a simple home on a side street and no one would have ever suspected his connections to the underworld. He asked David a lot about his new life and was interested in my father and the message he preached. We sat around until late that night eating cheese from one of his factories in Wisconsin and drinking Sicilian wine.

After David left the Bonanno family, he became entwined in the occult and wound up in the Andes Mountains of Peru, studying the religion of the ancient Indians. When he came to his senses and realized the spiritual grip the occult had on him, David cried out, "Jesus Christ, if you're the Son of the living God, save me now."

"I was saved that very moment," David told me, tears streaming down his face. "Kid, I didn't deserve it, but He took me just the way I was, and He cleansed me. Now I have a new life."

By the time David returned home from Peru, his grandfather had died. That's when David turned to my grandfather—Dr. Bell. He ended up in Montreat, and that's where we met.

When I first laid eyes on David, he was a stunning man to behold. Stepping out of a long, black, 1957 El Dorado Brougham Cadillac, he was dressed in designer clothes that fit his lean, long-legged frame like a glove. His pant legs were neatly tucked down inside handmade Lucchese alligator skin cowboy boots that towered up to his knees. The Spanish roping heels were as elaborate as the Oliver Cromwell logo—a cross encircled by a crown—stitched into the leather.

When the sleeve of David's silk shirt inched up his lanky arm, a heavy gold Rolex watch reflected the sun. Around his neck dangled the largest gold cross I had ever seen.

He wore his blond, sun-bleached hair shoulder length and combed straight back. With his arm propped up on the stainless steel roof of the vintage Cadillac, he looked like a cross between an old-time western movie star and a modern-day Las Vegas gambler.

As many Texans do, David loved his guns. His constant companion was a gold-plated hand engraved Browning .9 mm pistol. How could this guy not impress me?

Everything about David Hill was dazzling. I always wondered how and where he got the huge roll of one-hundred-dollar bills bulging in his jeans pocket. David didn't have a job, and he didn't have a bank account or credit cards. His daddy didn't bankroll him. Later I learned that he had made his money gambling before turning to Christ.

I can say for sure that when he arrived in Montreat, nobody in those mountains had ever seen the likes of David Hill. (And they still haven't, even to this day!)

We became fast friends. It didn't take long before his piercing eyes saw right through my hypocrisy. He was a straight shooter and never afraid to say what was on his mind, even as I blew smoke in his face and tipped the bottle in front of him.

"You know, you're going to have to get right with God some time, kid," he would say in that unmistakingly San Antonio drawl. "Otherwise, alcohol is going to do you in someday. You'll have to give it up."

I would tempt him—try to get him to smoke a cigarette or drink a beer. Down deep, though, I wanted him to be the real McCoy and not a phoney. David had been to the doorsteps of hell, and he didn't intend to go back.

Because of his distinctive appearance, people were attracted to him and were anxious to engage him in conversation. He took every opportunity to talk about what Jesus Christ had done for him. Even though he had not graduated from high school or attended college, he was a magnificent communicator. David had a photographic mind, and his recall of the Scriptures caused people to listen carefully to every word he said. Many times David had me nearly convinced to change, but I always managed to wiggle out by changing the subject. I just wasn't ready.

My two years at Montreat-Anderson College were a success. At last I had made it through a school without quitting or getting kicked out! I graduated in the spring of 1974. My cousin, John Somerville, graduated at the same time—with honors. My mother said I graduated "with relief!"

Jane Austin had already received her diploma and teaching certificate from Stratford College and returned to teach at an elementary school nearby in Black Mountain.

I was elated! Now I didn't have to worry anymore about her moving far away. I'd bought an old 1949 Jeep, and we spent many fun hours bouncing over the mountain trails.

Our relationship had grown more serious, even to the point of our contemplating marriage. Of the girls I had dated, Jane Austin was the one my parents loved especially. I was hopeful—I knew now that she was definitely the one for me. But I hadn't found the place, the time, or the nerve to pop *the* question.

In July of 1974 the BGEA sponsored the International Congress for Evangelism in Lausanne, Switzerland. About 2,500 Protestant evangelical leaders came from 150 countries to attend the ten-day conference.

I left for Switzerland in May, right after I graduated from Montreat-Anderson College, to help handle logistics for the congress.

I had spent the summer in that area when I was young, so it was familiar territory. I rented a small apartment for the summer; actually to call it "small" is being generous. It was more like a room, eight feet wide and fifteen feet long. The bathtub was so tiny that I had to sit on a ledge in the tub and use a long shower hose to rinse off.

Trying to cook was another hardship and a brand-new experience for me. I had watched Bea fry chicken enough that I didn't think there would be anything to it. So I went to the market and bought a whole chicken, which I had to cut up into pieces myself. I threw some flour, salt, and pepper into a paper bag along with the chicken parts just like Bea had done so many times. I shook hard, but I didn't remember Bea getting the flour all over the place like I managed to do.

But that wasn't nearly as big a mess as when I filled the frying pan with oil and turned the heat on high. I dumped the chicken into the hot grease and it spattered, popped, and smoked. (I usually liked things that popped and smoked, but not this time!) I was very discouraged five minutes later when I took the charred chicken out of the sizzling grease. I couldn't figure out why it was overdone on the outside and raw on the inside. So much for bachelor life!

When I returned to my apartment from work each evening, I had no TV or stereo to turn on, so I started reading my New Testament. Even though I was living one adventure after another, I felt such an emptiness. I had friends, but still I was lonely and unfulfilled. Something just didn't connect in my life. It was like having a television but not plugging it in.

The sinful life I was living was not satisfying me any longer. There was an emptiness—a big hole right in the middle of Franklin Graham's life—a void that needed to be filled. The truth was, I felt miserable because my life wasn't right with God.

During the Lausanne conference I celebrated my twenty-second birthday. Mama and Daddy wanted to take me to lunch. "Where do you want to go?" Daddy asked.

I chose a little Italian restaurant on Lake Geneva. Nothing much happened during the meal. It was pleasant and relaxed. We had a good time.

After that meal, Daddy and I walked along a pathway beside the lake. My father, who hates confrontation, turned to me and, somewhat nervously, said: "Franklin, your mother and I sense there's a struggle going on in your life."

I stared at him, but I didn't say anything. He had caught me totally off guard. *How does he know this?* I wondered.

"You're going to have to make a choice either to accept Christ or reject Him. You can't continue to play the middle ground. Either you're going to choose to follow and obey Him or reject Him."

My mind raced. *What was he going to say next?*

"I want you to know we're proud of you, Franklin. We love you no matter what you do in life and no matter where you go. The door of our home is always open, and you're always welcome. But you're going to have to make a choice."

I felt angry. Maybe I was mad because he had seen right through me. I'd always thought I was so clever and could fool my parents. After all, I went to church, sang the hymns, and said the right words. But my sinful life was no secret. I couldn't figure out how he knew about the struggle that had been going on inside me for some time. But he did. I knew he was right.

After he had his say, Daddy patted my shoulder and smiled. He said nothing more about it as we finished our walk.

But in spite of some of the most beautiful and inspiring scenery in the world—and near the man I loved and wanted to please more than anyone else on earth—I felt joyless, empty, lonely, and dirty. The clock was ticking loudly now on my own personal "hour of decision."

The congress ended a few days later. I bolted from Switzerland to help Roy Gustafson conduct the last summer tour. Daddy had paid for David Hill to come to the congress and wanted him to travel with me on Roy's tour to the Middle East. I think Daddy thought David was a young Christian who would benefit from Roy's Bible teaching, so David and I flew to Zurich to meet Roy.

The first stop on the tour was Rome. One evening, while we were at the Cavaleri Hilton, I went to David's room and found him reading his Bible.

"Hey, kid," he said, "what's going on?"

I said, "Not much. What are you doing?"

"Just reading what the apostle Paul has to say in Romans 7—want to hear it?" David asked.

"Guess so," figuring I didn't have much choice.

David read: "I have *the will* to do good, but not *the power.* That is, I don't accomplish the good I set out to do, and the evil I don't really want to do I find I am always doing" (Rom. 7:18–20 PHILLIPS, italics added). David paused.

I felt like that deep down inside. I couldn't believe that the apostle Paul had had the same struggles.

"No Christian is perfect," David said. "We struggle with sin. None of us has the power or the ability to live a life of perfection—not even Paul. But when we let Jesus Christ come into our hearts and we surrender our lives to Him, He gives us the power to live the Christian life because of His Spirit living within us."

David had my attention. He went on: "I *want* to do good, but in *practice* I do evil. . . . This is in continual conflict with my conscious attitude, and makes me an unwilling prisoner" (Rom. 7:21, 23 PHILLIPS, italics added).

This was me! I wanted to do right. I wanted to get my life cleaned up—but how? Daddy had told me a few days earlier that I had to make a choice. But how could I? The apostle Paul confessed his weakness. Could I?

David continued: "It is an agonizing situation, and who on earth can set me free from the clutches of my own sinful nature? I thank God there is a way out through Jesus Christ our Lord" (Rom. 7:24–25 PHILLIPS).

I felt frustrated as I listened, wondering how to overcome such a struggle. I broke out in a sweat and lit a cigarette to ease the tension.

David didn't say another word at that moment—he just stared at me. I think he knew that God was speaking to me. I made some excuse to leave, but I couldn't forget the words David had just read.

How many times had I heard these verses? But this time they sounded as if the apostle Paul had written them in a personal letter to me. I realized for the first time that sin had control over my life. Franklin Graham was not in charge, but sin was. And there was absolutely nothing I could do in my own power to overcome it. I went back to my room and fished through my luggage for my New Testament and turned to Romans 8:1: "There is therefore now no condemnation to those who are in Christ Jesus."

No condemnation, I thought, *for those* in *Christ*. I was condemned; I had broken God's law in every conceivable way, and it troubled me. I wanted what David Hill had; I wanted what Roy Gustafson had; I wanted what my parents had.

That night instead of going to the bar for a couple of beers, I found myself alone in my room reading through the gospel of John.

When I came to the third chapter, I read not just that Jesus told Nicodemus he had to be born again, but I also grasped that Franklin Graham had to be born again as well. (See John 3:3–7.)

I don't remember all that happened that night, but when I went to bed, I knew that all was not well with Franklin Graham. Something was missing in my life. I felt I was a Christian. I was the son of Billy Graham, I went to church, and I memorized Scripture. What more did it take? My mind raced, and I found myself talking as though there were two people struggling inside of me. I don't remember getting much sleep.

For the next several days I didn't have much time to myself because of the demands of the tour. We had gone on to Israel, and on our fourth night in the country, we were at a hotel in Jerusalem.

I went to my room early. I sat on my bed and smoked a cigarette, picked up my New Testament, and re-read John 3. The words of my father a few weeks earlier haunted me: "Franklin, you are going to have to make a choice to accept Christ or reject Him." I thought back to the time I had made a decision for Christ at age eight. I'm not sure I really understood what I had done. All I knew was that Franklin Graham was a sinner who had been running from God. Suddenly, I had an overpowering conviction that I needed to get my life right with God.

I read John 3 again where Jesus told Nicodemus, "You must be born again." Nicodemus was a respected religious leader in his city. Yet, all of his religion and learning were not enough to gain entrance into heaven. Nicodemus had to be born again. All I knew was that I wanted the big empty hole inside of me to be filled. I was tired of running.

I read Romans 8:1 over and over, and I realized that I was not "in" Christ. More than anything else, I wanted to be, but didn't know how.

I put my cigarette out and got down on my knees beside my bed. I'm not sure what I prayed, but I know that I poured my heart out to God and confessed my sin. I told Him I was sorry and that if He would take the pieces of my life and somehow put them back together, I was His. I wanted to live my life for Him from that day forward. I asked Him to forgive me and cleanse me, and I invited Him by faith to come into my life.

That night I had finally decided I was sick and tired of being sick and tired. My years of running and rebellion had ended.

I got off my knees and went to bed.

It was finished.

The rebel had found the cause.

Cigarettes, the Altar, and the Snake

The night I prayed and surrendered my life to Jesus, I had an overwhelming conviction that I should quit smoking (not drinking—that came later in life). But at that moment, I felt the Lord dealing with me about my cigarettes. This doesn't mean that He deals with everyone the same way. But I felt He was asking me to prove my dedication to Him: Was I willing to give cigarettes up?

I took the two or three packs I had in my room, wadded them up, threw them in the wastebasket, and went to sleep—but not for long. About two in the morning, I woke up with terrible abdominal cramps. Bad food, I guessed. I sat up in bed, moaning in agony. I was in such misery my face was wet with sweat.

After nearly an hour, the cramping began to subside, but I either grew weak or fainted and fell backward. My head struck a sharp corner of the bedside table, and I was knocked unconscious.

What a unique way to begin my new walk with Christ!

In the morning, my pillow was soaked with blood. Groggily, I tried to figure out what was going on.

David took me to a doctor who put several stitches in the back of my head. During most of that day, my head throbbed and I didn't move around much. I felt so lousy I didn't even think about my cigarettes.

But by the evening, I was feeling better and wanting to smoke. A struggle mounted within me.

I was aware—boy, was I aware—that in evangelical circles smoking was frowned on. I knew that smoking was far from the worst thing I could do, and there wasn't near the awareness then of the health hazards and addiction to nicotine that cigarettes bring. But after being a heavy smoker for years, smoking represented something very special to me.

So there I lay on my bed alone in my room, staring at the ceiling. It dawned on me that I had not really desired to smoke all day. I had made a bold move the night before when I trashed the cigarettes. A sense of relief came over me because I knew I had done the right thing, but I was addicted and wanted a cigarette—now. Somehow, though, I managed to fall asleep.

The next day the ache in my head was nearly gone. I was feeling more like myself, and I began to long for the smell and taste of a cigarette. "No," I said out loud to myself, "I'm through with them. I surrendered every part of my life to Christ. That includes cigarettes." I made it through that day without giving in.

I didn't know it, but Roy was already manning the prayer guns on my behalf. He told me later that he had immediately noticed a difference in me. The day after I had turned over my life to Jesus, Roy came into my room. My Bible was open on the bed next to me. He had never seen that before!

I shared with him then what had happened the night before. He was overjoyed, and we prayed together. Of course, he was an old pro in the Christian life, and he knew I would be tempted by many things—including smoking. So he began to pray.

On the third morning after quitting smoking, I woke up with an absolutely overwhelming—almost terrifying—desire for a cigarette. I wanted to smoke so bad that I couldn't think of anything else. But I had determined I wouldn't given in, so I stuck it out. But the desire would not leave. If anything, it intensified with each passing minute. Throughout the day, every chance I had time to be alone and think, the yearning for a cigarette grabbed me like the jaws of a junkyard dog.

Knowing I had to do something or I'd give in, I finally decided to talk with Roy. I found him eating a hamburger in the coffee shop at the Intercontinental Hotel. I sat down at the counter next to him.

For a few minutes we did the normal small talk. Finally, I blurted out, "I don't need cigarettes anymore. I'm going to quit. I'm going to let God free me from this nasty habit. I gave Him my life, and I'm going to give Him every bit of it—including cigarettes."

Without giving him a chance to say a word, I kept on talking. "Roy, I gave my cigarettes to Christ. I quit smoking. But I don't think I can hold out. I just don't think I have the power to say no any longer."

Roy looked at me while he finished chewing a bite of the hamburger. "Oh, you don't, huh? Why don't you just get down on your knees and tell God He's a liar?"

"What? I can't do that!" *What's* he *been smoking?* I thought.

"Sure you can. Tell God He's a liar."

"What do you mean?"

Roy quoted 1 Corinthians 10:13:

There hath no temptation taken you but such as is common to man: but God is faithful, who will not suffer you to be tempted above that ye are able; but will with the temptation also make a way to escape, that ye may be able to bear it. (KJV)

"That's great, Roy, but I want a cigarette so bad—"

"See, you prayed and committed yourself to God, but it didn't work," Roy said. He stared at me and paused before he leaned forward and said, "So you need to tell God He's a liar. You claimed that verse and it didn't work."

"I'm not going to call God a liar! Besides, I haven't claimed that verse yet!"

Now Roy had me right where he wanted me, "You haven't?" he said, his voice full of surprise. "Why don't you do it, then? Try it and see if it works. What have you got to lose?"

I stared at him. He was right. I had not really wanted an escape—just an excuse to smoke a cigarette.

Roy's blue eyes held mine. They were full of love. I swallowed hard and looked away. I had nothing else to say. I had only fifteen minutes before I had to meet the tour group. I rushed upstairs to my room and knelt beside my bed and prayed: "Lord, I've been wanting a cigarette all day. I don't want to smoke again, but I don't know if I can make it through this day. Will You take this overpowering desire from me?"

I prayed until I had to hurry down to the lobby and meet the tour group.

I didn't smoke that day. The desire didn't leave, but I had the strength to resist.

The next day, we boarded a plane for our last stop—Athens. In the middle of the flight, a desire came over me for a cigarette. This time I couldn't fight it anymore. I was willing to do anything for a smoke. I bought a pack of French cigarettes from the flight attendant and walked to the smoking section in the back of the plane.

I lit up and took several puffs. Instead of the usual satisfied feeling I would get, the cigarette left a bad taste in my mouth. I snubbed it out, wadded up the pack, and threw it on an empty seat. I couldn't believe it. God had taken the taste out of my mouth—but not the yearning. That would come later.

I felt guilty for giving in to my temptation. I quietly bowed my head and said, "God, forgive me. I haven't trusted You today the way I should have. I've allowed temptation to overcome me. I'm sorry." To this day I've never smoked another cigarette.

That doesn't mean the desire left for good. For months after that, I frequently wanted a cigarette. But each time I said no, I got a little stronger. Even now I sometimes have a nightmare about smoking. I dream I have started to smoke again, and I'm saying to myself in the dream, "How will I tell my family? What will they think of me? What will my parents say?" Then I wake up in a sweat.

After a few moments, my heart rate slows, and I realize it's just a bad dream. Then I thank God for the strength He's given me and go back to sleep.

Earlier in the summer of 1974, before leaving on the Middle East tour, I had decided to ask Jane Austin to marry me. I wasn't ready to actually *ask* her yet, but at least I had made my decision.

A few nights after I surrendered my life to Christ, I was having dinner with Roy Gustafson when I asked, "Could you go with me to a jewelry store and look at some rings?"

He gave me a puzzled look, but agreed to go. We found a store, and I asked to see the women's wedding bands. The clerk pulled out several velvet-lined boxes with rows of rings. "What's this for, Franklin?" Roy asked with a smile.

"I'm going to ask Jane Austin to marry me when I get home. I don't have enough money for a diamond, but I want to get her a real nice wedding band."

"Oh? Is that so?" For once Roy, who had a wisecrack for every occasion, didn't seem to know what to say.

After about forty minutes I'd found a beautiful handcrafted gold band that I thought Jane Austin would like.

Jane Austin and I had been dating for four years, and during that time my mother had made quite an impact on her. She and Jane Austin would often sit at the big round table where our family ate meals at Little Piney Cove and, over a cup of tea, talk about everything. Unknown to me, Jane Austin had quietly asked Christ into her own heart months before.

I knew her about as well as anyone could know another person. There was no doubt she was the one for me. When I returned from the Middle East, I finally got my courage up and said, "Will you be my wife?" To my joy, she said yes.

True, I was a believer now, but my basic personality and style hadn't changed. God saves and changes us, but He doesn't throw away the person He made and has been shaping for years! I was still "good ole boy" Franklin Graham, which meant that right or wrong, I had my own ideas about everything—including weddings.

My three older sisters had all married ahead of me—each in a church wedding. That had been well and good for them, but I didn't want to go through all that formal stuff. "Do it simple and quick" was my approach.

Jane Austin and I talked it over, and we agreed to have a small outdoor wedding at Little Piney Cove. We were married on the morning of August 14, 1974, by my father. Those in attendance were our families and a host of close friends.

Immediately after the ceremony, I said a few words to our guests. "This is a new beginning for Jane Austin and me, and we want you to know we're going to follow Jesus Christ. Both of us have committed ourselves to serving Him, wherever that path takes us."

After the reception, Jane Austin and I left on our honeymoon. We drove to Walterborough, South Carolina, and stayed free at a Howard Johnson's owned by Jane Austin's father and some close friends.

Mama and I had never stopped playing jokes on each other, so she had to find a way to pull something on Jane Austin and me. She enlisted the help of George Burgin, who was then the caretaker at Little Piney Cove and also provided security for the family. He was like a big brother and would have done anything in the world for me. Only Mama could have coaxed George into catching a snake. The idea had been to slip the snake into my suitcase so that when Jane Austin and I arrived at our hotel, we would have an unexpected surprise to deal with on our wedding night.

Another friend of mine, Preston Parrish, had a joke he wanted to play too. He talked Mama into letting him open my suitcase and steal all my underwear. But she forgot to tell Preston about the snake. When he slipped into my room and opened up the suitcase, the snake started to slither out. Preston slammed the lid shut, jerked back, and nearly had a heart attack! It scared the stuffin's out of him!

Unknown to either Mama or Preston, the lid caught the snake's head, mortally wounding the poor thing. The snake crawled into a corner of the suitcase, curled up under my folded underwear, and died.

Jane Austin and I didn't know any of this until several days later when I began to wonder why my underwear had sort of a musty smell. I found the decomposing snake and immediately knew who was responsible. I called Mama to let her know what I thought about the joke. She was still laughing when I hung up the phone.

Before the wedding, Jane Austin and I had decided we wanted to get some Bible training. We realized we might never have a better opportunity since there were no commitments to hold us back.

I wasn't interested in seminary training, and I didn't care about degrees. I just wanted a practical, working knowledge of God's Word.

We had become aware of a Bible school called Raven's Crest that would hold its first classes that fall in Estes Park, Colorado. It was run by a friend of my father's, an Englishman named Major Ian Thomas. The major's son, Mark, was the school's director.

We headed west, pulling a U-Haul behind our old Jeep, and arrived in Colorado about a month early. Daddy had wanted us to spend some time with the Navigators at their headquarters in Colorado Springs. The Navigators' founder, Dawson Trotman, had helped with follow-up at Daddy's crusades in the early years, and my father knew "the Navs" could help both Jane Austin and me establish some good spiritual habits as "baby Christians."

The Navigators owned an old castle named Glen Eyrie, which was nestled in a mountain canyon. For Jane Austin and me, staying in such a spot was like an extension of our honeymoon. And we did learn much about the basics of the Christian life.

In early September we moved deeper into the Rockies to Estes Park and started our studies at Raven's Crest. Although I had lived away from home several times before, this was the beginning of a grand new adventure for me as a married man.

The courses were a challenge—I still wasn't really the "student type," but learning more about Scripture was a fantastic experience. Both of us absorbed the Word like dry sponges.

Except for a month off in the spring of 1975 to help Daddy with his crusade in Albuquerque, we spent the entire school year in Estes Park. In June we packed up and headed home to Montreat.

When we left Estes Park, I had no strong sense of just what God wanted me to do. One thing I was certain of: I didn't want to preach. Maybe I was just afraid of being compared to my father. I did have a strong desire to serve Christ, but how?

For now, Jane Austin and I were just happy to be together. The future could wait for awhile. We had Christ and each other. Life could only get better.

"God Room"

H ey, Buddy, I want you to take a trip with me," the man said on the other end of the phone. I didn't need him to tell me his name. Bob Pierce had a distinctive, rough-edged voice that could not be mistaken.

"Sure, Dr. Bob," I said. "Where you going? And how long?"

"We'll be gone a couple of months, but we'll be back right before Christmas. I want to take you around the world so you can see what God has allowed me to see all of these years. You'll see for yourself the poverty of pagan religions and the hopelessness and despair of the people. Then you can see the contrast when the light of the gospel is introduced."

I couldn't get a word in. When Bob got on a roll, you just listened.

"I want you to feel it, Buddy. I want you to smell it, taste it, and see it. We'll go to places like Bhutan in the Himalayas. I want to take you to the jungles of Borneo. I want to take you to the banks of the Ganges River in India. You've got to see it for yourself."

Bob gave me such a first-class sales job that I would have been ready to go tomorrow. But I needed to talk to Jane Austin. I told Bob I would call him back.

Jane Austin and I had been asking God to show us what to do next. We were back in Montreat, and except for working with my father on some of his crusades, I didn't have a full-time job and was in a kind of limbo.

After Jane Austin and I prayed about the trip, we became convinced that God wanted me to go. Her parents and mine would help with our living expenses while I was gone. Once the decision was made, I really got excited. I knew I could learn a lot from Bob. This would be the experience of a lifetime.

In October of 1975, I met Bob in Los Angeles. The night before we left for the Orient, we had dinner together at the Luau Restaurant located on Rodeo Drive. Dr. Bob told me what to expect on the trip—what we would see. That night I was so excited I could hardly sleep.

Bob had struggled through tragedies in his own life: A rocky marriage; discord within World Vision, the organization he had founded—and later lost; a nervous breakdown; and the tragic suicide of a daughter. Although these events might have destroyed others, Bob refused to give up on life. He wanted more than anything to serve Christ with all of his heart, soul, and body.

Bob was a complex person. At times he could be warm and tenderly sensitive, then brazen and abrupt.

I had learned that few people felt neutral about Bob. People either loved the guy or had little use for him. I liked him because he was so unorthodox. He just didn't do things like everybody else.

Bob really cared for the hurting and downtrodden, but as I would learn on the trip, Bob could easily become angry and demanding. Yet, minutes later, he would realize what he had done and humbly ask for forgiveness.

More than anything else, though, Bob was a passionate evangelist. When Bob gave food, provided medicine, and offered other assistance to those in need, he did it in such a way that they understood that the "good works" were done in the name of Christ—the same One who had come to die for their sins. Bob always urged people to repent of their sin and invite Jesus into their hearts by faith.

During the early part of our globe-trotting trip, Bob told me that he had leukemia. "The doctors don't know how long I've got to live. But I want you to see the things that must break the heart of God."

I didn't know what to say to him, but this revelation about his health gave our entire trip a sense of urgency. Obviously, time was precious. Every minute counted in Bob's life.

We flew first to South Korea, a country where Bob and World Vision had done a major relief effort in the dark days following the Korean War. The leaders of the Korean government wanted to honor Bob for his twenty-five years of service to their country. Since most of that work had been done when Bob was president of World Vision, the ceremonies were awkward for him. But he was gracious and careful not to say anything negative about his former organization, even though he was brokenhearted at the changes the new leadership was making.

Bob and I attended banquets and formal dinners with many dignitaries, people like the vice president of Korea, as well as Korean and U.S. Army generals. All the church leaders in the country came out too. At every occasion, people would hug and kiss Bob. Many people in tears told how Bob and his ministry had saved their lives.

I was very touched by what I saw. I've never forgotten this experience, because I observed what one man could accomplish if he trusted God and remained faithful to His Son Jesus Christ. Even an entire nation could be impacted. I began to appreciate in a different way my own father and the impact that his life had made not in just one nation but the entire world. Wherever I went, I met people who had given their lives to God under my father's ministry, many of them men and women who were now in high places in many walks of life—serving Christ. It made me proud.

From Korea we went to Hong Kong. Bob made sure we visited the border between Hong Kong and mainland China. The British Army had an overlook where we could actually see into China, which was still closed to the gospel. With tears in his eyes, Bob said, "I will probably not live to go back to that country I love so much. But, Buddy, someday you will go. The Christians in China need our help."

As I stood gazing into China, I thought about my grandfather who had given the best years of his life as a missionary doctor for the Chinese people. My mother had been born there. I thought of the hundreds of missionaries who had died while taking the gospel of Jesus Christ to that land.

Before we left, Bob made sure that we prayed for the church in China and for the many friends he still had there.

Our trip took a dramatic turn. Up to this point, we had stayed in modern cities—Seoul and Hong Kong. Now we headed to the jungles of Indonesia, to the island of Borneo.

"I want to show you where the people still run around naked, living the way they did a thousand years ago in a Stone Age culture," Bob said. "These are the places we need to visit, because this is where the gospel is on the cutting edge."

He told me about Mission Aviation Fellowship (MAF) and the unique contribution they were making to world evangelism. "They fly small airplanes and carry missionaries into the jungle. These trips used to take months; now they take just hours. We're going to go in one of their little Cessnas, and you can see these folks for yourself."

We flew deep into the jungle of former Dutch Borneo, now called Kalimantan, staying with missionaries along the way, then moving on.

One day as we flew, down below Bob saw a small, crude landing strip that ended at the edge of a deep ravine.

"That's it!" Bob said. "That's where we want to go!" He tapped the pilot's shoulder and pointed. "Right there!"

The pilot said, "No way, Bob! With this load I wouldn't be able to get out."

"I don't care," Bob said. "That's the village. I want to see that one. We'll worry about how to get out after we go down."

The pilot smiled and quietly said, "Okay" as he began to circle to land. "Bob, we'll probably have to make a couple of trips to get everyone out of here when we leave." That was no obstacle to Bob.

The airstrip had been cut into the side of the mountain with a ravine on either end. The pilot had to make his approach along a narrow river valley. I could tell he still wasn't thrilled about having to land a loaded Cessna 185 on such a short strip. Huge beads of perspiration formed on his forehead. Bob was grinning now.

This guy's got leukemia and he's dying, I thought. *He probably would want nothing more than to go to heaven by dying in a fiery plane crash in a jungle. But how about me? I'm not so sure I want to go yet!* I thought about Jane Austin, waiting for me at home.

Bob just kept smiling, loving every minute of it.

The pilot didn't make the best landing. The plane bounced, which ate up valuable runway. By the time he got it down and stopped, we were within a few feet of the precipice.

We piled out and Bob said, "This is what I want you to see."

The village was about a mile away on the other side of the ravine, so we started to walk along the jungle trail. We had to slide down and walk over a slimy wet log bridge, then go back up the other side.

A witch doctor ruled that particular village, and I could sense an evil presence. Yet the people were friendly enough and allowed us to walk into their village to see how they lived. The villagers live in traditional "long houses"—a long house starts out as one family's dwelling. As the children marry and have children of their own, the house is expanded to house everyone. The houses can grow as long as forty to fifty yards with several generations, but the entire family unit stays together under one roof. Of course the villagers had no modern conveniences. Their only mode of transportation, other than their legs, were dugout canoes, which were beached on the river bank.

Bob kept pointing and tapping me on the shoulder. "Buddy, these people need to hear about Christ. That's why mission aviation is so important. The pilot just told me this is one of their newest airstrips. They're going to bring missionaries in here next month. If it wasn't for these pilots and their little airplanes, the gospel of Jesus Christ might never reach an area like this."

I nodded my head. It was a fascinating stop, but I was glad when the small plane took us out—and it did take two trips, but we finally made it!

Now I began to sense what Bob was trying to teach me. Up until this point, when Bob talked about the gospel being on the cutting edge, I hadn't understood. He wanted me to catch the vision of meeting people along life's road, right where they were, and to see for myself what it was like when people lived in total spiritual darkness.

From the jungles of Indonesia we went to Bangkok, Thailand, to observe the refugee crisis that had engulfed that area. The Vietnam War was finally over, and the Communists were solidifying their hold on Indo-China. Tens of thousands of people had fled Communist rule. They went by whatever route they could. Thousands went by sea. Others risked their lives to cross through the jungles of Cambodia to the border of Thailand. Many never made it.

The living conditions were abysmal. All these people wanted was freedom. Many of them eventually came to the United States.

From the refugee camps we traveled to the subcontinent of India, with its hundreds of millions of people locked in the darkness of Hinduism.

It was an unbelievable eye-opener for me to see how pagan religion blinds and enslaves people. Here I saw Hindu priests sacrificing live animals. Blood gushed from severed heads and flowed over the altar. The priest would sprinkle the crowd with the blood as people cheered.

These scenes reminded me of Old Testament accounts and helped me to understand in a deeper way that Jesus Christ is the Lamb of God, who takes away the sins of the world. I began to understand what Bob was teaching me. These people were bound by Satan's power. If they only knew that two thousand years earlier on a Roman cross, God had provided the ultimate sacrifice—His Son who with His life paid the debt of sin for everyone.

From India we went to Katmandu, Nepal, and Iran. While traveling with Bob, I learned many of life's lessons. But the lesson Bob taught me that stands out above all else is what Bob called "God room."

"What do you mean?" I asked him once when he started talking about "God room." He gave me a glance that was close to disgust, almost as if to say, "Don't you know?" He took a deep breath and sighed before he said, "'God room' is when you see a need and it's bigger than your human abilities to meet it. But you accept the challenge. You trust God to bring in the finances and the materials to meet that need.

"You get together with your staff, your prayer partners, and supporters, and you pray. But after all is said and done, you can only raise a portion of the resources required.

"Then you begin to watch God work. Before you know it, the need is met. At the same time, you understand you didn't do it. God did it. You allowed Him room to work."

Bob was on one of his rolls. His eyes sparkled and the words tumbled out: "Many times I went to places like Vietnam, where I'd see people who needed help. I would commit a hundred thousand dollars for the project. Then I'd go home, knowing that Samaritan's

Purse didn't have the money. I certainly didn't have the money. But I believed that through praying and trusting God, He would provide.

"You know, Franklin, you always have to have 'God room'!"

I stopped him and asked, "Does this always work? I'm not sure I've got that kind of faith."

Again he flashed a look that seemed to say, "Aren't you listening?" He smiled and said softly, "Listen, Buddy, 'God room' is when you have seen a need you believe God wants you to meet. You try, but you can't. After you've exhausted all your human effort, there's still a gap. No matter what you do, you just can't humanly bring it about. That's when you pray and leave room for God to work. You watch God close that gap.

"That's why I keep saying we need always to operate on 'God room.'" He paused and grinned. "When you go back to America, Buddy, commit yourself to bigger things than you can humanly do. Then you can watch God work a miracle."

I finally understood. In some ways I had already seen this principle at work in Mafraq at the hospital when the missionaries there got down on their knees every Friday to pray for their needs.

But Bob pressed on, wanting to make sure I got exactly what he meant. It seemed extremely important to him that if I didn't get anything else out of this trip, I would at least understand the "God room" principle.

"You see, Franklin," Bob continued, "faith isn't required as long as you set your goal only as high as the most intelligent, most informed, and expert human efforts can reach."

Bob illustrated what he meant by telling me of a church in the United States that had set a goal to raise one hundred thousand dollars to refurbish the church. The church leaders appealed to the congregation and collected seventy-five thousand. They still needed twenty-five. So what did they do?

"They formed a committee, and members of that committee visited each church member and encouraged them to give more so they could meet their obligation. And they met it. Okay, that's what human strategy and planning can do. Nothing wrong with that, Buddy, but just don't call it faith."

"They reached their goal, didn't they? Wasn't that faith?" I asked.

"Naw, that's just good sense at work. Now, here's how faith works." He told me about another church, which outgrew its building and needed to enlarge. Members pledged two hundred thousand dollars for the expansion.

"About that time, a missionary couple from India came home on furlough and worshipped with the congregation. They told about the hellhole of Calcutta. The people could hardly believe what they heard. The couple never asked for anything, just shared the needs of the homeless, starving children they were trying to care for.

"You know what, Buddy? The board of the church got so involved with that vision, they voted to take the entire two hundred thousand dollars and give it to the missionaries for their work." (Later on I learned that this church became one of the fastest growing congregations in the United States and completed several building programs.)

"Their giving the money to the missionaries—that was faith." Then Bob got to his point: "That's where 'God room' comes in. Nothing is a miracle until it reaches the area where the utmost that human effort can do still isn't enough. God has to fill that space— that room—between what's possible and what He wants done that's impossible. That's what I mean by 'God room.'"

Bob stood up and faced me. He tapped me on the chest, emphasizing each word with a thump of his index finger: "You don't exercise faith until you have promised more than it's possible to give."

Bob lived by the "God room" principle, but it caused him many problems. Some people who worked with him from time to time just couldn't accept it. They wanted everything written in black and white with a five-year plan and detailed budget. Bob just couldn't work that way.

People like Bob remind me of the words Jesus spoke to Nicodemus: "The wind blows where it wishes, and you hear the sound of it, but cannot tell where it comes from and where it goes. So is everyone who is born of the Spirit" (John 3:8).

Bob was definitely one of those "unpredictable" saints who responded on a moment-to-moment basis to the Spirit of God.

Bob Pierce was a spiritual giant to me. Next to my father, few influenced me and set the course of my life more than my buddy, Bob.

As promised, Bob and I arrived back in the United States just before Christmas. I shared with Jane Austin all I had seen and learned, including all the funny stories about Bob.

Only later did I realize that Bob had a motive for wanting me to go with him on the tour. For some reason Bob saw something of himself in me. What he had in mind would drastically affect my future. Maybe that's why he spent so much time making certain that I really understood "God room."

A Grandfather's Prayer

One thing you can be sure of with God: He always gets His way.

Until I accepted Christ, I had run as hard as I could from anything to do with full-time Christian service. The last thing I wanted to be was a pastor or missionary. It wasn't that I didn't respect them; I just didn't want to be one of them.

God had other ideas. Plus, missionary service was such an important part of my family heritage that I may have been born with a medical missionary gene or two.

My maternal grandfather, Dr. Nelson Bell, for example, had a lot of vitality in his blood, as did all the Bells. (Take Mama for instance—she can go night and day. I'm glad I inherited some of that stamina.)

When I was a boy, my mother's parents (Nelson and Virginia Bell) lived in a small house in Montreat. We children called them Lao E and Lao Niang (Chinese family names for Grandfather and Grandmother). Almost every Sunday we had dinner with them as a family, and they were included in most of our life's activities.

When any of us kids got sick, Mama or Bea took us to Lao E. I didn't realize until I went to Stony Brook that people actually paid to see a doctor! Lao E did everything for us, from sewing up cuts to treating infections with antibiotics.

My grandfather was an extremely proper man. I can't think of a time when he didn't wear a coat and tie. He was diligent at his work—some might say he was a workaholic. This is another gene I certainly inherited.

Regardless of how else you might describe him, above all Lao E was a Christian gentleman who always put God first. My grandfather gave the best twenty-five years of his life as chief surgeon at Tsingkiangpu Hospital. His life was written up in the book *Foreign Devil in China* by the English author, John Pollock, and on his fortieth birthday he was honored by the Fellow American College of Surgeons (FACS).

As is typical of surgeons, Lao E's approach was to go right to the source of a problem and take care of it. Usually, that meant cutting something out. He was decisive and said exactly what was on his mind—even at the dinner table. He didn't hesitate to talk about his latest operation in full detail. We kids hung on every word. Lao Niang didn't find it very humorous at all, and a couple of sharp kicks under the table and a quick "Nelson, Nelson, Nelson" only egged Lao E on as he acknowledged her reprimand with a smile, then added a few descriptive points.

I remember that Lao E was a fighter. If he believed in something, he didn't care who opposed him. "Right is right, wrong is wrong, and wrong is never right," he used to say.

When I attended Stony Brook, and later when I was away at LeTourneau, he wrote a family newsletter once a week that he sent to all his children and grandchildren. I looked forward to reading those letters, which kept all of us informed on what everybody was doing.

Several times he stopped in Texas to see me. His daughter, Rosa, lived in Los Alamos, New Mexico, at the time. Even when he was well into his seventies, he would drive his Oldsmobile 98 cross country to visit me at LeTourneau College in Longview, then go on to see Aunt Rosa. Longview was not on his direct route, but he drove hundreds of miles out of his way to stop by and find out how I was doing. He had a real sense of family loyalty.

Although I spent time with Lao E, I didn't really know him. He was the grandfather I was a little afraid of, because he was a disciplinarian. As I got older, I was smoking, drinking, and running with the wrong crowd. I felt guilty and ashamed when I was around him, so I kept my distance.

He tried to reach out to me, but I didn't want to get too close in those days. I guess I feared a lecture. The lectures never came, but I still didn't feel comfortable around him. The problem wasn't Lao E, it was Franklin.

Not until after he died did I realize just how much I missed him and wished I had taken more time to be with him.

It wasn't long before I saw Bob Pierce again. He caught up with me at my father's Seattle crusade in 1976.

Shortly after my return from the long overseas trip with Bob, my father had asked if I would move to Seattle for six months to help with preparations for his upcoming crusade there the next spring.

Jane Austin and I were excited about the opportunity and moved right after Christmas in 1975. I enjoyed the work, which included speaking at churches, helping with administrative chores at the local office, and being basically a gofer ("go for this, go for that") for Daddy's team. Daddy made sure that he started me out at the bottom and that his team didn't give me any special treatment.

As I already knew, crusades just don't happen. They require a lot of organization, prayer, and the support of local churches, along with hours of counselor and usher training and choir rehearsals. It was a tremendous amount of work. The set-up team even put me to work on Saturdays, leading counselor-training courses in a small downtown Tacoma church. Crusade preparation was a whole new experience, which is invaluable to me today.

When Bob arrived in Seattle, he wanted to meet Jane Austin and take us to dinner.

By this time I knew Bob wanted me to work with him, but I just wasn't sure I wanted to work with Bob. I loved and respected him, but our personalities and styles were miles apart. Yet I admired the work he was doing through Samaritan's Purse, and in my heart I prayed, "God, if You will allow me, this is what I want to do with my life."

My biggest problem with Bob was his temper, which I had observed during my first trip with him overseas.

Before he died, Bob once told me, "One of the hardest things I've had to endure all my life is my temper. It's kept me busy saying, 'I know I did it, and I'm wrong; I have nobody to blame but myself.'"

Bob had his moments, but he was full of fun. He was one of the most entertaining men I've ever known. (Grady Wilson was number one—but that's another book!) When Bob told a story—and he had an endless supply—he spun it with such colorful intensity that I hung on every word. Sometimes he would repeat himself, telling the same story only a couple of days after I'd heard it the first time. It didn't matter. He was so dramatic and, of course, he embellished the story each time he told it. I would listen again just as intently.

I had told Jane Austin about Bob's explosive temper, especially with waiters, so she was nervous about having a meal at one of Seattle's best-known steak houses. After we met Bob at the restaurant, I think he sensed that Jane Austin was uptight. He flashed that infectious grin of his and said, "Don't worry, honey, I'm not going to embarrass you."

Bob could really turn on the charm when he wanted to, and he was at the top of his game during our dinner. He won Jane Austin over. By the time the evening ended, she probably felt she had never met a more entertaining, lovable, distinguished, and gracious gentleman. I just shook my head; Bob was something else!

During our time in Seattle, I decided to go back to school. Since we would be in the city for six months and I had a flexible work schedule with the crusade, I enrolled in several business courses at Seattle Pacific College.

I chose business because I felt that no matter what my life's work, whether with my father in his crusades, leading Samaritan's Purse, or being involved in any other type of ministry, I needed to understand fundamental business principles. I felt this was a must for ministry leadership in the future.

When the crusade was over and I had finished the college semester, Jane Austin and I packed our bags and headed back across the country to Montreat. That summer we decided I should set a goal to complete my college education while Daddy was still in the frame of mind to pay the bills. I enrolled in Appalachian State University (ASU) in Boone, North Carolina. The school was known for its strong College of Business.

We moved to Boone, and I was thrilled to remain in the western North Carolina mountains, only ninety miles from my beloved Little Piney Cove.

The first of four children, a son, had been born and made Jane Austin and me proud parents. Because my own rebellious teenage years were a fresh memory, I had some anxiety about being a father. I still felt, at times, like a kid myself.

But with one baby at home and another on the way, I certainly plunged into my college courses with a new level of commitment—I wanted to get out of school before my kids did!

In the spring of 1978, just before I graduated from ASU, I received an interesting phone call from two local surgeons in Boone—brothers, named Lowell and Dick Furman.

The Furmans asked if I would meet with them about setting up an organization that would send Christian physicians to missionary hospitals around the world for short-term voluntary service.

"Why in the world are you calling me?" I asked. "I don't know anything about that."

"Well, your grandfather was a surgeon in China . . ."

That qualifies me? I thought.

"And you've been overseas with Bob Pierce," the doctor continued. "We also know you visited several mission hospitals on that trip. Besides that, we heard about the help you gave in building that little hospital in Jordan. We figured you'd be the best man for the job."

"What I know about missionary medicine you can put in a thimble," I said with a laugh. "Sure, I worked at the hospital in Jordan. I did maintenance and construction! When I traveled with Bob Pierce, I followed him around and looked at what he pointed to. So what do I know?"

"You know more about this subject than we do."

I thought about what he'd said. I probably did know more about mission hospitals than these men in the sense that I had visited mission hospitals—they hadn't. I also knew there were scores of Christian organizations probably doing the same thing they wanted to do.

"I think you're reinventing the wheel if you try to start a new organization," I said. "The last thing God needs is another Christian organization. Why don't you join up with somebody who is already doing it?"

"Fine. Who's doing it?"

"You might contact the Southern Baptist Foreign Mission Board. They send a lot of doctors overseas."

"We did," Dick said. "The head of their board told us, 'We can't take you unless you go for a minimum of two years.' That's their definition of short-term."

The Furmans' definition of short-term meant sending volunteer doctors, at their own expense, for four to six weeks. The short-term physicians would provide relief for the missionary doctors so they could get some rest, spend more time with their families, or get away for a furlough.

The goal was to send doctors with a servant's attitude. Two years was too long to ask a person to go. But four to six weeks was reasonable. The Furmans believed a doctor could get a lot done in that period of time.

I could see that they were sincere and meant business. I contacted Bob Pierce. "What do you think about this?" I asked.

His response was, as usual, colorful and to the point: "Just be sure what you want to do," he said. He obviously believed in helping, but he expressed concern about the way to go about it. "If the doctors are not willing to go into the jungles and find out what's really making people sick, and if they're not concerned about how the people live and the things that are killing them, Buddy, then I wouldn't give you a nickel for the whole thing."

That makes sense, I thought.

"Listen, Buddy, if they're willing to go into the jungles, I'll tell you what, God can use them. I'll be honest with you. I know there are some fine Christian doctors out there, but what I'm really concerned about are the guys with big egos and pompous attitudes going overseas and causing more trouble for missionary doctors than they're worth. Then they go back to America after their adventures and leave the missionaries to pick up the pieces. The Christian world doesn't need this."

I nodded in complete agreement.

Bob wasn't through yet: "These two doctors you're telling me about sound like they're different. Maybe the Lord is in this and leading them."

"I've got an idea," I said. "One of the doctors, Dick Furman, is headed to India soon. This will be his first time out. Would you be willing to meet him, take him around, and show him some of the places you've been—like the jungles of New Guinea? Places where he can really see human suffering and the need for the gospel?"

"I don't know about traveling with these doctors," Bob said. I could tell he was reluctant. "Buddy, they're a funny breed—arrogant, egotistical . . ."

"Not Dick Furman," I said. "Look, Bob, if I called him and got him to meet you somewhere, would that be all right? Would you take him around for a week or so and show him the kind of places you took me. How about it?"

"If you'll go with me, Buddy, I'll do it."

"Sure, why not?"

Bob and I flew to New Guinea several days later and waited for Dick Furman to arrive from India. Then Bob took us to the places few westerners ever see, because New Guinea is one of the most primitive spots on earth.

It was an eye-opening experience for Dick and me. Bob and Dick hit it off like two peas in a pod. Bob agreed that, despite his prejudice against most doctors, Dick was okay.

When I got back home, I felt in my heart that I should try to help the Furmans any way that I could. They were sincere about starting a new organization to send short-term physicians, but I wasn't convinced of the need.

"I'll tell you what," I said, "I think I can help you if you'll help me." The wheels were spinning inside my head. The university had told me I would have to attend summer classes if I wanted to graduate in August of 1978. The school did provide an alternative to class work. I could set up an internship with a local business and write a paper at the end of the summer.

I asked Lowell and Dick, "If I help you get this started, do you think you could arrange with the university to give me credit for this as an internship?"

"We know the chancellor," Lowell said. "No problem. I'm sure we can work it out." And they did.

I worked out of my father's office in Montreat. My plan was to write all the mission organizations that had hospitals and ask them the following: (1) If we could provide short-term doctors for four to six weeks, could you use them? and (2) Do you know of any organizations currently sending, on a nondenominational basis, short-term Christian physicians? If so, who?

I figured I could get these letters off in the mail and go to the beach for the rest of the summer while I waited for their responses—and get college credit for my hard labor! In spite of my intentions, God was intervening once again and working behind the scenes. I never expected to get the overwhelming and quick response I received. And I never dreamed that this school project would become a foundation of my life's work.

Through the responses, I learned about three organizations that sent out doctors. Although I liked what they were doing, their scope was smaller than what the Furman brothers had in mind. Except for one organization, all of the mission organizations responded. Nine of them requested doctors right then! The problem was we didn't have any doctors to send—we were just asking if they needed help!

At the end of the summer, I made my report to the Furman brothers and shared with them the statistics about what the other organizations were doing. I concluded, "Gentlemen, when you asked me last spring to help you, I didn't know if you were sincere. I also believed that there were other organizations already doing what you wanted to do. To my surprise, from my research, there are no organizations sending out short-term doctors in the way you envision. I doubted you, but I was wrong.

"So, where do we go from here? I believe if God reveals a need to you, He expects you to do something about it. Are you prepared for this? I believe that if you're not willing to make the commitment, don't get involved, because God will hold you accountable."

Lowell and Dick looked at each other. I could tell they had put a lot of thought into this.

Dick nodded his head with assurance. "We're committed. Show us how to get started."

"What do we do first?" Lowell asked.

"To begin with," I reminded them, "you don't have any office space."

"We'll take care of that," Dick said. "If you'll agree to set it up and run it."

To set it up was one thing, but run it? I felt I might be getting trapped. This was just supposed to be a summer project so I could graduate! True, I didn't have any firm plans. Jane Austin definitely wanted to move back to Montreat, and Bob Pierce wanted me in California. I didn't have peace about either choice.

Running the medical project for the Furmans was a completely new option. The more I thought about it, the more interested I became. We wouldn't have to move right away, and I could wait and see how things worked out with Samaritan's Purse.

The trust fund Daddy had set up for me to go to school would continue for another six months. That meant I could help the Furmans but not be financially obligated to them. I could help start the project, then if the Lord opened up another door later, I could say *adios* and move on.

The Furmans agreed to a six-month commitment and we got together to discuss the details. I told them I didn't want to take a salary. "I don't want to owe you guys anything," I said. "I am willing to work and pour myself into this project for the next six months. I am willing to test the waters. If God is in this, God will build this organization."

I knew from working with my father that it takes a lot of resources to run a ministry. We would need telephones, furniture, supplies, and some office help. All that would take money. I was going to have to test the "God room" principle. Inside my soul I was searching for God's plan for my life.

The first need was some office space. The Furman's one-story clinic had a flat roof that constantly leaked. They had already decided to make it a pitched roof and were putting in the rafters when it occurred to them, why not build office space upstairs for Franklin?

Within weeks, I moved in, and World Medical Mission was born.

For graduation from ASU, Mama gave me my grandfather Lao E's *Cruden's Concordance*. When I opened the leather book, I understood why she wanted me to have it. On the front page he had written his prayer requests. My eyes skimmed down the list, and the last item read: "Pray for Franklin's education." My grandfather had died August 2, 1973—five years to the day of my graduation (August 2, 1978).

Lao E probably had feared that I would never get out of school! Even though he was now in heaven, God had answered his earthly prayers.

I sometimes wonder: In addition to pleading with God to help me finish my education, what else did Lao E ask God to do with my life?

"Guts for Jesus"

Bob Pierce was a person given to drama. He was near death from leukemia, and everyone he met found out about it. He talked about his illness in such a way, though, that you were not offended by the personal details. Instead you were moved to sympathy.

Several times he called me and whispered into the phone, "I'm dying, Buddy. I don't have long to live." He would ask me for help. How could I refuse? When Bob called, I would drop everything and run to his side. So did others.

But after this happened several times, I began to wonder, *Is Bob faking this?* I felt guilty about having such a thought about a godly man like Bob, but I learned I wasn't the only one who had entertained the idea.

When he would reach a very low point physically, Bob would take treatments for the leukemia. I would think he might die that very night. But almost in a flash he would go into a period of remission and tear off somewhere across the world to visit missionaries and look for those he could help. I would learn about his latest trip and think, *Wait a minute! I thought he was dying!*

Bob felt in his heart that I was God's man to succeed him. However, at this time he had never really discussed it with me; he just dropped hints and told others what was in his mind. I guess he figured that somehow it would all work out.

In late summer of 1978 I visited Bob in southern California, where we had our first serious conversation about the future of Samaritan's Purse. For the first time I began to sense Bob's heart.

In a phone conversation shortly after, I told him that deep down in my heart I felt God was calling me to this ministry, but I had two serious questions.

First, the location. His office was in downtown Hollywood, near the corner of Hollywood and Vine—close to the famous Mann Theatre. Outside the office building, drug dealers and prostitutes congregated. Instead of Hollywood, I thought it should be renamed "Helly-wood." No way on God's green earth did I want to give up the mountains of North Carolina to move my wife and family to what I perceived was a modern-day Sodom and Gomorrah.

I was up front with Bob. I explained that Jane Austin's family and mine were from the Southeast. "I have no family connections out West. Do you object to my moving the office one day to the East Coast?"

My mother had decided early in her life to be close to her family in Montreat since Daddy was away so much of the time. Likewise, Jane Austin wanted to be close to her parents if I was going to travel and be gone on long trips. She needed that kind of support in raising our children.

I expected Bob's volcanic temper to explode, but to my surprise, he had no objection. Even more surprising, he agreed that Samaritan's Purse should be moved.

Then I expressed my second concern. "Bob, a few years ago you asked me to serve on your board of directors, which I have done because I believe in what you are doing and want to back you. But the present board is your board, Bob, and they don't really know me. If I were to take over, I would be subjecting myself to the leadership of people I don't know that well. Would you be willing to ask them to step aside so I could appoint my own board?"

I held my breath and waited. If this didn't set off an explosion from Bob, what would? I just knew he would resent this.

Again, to my surprise, he said, "Buddy, if that's what you want, that's what we'll do. Give me a few weeks to call each of them and explain the situation. I'll get back in touch with you."

Jane Austin and I talked about this matter for a long time. We decided to put a "fleece" before God: If God really was leading me to Samaritan's Purse, He would remove all the obstacles.

We were at a major crossroads in our life and couldn't afford to make a wrong turn. I had just graduated from ASU with a degree in business. For the next six months, I had committed to help Lowell and Dick Furman with their short-term medical missionary program. That project needed to be completed first. Jane Austin and I prayed fervently. Our future, and how it might relate to Samaritan's Purse, was in God's hands.

Several weeks later, Bob called. "I'm getting weaker," he said on the phone.

I flew to California thinking it might be my last opportunity to see him.

This time he really looked rough. It was obvious he wouldn't last much longer. I sat beside his bed and listened to his labored breathing.

Bob hadn't written his autobiography and now realized he probably wouldn't. So he had been collecting papers and making tapes for whoever would finally write such a book. He taped our entire conversation—more material for the book.

Many emotions washed over me. I deeply loved him. Few men had influenced me so strongly or done so much to shape the course of my life as had Bob Pierce.

"If I had a dying blessing to give you as they did in Old Testament times," he said, "it would be a prayer that God would grant to you the highest, noblest aspects of the vision He gave me for a dying world."

Bob stopped and prayed for me. Then he said, "I want you to follow me and earn the right to be heard for Jesus and His cross."

We both knew what he meant: He wanted me to head Samaritan's Purse. His words overwhelmed me, and I felt inadequate. I asked him to explain how he saw the future of Samaritan's Purse. Since he was putting all this on tape, these would be important words for those involved in the future of the organization.

"I want Samaritan's Purse to be exactly what Jesus said it was to be. If we stick to the facts of the story Jesus told, we'll keep right on track. [See the parable of the Good Samaritan in Luke 10:29–37.] Now, who was the Samaritan? Likely a layman. The professional religionists—the priests and the Levites—had taken a casual look at the wounded traveler and gone on their way quite unaffected by his critical need for help. Then along came a Samaritan whom the religionists despised. He, too, looked. But when he looked, compassion welled up in him."

As Bob went on with the story, he recounted that the Samaritan put the wounded man on his own donkey and took him to an inn. "The Samaritan inconvenienced himself. Not only that, but he committed himself financially. He paid the innkeeper the equivalent of a day's wages for a skilled craftsman."

I listened carefully, grasping what he said. Of course, I had heard it before, and from Bob himself as well, but these might be his final words, the most important things he wanted to say to me.

"Franklin, the Samaritan assured the innkeeper that he'd be back. 'Keep track of your costs; I'll take responsibility for this man,' he said and went on his way. That's the kind of people we want on the board of Samaritan's Purse—those who will put a wounded man on their own donkey and then walk themselves."

Bob explained that the wounded man would have had no way to repay the kindness shown to him. The Samaritan hadn't expected repayment. "This is the story of a real Samaritan. He did something that cost him, and it was something he couldn't get back."

I nodded as I listened. Many times I had seen Bob himself give generously to needs. Not once had I ever sensed that he wanted or expected any repayment. Yes, I understood his heart as he continued to talk.

"There was no way this victim of robbers could repay the Samaritan. That didn't enter into the Samaritan's thinking. The need of the hurting man was what grabbed him and moved him to action. It cost him time and money. And notice, it wasn't an ongoing thing. It was a one-time stepping in and meeting a critical need." He went on to say that this was the difference between Samaritan's Purse and traditional relief organizations. "This is our reason for being."

As he spoke, I decided that as long as I had anything to do with Samaritan's Purse, I would respect those principles. I might do things differently, but the goal would be the same.

"Another point I want to make is this," Bob continued. "I would not want anybody on the board of Samaritan's Purse who is not willing to go at least once a year to a mission field, at his own expense. What I mean is, the man has to have it in his heart—a genuine commitment to God. It may be for just two weeks, but let him go where the need is the greatest at the moment, and let him come back knowing what we're all about and why we do what we do."

Bob talked a long time, perhaps wanting to make certain that I understood clearly the principles by which he had operated. Then he said, as if he meant it as the final and most important thing for me to hear, "Keep the flag of Jesus Christ flying high. That is what will characterize us. Whatever Samaritan's Purse does—whether helping lepers in India, the sidewalk dwellers in Calcutta, victims of flood or earthquake or famine in Guatemala, Africa, or Bangladesh—anything we do or have a part in doing—we do in the name of Jesus Christ.

"The gospel has to be at the core of everything. Buddy, when we help somebody, like the Samaritan did, we then earn the right to be heard. We must take advantage of that right to present Jesus.

We have to keep it simple so they can understand. We have to give them enough information so that they can not only understand, but make a choice to accept Christ or reject Him. But we've got to make it clear. Repeat it often, every chance you get."

I'll never forget his words. I flew back to North Carolina wondering if I would ever see him again.

A few days later, Bob called. Though he was much weaker, he seemed obsessed about the future of Samaritan's Purse. I think he wanted to hear my voice and be assured of my interest in seeing that the work continue.

"I'll tell you what," he said thoughtfully, "I'm not going to name my successor. I'm going to ask the board to take eighteen months to search. If they can't name a successor within eighteen months, then they have to promise me that they will close Samaritan's Purse and seal the name forever so nobody else can ever use it."

"Maybe that's the way to do it," I said.

"I'm doing it this way because I believe you're God's man, and Buddy, I love you. During the next eighteen months after my death, you are going to get to know the board of directors and they are going to get to know you. I know that's one of your concerns, but I believe that God will answer that concern for you—in His time—in His way.

"Buddy, I'm getting weaker. I don't have much more time. I just don't have the energy for this."

As we hung up, I assured him that I loved him too.

That was the last time we spoke.

The next week, on the morning of September 7, 1978, the phone rang. It was Fred Dienert. "I guess you've heard. Bob Pierce died last night," he said.

"No, I didn't know." My heart sank. Even though I had expected it, I still wasn't ready. Fred kept on talking, but I had trouble concentrating. I felt numb.

"The funeral's going to be in California in a couple of days," Fred said. "I'll pay for your ticket and hotel—we'll stay at the Hilton."

"I'll meet you there," I remember saying. As I hung up the phone, a heaviness came over me. I had lost a very special friend.

I didn't know until later, but just a few months before his death, Bob had visited my parents. I think he had wanted Mama's and Daddy's blessing on his decision to offer me the leadership of Samaritan's Purse. Maybe he also wanted them to put pressure on me to say yes. But Daddy wouldn't interfere. He wanted to let God call me if that was His plan and purpose.

People from all over the world came to Bob's funeral.

As I listened to the eulogies and struggled with my sense of loss, questions gnawed at me: What's going to happen to Samaritan's Purse? It just can't stay in limbo. His secretary can't be expected to run it. Without leadership it will fall part.

Bob's attorney, Roger Arnebergh, had suggested we have a board meeting immediately following Bob's funeral. Mr. Arnebergh had once been the city attorney for Los Angeles. He was well-known, highly respected, and one tough lawyer. The purpose of our board meeting was to figure out what to do with Samaritan's Purse.

I found it interesting: To my knowledge, it was the first time the board had officially met. In the past, Bob had conducted our board meetings by telephone. He would call each of us from some place like Calcutta and say, "I've just given Rose and Wai Hu [they were longtime friends who ran a small orphanage] ten thousand dollars, and I want board approval." Or he would call from Korea, on an around-the-world journey, and want approval for the trip he was already on.

We would chuckle during these phone conferences. We loved Bob and accepted his way of doing things. Plus, we also had total trust in him. His practices were not what I'd been taught in business school, and I would have done things differently. Yet with all the tens of millions of dollars that passed through his hands in his lifetime, none of it had ever stuck to his fingers.

I looked around the room at the interesting group. Bob's secretary was very capable in her clerical work. Dr. Robert Thompson, a distinguished Canadian, had been a missionary to Ethiopia and had served in the Canadian Parliament for a number of years. I smiled at Guy Davidson, the pastor of Grace Community Church in Tempe, Arizona. Next to me was Ted Dienert, son of Fred Dienert, who owned an advertising and public relations agency that handled a number of Christian ministry accounts. Dr. William Roberts, a retired minister from the West Coast, was also present.

During our board meeting we found out exactly what earthly possessions Bob had accumulated in his lifetime. He owned a small home, which went to his wife, a modest life insurance policy divided between his wife and daughters, his clothes, and a few special pieces of furniture that had been given to him by people from around the world. That was about it.

We discussed a lot of business details. Bob, in his heart, had named me his successor at Samaritan's Purse. And I sensed that this was a work God wanted me to do. I believed I knew the needs that Samaritan's Purse could meet. But I had an uneasy feeling in my stomach that I might have lost my opportunity. Though Bob had told the board that he believed I was the man for the job, he wanted them to confirm it.

A couple of board members had other ideas. To my surprise, Bob's secretary expressed interest in running the organization. She argued that she had been the person closest to Bob. That was true, but that in itself didn't qualify her to run an organization. There was another who felt we should close it down and give the assets to other organizations. My heart really sank at this point. I prayed hard as the meeting progressed, "Lord, if this is Your will, You're going to have to make it clear to these people." Bob had asked the board to search for a successor for eighteen months, so that did buy us some time.

Over the next few months, we had several board meetings. In the meantime, the secretary continued to run the office. My biggest concern was that whoever headed Samaritan's Purse needed to be in the field, out in the middle of human need, not someone who sat in an office and wrote reports. I knew that if the board ever offered me the leadership, I would go spend time and assess the needs for myself—just the way I had seen Bob do it.

My inner struggle about assuming the leadership of Samaritan's Purse was intense. I kept thinking of the fine work Bob had done, of his sacrifice, and of the needs around the world. Lebanon was in the middle of a bloody civil war. There were thousands of refugees pouring out of Vietnam, Cambodia, and Laos over land and by boat into the South China Sea. Africa was experiencing some of the worst famine in modern history.

There was so much opportunity for ministry through Samaritan's Purse. But if something didn't happen soon—if someone didn't lead the way—Samaritan's Purse would die. I've always been action oriented and never liked to beat around the bush. I was ready to take the bull by the horns at Samaritan's Purse and go to work.

I became increasingly apprehensive that what Bob feared most could happen; Samaritan's Purse would fall into the hands of someone or a group of people who would tear the heart right out of it. They would turn Samaritan's Purse into a Christian bureaucracy and strip away the uniqueness of a ministry that could move quickly and provide support and assistance without a lot of meetings and special studies. Most of all, I feared that they might take away the flag that Bob had instructed me to carry—that the Lord Jesus Christ would be foremost in everything Samaritan's Purse did.

In those gut-twisting months, I talked with Roy Gustafson almost every day because he was one of my closest friends and a very wise man. He was a good listener, and I could discuss every detail with him.

In one of those conversations he said something I'll never forget: "It is better to be worthy and not have Samaritan's Purse than to have Samaritan's Purse and be unworthy." As soon as he said this, it was if a branding iron burned the words into my brain.

Following a trip to the California office, I drove the two-hour trip back to Boone from the airport and had a long conversation with God. It began with a recommitment of my life to Him, and then I asked for His will in my life. I surrendered my future with Samaritan's Purse to Him.

"Lord, if You want me to lead this ministry, then You have to open the door. You have to work in the hearts of the board of directors. I can't do that. I take my hands off." I kept thinking of Roy's words: "It is better to be worthy and not have Samaritan's Purse than to have Samaritan's Purse and be unworthy."

If God intended for me to lead Samaritan's Purse and someone else took it, they would have to be accountable to Him. Then He would have something better for me.

I finally had a sense of peace, knowing that God would work all things together for my good and His glory.

In early 1979, income was beginning to fall off at Samaritan's Purse. I called Ted Dienert and Guy Davidson to ask them what they thought about my taking a trip to Lebanon and Southeast Asia on behalf of the ministry. I had been in these places with Bob Pierce and knew the people. I told them, "We need to get on track and do the work that Samaritan's Purse is meant to do." They agreed, and I packed my bags and headed out.

My first stop was Lebanon. As the plane approached Beirut, I became increasingly eager to see Sami Dagher's smiling face again. Sami was no longer working at the Phoenicia Hotel. He had left before the war started to begin a small church in one of the poorest areas of the city. Sami had shared with me the difficulty he had when he approached the manager of the hotel to inform him he was resigning to start a church.

"God has called me to preach," Sami told the manager. "I'm leaving the hotel."

"Leaving? You're a fool! You're crazy! A man in your position making good money, and you quit?"

"I leave for something more important than money. I'm going to preach the name of Jesus Christ."

"You're going to give up this good position to preach for some god? You must be crazy. No! I tell you the right thing to do. You stay here and make money, Sami. I need you."

"No, I can't stay any longer. I've prayed and this is what I must do."

The manager argued with Sami, but he didn't relent. Then the man grew angry and shouted, "I curse you! One day, Sami Dagher, you will come to the threshold of my door, and you will beg for a crust of bread, and I won't give it to you. I will let you starve! Do you hear my words? Not a crust!"

"I must obey God," Sami said gently.

The church was started with five or six converts in a room that measured thirty feet by twenty in Karantina, the poorest part of the city.

The tensions between the Lebanese and the Palestinian refugees living in Lebanon grew. Eventually, fighting broke out between the two groups and soon engulfed the entire city. The world-renowned Phoenicia was at the front line between the warring factions, and the city lived through some of the most vicious street fighting since World War II. Block after block began to crumble. Within days, the hotel burned and was completely destroyed. All the former staff were without jobs.

By that time Sami's church was growing, and people filled the little room as shells rained down all over Beirut. Bullets often whizzed through the windows of the church. No place was safe.

At one point I even offered to find a way to bring Sami to America, but he would not leave his country or his people.

"Franklin," he said, "how can a shepherd run when there are wolves attacking the flock? If the shepherd runs, then the flock will be scattered. It is more important that I stay now more than any other time. My people need me.

"It's very kind of you, my dear brother," Sami said, "but no. This is where God has called me to live and to preach. This is where I stay."

Late one night, during some of the heaviest fighting, Sami heard a knock at his door. He told his wife and children to stay in bed. He answered it himself.

Sami opened the door. Before him stood the former manager of the Phoenicia Hotel. "My friend, it is late, but please come in," Sami said. He took the man's arm and brought him into the house.

"I couldn't sleep," the man said. He kept his head down, as if unable to look Sami in the eyes. "I wanted to see how you were doing and to talk."

Sami made coffee and they discussed the old days and how much they had enjoyed the Phoenicia. Sami sensed his former boss and friend had come for a specific reason, but the man wouldn't say. Long past midnight, Sami finally said, "My friend, it is late. Why have you come to me?"

"Oh, nothing, Sami. Just to talk of old times."

The man walked to the door and opened it. As he stood in the doorway with his head hung low, he turned to Sami and said, "I have no food. I have not eaten for two days. Do you have anything that you could spare?"

Sami stared at the man and remembered how he had cursed him—threatening that one day Sami would come to his door and beg for bread, and he would not even receive a crust. Now the man was standing in *his* doorway asking for bread!

"I felt God had brought him to that very place," Sami told me. "He didn't ask while he was sitting at my table, and he didn't ask for food in the hallway. He did not ask until he stood right at my door."

"What did you do, Sami?" I asked, when he told me the story later.

"I fed him," he replied and smiled. "Isn't that what the gospel tells us to do?"

As I walked through the airport in Beirut, I reminisced about the trip when I had introduced Bob to Sami. I knew Sami would be Bob's kind of man, or—as he used to describe people he really admired—a man with "guts for Jesus." I was right. Bob loved Sami.

After that visit, Bob had gone back on his own several times to see Sami. Only one month before his death, on his last trip abroad, Bob had been to Beirut to visit and encourage Sami. They had attended a Wednesday night worship service at the Karantina Church, and just as the service was ending, the Syrians and Palestinians started to shell East Beirut, where the church and Sami's home were located.

The shelling became so heavy that Sami decided to take Bob back to his hotel in West Beirut, which was under Syrian/PLO control. To cross from East to West was tricky. They had to go through a kind of no-man's-land, an area often referred to as Sniper's Alley.

Bob's leukemia was so advanced that he was in a wheelchair, which caused problems in dodging the shells. Somehow Sami got him through. Once they reached the hotel, the shelling had become so intense that Sami didn't dare return to his own home in East Beirut. The hotel was already filled with people stranded because of the shelling, so without a word of complaint, he was forced to sleep on the floor in Bob's room.

"That night I learned how to die," Sami later told me. "I listened to Bob talk to God all night, hour after hour, praying for other people. He poured out his heart before God for missionaries in foreign lands, national pastors and their burdens, his family.

167

"The presence of God was so real in that room, I couldn't close my eyes. In the midst of my thoughts about the safety of my own family, I felt a calmness. God would take care of them.

"As I listened into the wee hours of the morning, I learned how to face death and not to be afraid."

The Karantina Church had become a very special project for Bob and Samaritan's Purse. As the war had raged and people's lives were shattered, Sami and the members of his church had fed and clothed the refugees. As the aid was given, Sami presented the hope of the gospel of Jesus Christ. Many responded and Sami's church flourished.

Today, Karantina Church is one of the largest evangelical congregations in Lebanon, and it has started numerous other churches. And Sami is still faithfully preaching the gospel, giving the bread (of life) to all who seek.

Hard Lessons

The schoolbooks were now closed. The lessons I would now learn would come from life's experiences.

A year after Bob died, the Samaritan's Purse board met in California to discuss the leadership issue. I still felt with all my heart that God was calling me to this ministry, but I had no idea what might happen.

After my trip in 1979, I had written a lengthy report detailing my experiences with Sami Dagher in Lebanon, as well as my first-hand look at the refugee camps in Thailand. The board asked me to write the next newsletter for Samaritan's Purse.

Bob Pierce had always written newsletters about his travels and the needs he observed. The readers loved his "on-the-scene" reports and gave generously. Bob then channeled the funds expediently to the people overseas he had promised to help.

When the newsletter I had written went out, I had no idea if anybody would give a penny. All I did was honestly tell about what I had seen. I prayed that the Lord would touch the readers' hearts. God seemed to bless that letter: It generated the largest financial response Samaritan's Purse had seen since Bob's death.

Maybe the letter is what prompted Dr. Bob Thompson to stand up during the California board meeting and say, "Bob Pierce asked all of us to take up to eighteen months if need be to find his successor. If we couldn't, he instructed us to close down Samaritan's Purse and seal the name so nobody can use it. We are approaching his deadline. Who can lead this work? I'm too old; I can't do it."

He then turned and said to the office manager, "You are a great administrator—but not a leader." She stared straight ahead in blank silence. She was still supervising the office in California.

Dr. Thompson continued to scan the room, pausing to look directly at each person. "Ted Dienert, you're not going to leave your office in Dallas. Guy Davidson, you're not going to leave your church in Arizona. Bill Roberts, you're like me. We're both too old. Now there's Franklin. He was Bob's choice. I see what Bob saw in him. He's got what it takes."

Dr. Thompson looked around the table and continued. "Bob came to Canada not long before he died and personally told me this was his desire." Ted and Guy nodded in agreement. Then Dr. Thompson looked right at me. "Franklin, do you feel God is calling you to lead Samaritan's Purse? I think you're the man."

Before I could answer, others on the board voiced their approval.

I hadn't expected to be chosen in quite this way, but I said yes with a smile. That day I was elected president and chairman of the board at the ripe old age of twenty-eight. How much did I know as such a young man? To be honest—not much. But I was willing to try and to give my best to the Lord. Later God would send older men into my life to help me, like George Johnston, who had spent most of his life as an executive with U.S. Steel. I also learned to rely on my board of directors for their advice and counsel.

Although I was now officially "in charge," I sensed it was too early to ask the board if I could move the headquarters to Boone. I did ask if we could begin to bring Samaritan's Purse and World Medical Mission together. They liked that idea very much. I agreed to work from my office at World Medical Mission and make occasional trips to California. This arrangement would have to be temporary.

I talked at length with Lowell and Dick Furman about my new role with Samaritan's Purse. They and the entire World Medical Mission board of directors were in total agreement that I should give leadership to Samaritan's Purse. They still wanted me to continue with my work at World Medical Mission, because they felt the two organizations complemented one another so well: Samaritan's Purse providing funds and resources in times of crises and World Medical Mission providing doctors and nurses to meet medical emergencies and serve in mission hospitals.

I just had to find a way to get both organizations under one roof—in God's time.

Following in anyone's footsteps isn't easy, especially a tremendously unique and colorful person like Bob Pierce. I certainly wasn't Bob.

My leadership style would differ from Bob's, but one thing I knew: Samaritan's Purse would continue on the same course Bob had set years before—searching for those who had fallen into the gutters and ditches along life's pathway. We would continue to follow the example of the Good Samaritan, and I wanted this organization to be a cutting-edge operation for spreading the gospel.

There were fundamentals we would not compromise. Samaritan's Purse would not use gimmicks or professional fund-raising agencies to write our newsletters.

I vowed to communicate to our donors what God allowed me to see and experience so that the needs would be seen as opportunities to invest in God's kingdom. I never wanted to be guilty of manipulating people to give. I felt that if we were not careful, Samaritan's Purse could be guilty of robbing God. I was keenly aware that there were many fine Christian organizations. God didn't want everyone to support Samaritan's Purse. Maybe He wanted some of them to give to another ministry or their church (above their tithe).

I expected difficulties during the transition from Bob's leadership to mine. People who had supported Bob's work did so because they knew and trusted him. At first, my only communication with Bob's donors would be the monthly newsletter. As I labored over the stories of needs to fill those pages, I prayed that the readers would sense that, like Bob, I had a burden for the hurting of the world.

I had learned through my experiences at the hospital in Jordan that when God wants something done, He will provide the resources. I knew our success at Samaritan's Purse would come only if God placed His hand of blessing upon us.

We stuck to our original plan: Present the facts, let people know the need, and then back off. We would let the Holy Spirit do the rest. We learned that it works.

A year after Bob's death, the refugee crisis really exploded in Southeast Asia. The Christian and Missionary Alliance Church, the Southern Baptists, and others got right to work and did a tremendous job—with extremely limited resources—providing food, medicine, and housing, as well as spiritual comfort, to the refugees.

I made a number of trips to that part of the world to visit refugee camps, especially those of the Hmong people from Laos. There I surveyed what the missionaries needed to do their job.

The missionaries were grateful for the assistance Samaritan's Purse could give, and we helped with doctors and nurses from World Medical Mission. (Lowell Furman was one of our first doctors to respond to the crisis in Southeast Asia.)

I was determined that Samaritan's Purse be involved in a crisis like this. If the United Nations and other humanitarian agencies could be there to help, I wanted to be sure that we were there on behalf of Jesus Christ and His Church.

One evening I was watching Ed Bradley of *Sixty Minutes* do a special report on the boat people. He was standing on a beach speaking, and behind him you could see a boat coming ashore.

Then the breakers capsized the boat. The refugees from the boat frantically swam for shore. Bradley saw what had happened, left the cameraman, and jumped into the surf to pull people to safety. As the camera focused on him, I could sense his compassion—a tough correspondent who had seen just about everything. But there he was, down in the waves, pulling people to safety.

If that correspondent could risk his life to save a handful of people, I asked myself, *could I do less?* I prayed right then, "Lord, if You can use me just to save one, I'll go anywhere."

Not long after that incident, I heard of an interview with Sir Lionel Luckoo, a Christian from Guyana and a world-renowned attorney who had represented Jim Jones, the cult leader who had moved to South America and built Jonestown. Later Jones had led more than nine hundred of his followers (including 276 children) into a mass suicide.

Thoughts of Jonestown started to whirl through my brain. *What about all that land? Wouldn't it be great if we could take that place of human tragedy and turn it into something that would give glory and honor to Jesus Christ?* I thought. *Would it be possible to transplant refugees from Southeast Asia and give them a new home in South America?*

I learned that the government of Guyana had done nothing with Jonestown. It remained vacant, a facility that could handle more than nine hundred people.

Would it be possible to convert the buildings and the land into settlement centers for homeless refugees? Samaritan's Purse could take the lead and make this happen. If we approached it right, why wouldn't the Guyanan government appreciate some positive publicity by allowing refugees to resettle Jonestown?

A friend of mine, Chuck Ward, who was in charge of all of my father's television broadcasting in Latin American, put me in touch with Sir Lionel Luckoo. I asked him, "What happened to Jonestown? In your opinion, would the government be interested in using it as a government refugee resettlement site?"

He told me that the government had not used the land for anything else. Luckoo liked the idea very much and felt it would help destroy the memory of a great tragedy. He said, "I am personal friends with the president of Guyana, Forbes Burnham, and I will bring this matter to his attention promptly!"

In the fall of 1979, my father called a meeting of his board of directors and staff. He asked me to come too. We all congregated at Callaway Gardens in Georgia for a time of spiritual renewal. During this time, he asked me to serve on his board. I was honored.

While at Callaway, I spoke to my father about the possibility of using Jonestown. He thought it was an interesting concept, and when I told him that Sir Lionel Luckoo was arranging for me to meet the president of Guyana to present a proposal, he suggested that I take Allan Emery, president of the BGEA board of directors. Mr. Emery is a seasoned Christian diplomat, and I was grateful for his willingness to come and give me counsel.

The meeting was set, and we all flew down in a private plane provided by Walt Meloon of Correct Craft (the famous ski-boat company in Orlando, Florida). I met with President Burnham and his entire cabinet. They liked the proposal of using Jonestown as a resettlement site and asked that I personally visit and inspect the property.

Jonestown is in a remote part of the country near the Venezuela border. There's not a road that leads to Jonestown—the only access is by air. Two government helicopters flew me and the rest of the inspection party to the site.

For approximately five minutes, we circled above Jonestown. While we were hovering it dawned on me that the pilot had no intention of landing. I hadn't come that far and gone to that much effort to circle a thousand feet above the ground. "I want to land, and I want to land now," I said, shouting above the engine noise and gesturing toward the ground.

The pilot shook his head; he wasn't about to go down.

"The president promised me I could go inside and look around. You land this helicopter now!" I yelled.

Again, he shook his head.

"I want to see the place from the ground. I don't think the president will be pleased to learn you refused to carry out his orders."

The Guyanan officials looked at one another, then motioned for the pilot to land. We went down.

As soon as we got out of the copter, I realized that the government had done little to the compound except remove the bodies a year and a half earlier. Nothing had been touched. It was eerie.

Inside the houses, furniture was covered with dust and cobwebs. Clothes hung inside closets. I noticed a stereo with a record on it, as if someone might come in at any minute and turn it on. Children's toys were scattered in a playpen. In one room a bed was made, slippers neatly arranged on the floor next to it, ready for use.

I began to understand why the pilot had not wanted to land. Jonestown was different from what the media and the government of Guyana had described. It had obviously been a Marxist-Leninist commune. Posters of men such as Che Guevara and other Communist leaders or heroes littered the place. Socialistic slogans were written on the walls and on homemade billboards. They had obviously been there before the mass suicide.

After completing my inspection tour and returning to the states, I began to have second thoughts about Jonestown and the government of Guyana. The more I learned, the worse the picture got. The Cubans, East Germans, and Russians obviously had a definite influence in the country.

I was ready to abandon the idea, but then the UN became interested. I felt as long as they might get involved, I should pursue the Jonestown resettlement—maybe there was a chance we could work it out. The UN sent a delegation to Guyana made up of leaders from the refugee camps in Thailand along with a member of the Royal Thai government and representatives from the UN High Commissioner for Refugees (UNHCR).

Once we arrived in Guyana, the government was very cooperative in getting us out to inspect Jonestown. To my surprise, there was a lot of enthusiasm from the delegation about the resettlement possibility. However, it soon became evident that to some, the refugee dilemma was big business. Some wanted the refugees to stay in Southeast Asia. Others wanted the refugees to come to America and no other country. There was even one warlord who wanted the refugees to become an insurgent army to go back and fight the Communists. These groups with other agendas began to block the way; political maneuvering beyond our control was working against the project. When I sensed it wasn't going to work, I finally pulled back.

Something still had to be done, though, for tens of thousands of men and women living in those filthy camps in Southeast Asia. They wanted a new start. There had to be other places where they could find a home and not be used as pawns.

Over the next few years, Samaritan's Purse helped thousands of these people. Even though we couldn't give them new homes, we were able to ease the suffering in their camps. We provided food and clothing and assisted in spiritual outreach.

The U.S. government and other Western nations opened their doors. In later years, many Christian organizations in the U.S. and Canada were able to find homes for thousands of refugees in communities across North America.

Even though the Jonestown project didn't materialize, I learned a lot about facing political agendas and dealing with foreign governments as well as the UN. I also realized that, in doing the Lord's work, it doesn't hurt to be bold and consider "far out" ideas. With just a slight shift in circumstances, the tragic ruin that was Jonestown could have been reclaimed. This was just the beginning of many hard lessons I would learn along life's road.

Daddy's parents, Morrow and Frank Graham, known to their grandchildren as Mother and Daddy Graham.

Mama's parents, Nelson and Virginia Bell, known to their grandchildren as Lao E and Lao Niang.

Growing up, the woman I loved most next to my mother was Beatrice Long. Here she holds me along the road in Montreat (1954).

When Daddy returned from a long trip, he always scooped us up in his arms and held us as though he never wanted to let go (1955).

Taking aim at the window of my parents' log home in the mid-fifties.

John Rickman "Gizmo" displays to Bunny (holding our poodle, Cedric) a rattlesnake he had just killed with a hoe (1959).

Growing up, Daddy was gone most of the time, it seemed. This was a typical family picture—no Daddy. Left to right on the steps of our log house: me, Bunny, Anne, Gigi, and baby brother Ned on Mama's lap (1958).

Preparing to go camping with my cousin, Deryl Graham, and the best dog ever, Cindy. We got her free from the pound (1962).

The Ivy League look at Stony Brook. What can I say? (1966).

Dr. Calvin Thielman (left) in the Oval Office. Not only was Calvin my pastor, but on many occasions he served as special adviser to Lyndon Johnson during his presidency (1966).

WALT DISNEY STUDIOS   Used by permission

Aileen Coleman with Bedouin police in the desert of Jordan (1970).

Daddy took our family to California in 1966 and stopped by for a visit with Walt Disney. My younger brother, Ned, is to my right.

Lester Gates (left) and Mohommed Makki in Mafraq, Jordan (1970).

ROY GUSTAFSON

ROBERT JONES

My beloved Triumph TR6 (1971).

Bill Cristobal (center) double-checks our course to Texas. I'm on the left with Jerry Zabel, Bill, Lee Dorn, and Mama (1971).

Mark Taylor (whose father, Ken Taylor, translated The Living Bible*) stands in front of the Land Rover that the BGEA bought for the hospital in Mafraq, Jordan (1971).*

In Israel (left to right): David Schultz, Roy Gustafson, and yours truly with a hedgehog face (1972).

David Hill, gun in boot, prepares for his evening message during the Rhodesian War in Bulawayo (1973).

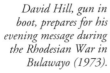

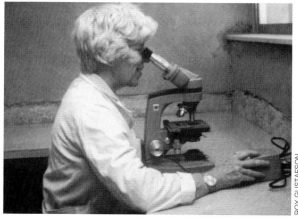

Dr. Eleanor Soltau at the hospital, looking for signs of tuberculosis through the only microscope in the lab (1973).

Jane Austin with her father and mother (Ned and Jane Cunningham) moments before we departed on our honeymoon (1974).

Bob Pierce (center) posing with Dr. Richard Furman and me in New Guinea, Indonesia. Behind us is Samaritan V, the fifth Cessna of thirteen that Samaritan's Purse bought for Mission Aviation Fellowship (1978).

Dave Mungenast, the 1967 and '71 gold medalist in the International Six-Day Trials, and me at the top of Poughkeepsie Gulch outside of Ouray, Colorado, during the Colorado 500.

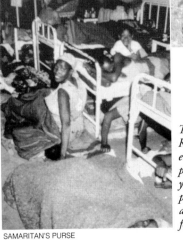

Tenwek Hospital in Kenya in the early eighties with 200 percent occupancy. As you can see, there are patients under the beds and on the floor at the foot of the beds.

In downtown Beirut (Lebanon) just off Sniper Alley with Dr. Ross Rhoads, vice chairman of the Samaritan's Purse board of directors (left), and Sami Dagher.

Roy Rogers cracks a joke with Mama (left) and Dale Evans in Los Angeles (1983).

When Daddy and I arrived in Russia, we were met by both Orthodox and Baptist leadership (1984).

In Jordan with two of my favorite gals, Aileen Coleman (left) and Eleanor Soltau, in the mid-eighties.

Dennis Agajanian entertains on a hospital ward in Nyankunde, Zaire.

With my parents at the home where my mother was born in Huaiyin, China (1988).

Members of the Contra Army Chaplain's Corps, men and women that we had the privilege of training during the late eighties.

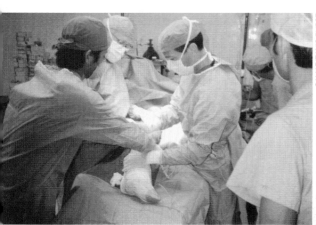

Dr. Lowell Furman (back center) and Dr. Richard Furman (front center) operate on a wounded contra soldier in the jungle of Honduras (1989).

Brother Ruben (Guerrero) (left) with Lazarus in Managua, Nicaragua (1992).

Roy Gustafson takes time to read the story of Gideon from the Bible to our boys (left to right) Edward, Roy, and Will at Gideon Springs in Israel.

In front of our home on the farm in Boone, NC. Left to right: Roy, Edward, Cissie, Jane Austin, me, and Will. Animals: Spankey, Dan, and Buford (how do you like that profile?) (1992).

Family portrait taken in front of Mama's log house at Little Piney Cove the day my parents celebrated their fiftieth wedding anniversary. Left to right: Gigi, Anne, Bunny, Mama, Daddy, me, and Ned (1993).

RUSS BUSBY

With Governor Walter J. Hickel, his wife, Ermalee, and Senator Loren Leman (1994).

Three generations of William Franklin Graham taken at my parents' home in Montreat (1993).

JOHN HENDRICKSON

RUSS BUSBY

With Johnny Cash in California (1993).

The Charleston, West Virginia, crusade in May 1994 was the first time my father heard me preach. Here the crowd of 12,000 that packed the civic center gave Daddy a standing ovation when I introduced him.

With former Joint Chiefs of Staff General Colin Powell (1994).

My sister, Anne Lotz, and I escort my parents from the plane during the Raleigh crusade in September 1994.

I explain to Pastor Dennis and our ministry team our plan for evangelism at the Central Hospital of Kigali in Rwanda (1995).

Youth Night at the Wilmington crusade (1995).

SAMARITAN'S PURSE

ANTHONY LOEW

The entire family loves motorcycles. Here, I take a moment to pose with Edward (left), Roy, and Cissie on the Harley (1995).

One of the greatest men I know— friends don't come any better than Dr. John Wesley White—in Bend, Oregon (1995).

JIM WHITMER

SAMARITAN'S PURSE

Ricky Skaggs on the platform at Trask Coliseum at my Wilmington, North Carolina, crusade in May 1995. That's Dennis Agajanian in the background.

COTSWOLD PHOTOGRAPHY

With Jane Austin and former President George W. Bush in Charlotte, North Carolina (1995).

The closing meeting of the Franklin Graham Triangle Area Crusade at Walnut Creek Amphitheatre, Raleigh, North Carolina. Twenty thousand attended (1994).

Shortly after my return from visiting Jonestown, I asked Dr. Lowell Furman to join me for a survey trip to visit mission hospitals in Africa that wanted our help. It was our strong conviction that before we sent a doctor overseas to work in a hospital, either I or one of our board members should go and see it firsthand so we would know what we were getting into. One of our stops would be at Tenwek Hospital in western Kenya.

To reach Tenwek, an extremely remote area, we had to fly in a small plane across the great Rift Valley and mile after mile of African bush. This was an exhilarating experience. Our pilot, Keith Jones, once had been with the Royal Air Force (RAF) and had flown planes off aircraft carriers in the rough waters of the North Sea. He handled the Cessna as if he were on a bombing mission.

As we approached Tenwek, Keith said, "We've got to let the hospital know we've arrived." He dived to treetop level and buzzed across the hospital compound with the engine wide open. It would have been a great strafing run—the only thing missing was the sound of machine guns. After terrorizing those below, Keith banked sharply to the right and climbed out. As we circled above, he said, "I think I'll go down one more time to make sure they heard us."

Lowell and I looked at each other. Neither of us said anything, but I knew what we both were thinking: *Make sure they heard us? That last pass was so loud, the dead probably heard us!* No question—we had a wild man at the controls!

Keith yelled at us again, "Write a note on the back of several of your business cards. Ask the missionaries to meet us at the airport." I wrote the message.

This time Keith cut the engine, slowing the plane's speed, and came in even lower—I felt like I could almost reach down and touch the heads of the people who were looking up, wide-eyed, at us. As the plane drifted over the hospital, I waited until our pilot yelled, "Now!"

I dropped the cards. They fluttered to the ground, and several children raced to pick them up.

We banked again and headed to the little grass air strip at Bomet, a few minutes from the hospital compound. From the air I could tell there wasn't much of a road connecting the airstrip to the hospital—it seemed like just a pig path cut through the heavy bush.

Keith set us down smoothly, and within minutes hundreds of people appeared out of nowhere and surrounded the aircraft. I was relieved to see that none of them were carrying spears. They were friendly and eagerly shook our hands.

Within half an hour, a VW van came bouncing down the dirt road that paralleled the strip. Out hopped a slender man of medium height. He greeted us with an infectious grin. "I got your card," he said. "My name is Dr. Ernie Steury."

Ernie, Lowell, and I immediately felt a common bond, and our visit got off to a great start. The hospital had an impressive, efficient ministry, and over the next two years I made several trips back to assess their needs. The hospital was seriously overcrowded with their 130 beds often filled to 200 percent occupancy!

Each time I visited I would ask, "Ernie, why don't you build a new ward? You need more space."

"Maybe someday," he would answer with that bright smile of his.

On one of my trips, Ernie told me they now had plans to build a new ward.

"How much do you think it will cost?" I asked.

"About four hundred thousand dollars," Ernie replied.

"How much money have you raised?"

"Nothing," he said with a laugh. "We don't have any money, but God knows our need."

I smiled, too, because I was remembering the missionaries in Jordan and others I'd met over the years who had the same confident attitude. That kind of faith always got my blood pumping. I really wanted to do something.

I took a roll of pictures and promised Ernie we would try to help them. When I left, I thought to myself, *What have I done? How in the world could I help them raise four hundred thousand dollars for a new ward?* Of course, I had used the word *help* not *promise,* which was a good loophole in case I couldn't deliver. But then I thought about Bob Pierce and his lectures to me on "God room."

"Lord, I have promised more than I can deliver," I prayed. "You know that! But these faithful servants of Yours have been working here in the African bush under such difficult conditions. They need Your help—now I leave You room to provide a miracle."

I went home, and within only weeks I received an invitation to be a guest on Jim Bakker's television program, *PTL.* In those days it was broadcast from Charlotte, North Carolina.

When I showed up at *PTL* wearing my best suit, one of the program directors informed me that Jim Bakker had gone out of town unexpectedly and someone else would interview me.

Maybe I looked nervous or something, but for whatever reason, the interview was a disaster. The host would ask a question, and just as I would lean forward, ready to speak, he would jump in and answer the question himself. In the half hour the cameras rolled, I hardly said anything at all!

"So much for *PTL,*" I said to myself as I left.

Two days later, Jim Bakker called me. He had heard about the "interview."

"I'm sorry I wasn't there, Franklin," he told me. He obviously felt embarrassed and invited me to come back.

I wondered if it would be worth the time, but I said, "Why not?" What did I have to lose?

It took several weeks for me to be rescheduled. When I arrived at *PTL,* Jim greeted me warmly. The program went smoothly, and Jim allowed me to talk at length about Samaritan's Purse. I was impressed with his interest in missions. One of the last questions Jim asked was, "Where have you just been, and what are you working on now?"

"I've just been to Africa," I said. I told about Tenwek Hospital and how they were at over 200 percent occupancy.

"How does that work?" Jim asked. "A hundred percent is full. What does it mean to have 200 percent plus occupancy?"

"It means they have more than two people in a bed." I handed him a photograph. It showed a narrow hospital bed with three people lying in it.

He became teary eyed and held the photo up. The camera zoomed in, and soon the photo from the hospital filled the screen. "Look at this, folks," he said. He turned to me, "Franklin, what can I do to help?"

"They need a new ward, and I'm trying to raise money to have it built."

"How much is it going to cost?"

"They think it's going to cost about four hundred thousand dollars." I almost could not say the amount; to me it was an enormous amount of money.

Jim turned to the camera and said, "Everybody watching right now, I want you to send Franklin Graham one dollar. Don't send it to me or to *PTL*." He then spoke to the people in the control room. "Put Franklin's address on the screen."

Next Jim spoke directly to the studio audience: "All of you in the audience—we're going to take an offering, and I want every one of you to put one dollar in the bucket right now."

Within seconds, ushers came down the aisles with huge buckets. Someone started playing the piano and a soloist sang. I was a little overwhelmed—everything was happening so fast. I watched the buckets going up and down the rows. Soon I could actually see the dollar bills rising to the top of all of them.

The ushers came forward and handed me the buckets. There were at least six of them, each one so full that the dollar bills were spilling off the top. Jim and others picked up the falling bills and put them in my lap. What a sight!

Although I was delighted and grateful for the money, I felt a little embarrassed—after all, Samaritan's Purse didn't do fund-raising this way. At the same time, I silently thanked God for providing the first funds for that new ward.

Though flustered, I reminded myself that I had not asked for this offering or expected it. God was doing this—He always does things His way. He had touched Jim Bakker's heart and was using him and the supporters of *PTL* to help build a hospital in Africa that would glorify His name.

My inner voice was saying quietly, "Thank You, Lord. Thank You." Jim Bakker wasn't the only one who had some tears.

In direct response to Jim Bakker's pleas, over the next month we received fifty-six thousand letters. Each of them contained one dollar or more.

Two more months passed. Jim Bakker called to find out how things were going. He invited me back to give a report to his viewing audience on the hospital in Africa. I was eager to thank all of those *PTL* partners.

After the program started, Jim reviewed the story of Tenwek Hospital for the audience. Then he asked me to talk about the response to his appeal.

"Money has come in from all over the country," I said. "We received more than fifty-six thousand letters." Then I turned to Jim and reminded him that the need had been four hundred thousand. "And, Jim," I continued, "God provided through you and your partners more than we needed."

I pulled a check out of my pocket and handed it to him. "We received a total of $409,000 dollars. Here is a check for nine thousand dollars. We want to give this back to *PTL*."

Now it was his turn to be flustered! He didn't know what to say. I knew that Jim was always helping other people, and not too many came back to say thanks. He had a tender side and loved missions and the Lord's work, but sometimes people took advantage of him. Later he told me I was the only one he could remember who had ever returned money to *PTL*.

This was my first real experience testing the "God room" principle Bob Pierce had so carefully taught me years before. Bob was right; it works. Franklin Graham didn't raise that money and neither did Jim Bakker. God did it, and I gave Him the glory.

It took several years to build that ward at Tenwek because of the hospital's remote location. It was difficult to get steel, concrete, and skilled laborers, but God provided.

When the hospital was completed, Kenya's president, His Excellency Daniel T. Arap Moi, came to the dedication and personally opened the new ward with a ribbon-cutting ceremony. In his address to the thousands who had gathered in the hot African sun, he reminded everyone that the name "Tenwek" came from the early missionaries who had come to the region at the turn of the century. They had walked "ten weeks" from the coast to reach that part of Kenya.

President Moi praised the early missionaries who had brought the gospel of Jesus Christ at great personal sacrifice. And he thanked the doctors and nurses of today for their service to the people of Kenya.

Shortly after the dedication at Tenwek, I learned about the hospital's need for Bibles. Of the thirty thousand patients who had been treated in twelve months time, eight thousand had made decisions to follow Jesus.

David Kilel, the hospital's evangelist, approached me with a real burden on his heart. "I want to give these new Christians something they can take back with them to their homes in the bush," he said. "I would like to provide everyone with his very own copy of God's Word. But we do not have money for this."

"How much do they cost?"

"They are very expensive."

"How much is expensive?"

He told me the amount—the equivalent of two dollars each.

I told him that Samaritan's Purse would buy a thousand—I was operating in the "God room" mode again, because we did not have money set aside for this. Just two days later, one of our Samaritan's Purse surgeons who was serving at another hospital offered to pay for the Bibles. Praise the Lord!

I was realizing more and more that when we faithfully present the world's needs to God's people, they do respond.

I supervised Samaritan's Purse from Boone while Bob's secretary and office manager handled the clerical work from California. I flew to California every six weeks or so and spent a week at the office. The remainder of the time, when I wasn't in Boone, I was usually on the road to Lebanon, India, Nepal, Africa, Hong Kong, and elsewhere.

I had fully expected the ministry's income to drop the first year, but to my surprise, donations actually increased, and Samaritan's Purse began to grow. The interview on *PTL* had not only brought in funds but had made an enormous number of people aware of Samaritan's Purse.

I began to get invitations to speak at various events. As I accepted those invitations, I decided I would never ask for money. Although it was tempting to change the strategy, I stuck to our policy of not giving emotional appeals or twisting the arms of God's people. If people offered to help, we would gratefully accept their gifts on behalf of the Lord. But I wasn't going to ask.

One evening I received a phone call at home.

"You need to come out here to California," said the person on the other end of the line, mysteriously.

"What do you mean by that?"

"It's just not right. Things are going on here that you need to know about." There was a sense of urgency in her voice. "Franklin, you don't understand. They are using the Samaritan's Purse mailing list for something else."

I couldn't believe what I was hearing.

"They are no longer sending your letters to the key supporters of Samaritan's Purse," my caller went on to say. "There are some who have started their own ministry and are using the Samaritan's Purse mailing list to send their own letters."

"I'll be out there as soon as possible."

The first thing I did was call Roy Gustafson and explain what I had heard. "What do you think I should do?"

Roy wasn't on the board, but he was a close friend. "The quicker you close the office in California," he said, "and move it to Boone, the better off you're going to be."

Maybe because I was still in my twenties, I was too naive to realize right away that a fight was brewing. Obviously, I knew about fighting from my past, but since becoming a Christian, that was a "talent" I had worked to retire. I was about to learn something that still breaks my heart, but it's true: Christians can viciously kick, claw, and spit on each other with the best of them. And Satan laughs the whole time.

I packed a bag and headed west. Was the future of Samaritan's Purse hanging in the balance?

Dodging Bullets

I called the Samaritan's Purse board and asked if we could meet on October 23, 1980, at the Hyatt Hotel near the Los Angeles airport. I talked to Bob Pierce's former attorney, Roger Arnebergh, and presented the problem we were facing, "Can you help us get to the bottom of this?" I asked. "I need to know what kind of ministry has been formed and who from our camp is involved in it."

Roger assured me that if papers had been filed in Sacramento, he could obtain copies with the names of the signatories. Sure enough, in time for the meeting, Roger supplied me with the ammunition needed to confront the problem at hand.

It was a complete surprise to me and most of the others on the board of directors that this had been going on behind our backs.

The board meeting was called to order, and we proceeded with the usual preliminaries.

When time came for me to give the chairman's report, I reached in my briefcase and pulled out the documents, feeling dismayed. I turned to the secretary and, pointing to the legal documents, said, "I understand that you and some others have started another organization. Is that right?"

She didn't deny it.

I held up the papers. "This is a copy of the articles of incorporation. Your signature is on them."

She just sat there and said nothing.

"Does anybody else on the board know anything about this?" I was angry. I looked from face to face.

There was silence.

Bob Thompson, who was visibly upset, spoke to one of the elder board members: "Did you have any knowledge of this?"

The elderly gentleman swallowed hard a couple of times but said nothing.

Bob persisted, "Is this your name and your signature on these documents?"

He couldn't deny it.

"What you did was wrong," Bob said. "You did this without our knowledge or approval. I don't see that we have any other recourse than to close the California office and move it to North Carolina so Franklin can oversee it on a day-to-day basis."

My feelings were mixed. On the one hand I felt betrayed, but I also knew how much these people had loved Bob Pierce and served him faithfully in the past.

There was much discussion that afternoon around the board table, but in the end, a consensus was reached: "Move the operation east."

The board decided not to take any action directly against the two members, but they were asked for their board resignations. I told the secretary that if she wanted to stay with Samaritan's Purse as an employee, she would have to move to North Carolina.

She decided against coming to North Carolina. "My family and friends are all in California. This is where I want to be," she said. Later she apologized to me for her actions.

With that settled, we packed the office equipment and files in the back of a Ryder truck with the help of old friends, Dennis Agajanian and Fred Durston. Then Fred and I drove the truck from L.A. to Boone.

The crisis had passed. The challenge of my leadership was behind me—for now. My longtime prayer was finally answered:

Samaritan's Purse would join World Medical Mission under one roof in Boone, North Carolina.

I was relieved to be over this first hurdle at Samaritan's Purse. It was my first intimate encounter with some of the fighting and foolishness that unfortunately goes on in the board rooms of many Christian organizations. But I've learned that Satan's attacks often come from within.

I turned my attention again to the primary goal of Samaritan's Purse—sharing the gospel. Some people are a bit surprised to learn that this is our main focus, but it's true: We are not just a Christian relief organization. We are an evangelistic organization that takes to the ditches and gutters of the world to reach out to those in need.

I personally believe that when we respond as Christians to wars, famines, natural disasters, and other tragedies with food, medicine, and clothing, we earn a hearing for Christ. When people are down and out—whatever their circumstances—and we stop and help, they will listen to what we have to say. We have earned their respect. I want to take advantage of such opportunities to do everything I can to clearly, convincingly present Jesus Christ and His claims.

Some people who hear this object: "That's not fair, Franklin. You shouldn't take advantage of people when they're hungry or cold—in their weakness!"

I answer that I would never take advantage of them for personal gain. But you better believe I will take advantage of each and every opportunity to reach them with the gospel message that can save them from the flames of hell.

If we provide suffering people with food and medicine and then walk away, what have we really done for them? They will probably still be hungry and sick tomorrow. The greatest thing I can do is introduce them to Jesus Christ. Then they have real hope to deal with the often difficult and tragic realities of life.

I continued to visit Sami Dagher in war-ravaged Lebanon and supported his efforts to relieve the suffering all around him.

It was hard to fathom that sophisticated, modern Beirut, once the crown jewel of the Middle East, had become nearly a pile of rubble.

In the early eighties, many radical Muslims based their operations in Beirut. Well-known groups like the PLO and the Iranian-backed Hizbollah, and other groups not so well known, did their dirty work right in the heart of this once beautiful city. The passions of all these factions were fueled by Islam, a shared hatred of Israel, and a mutual distrust of Christians.

Sami lived in this sea of dissension. In spite of the dangerous obstacles he faced daily, his faith grew strong and his witness was unmatched.

Sami was supported every step of the way by his wife, Joy. She never seemed to get rattled and always provided graciously for everyone who came to her door.

Sami discouraged me from coming to Lebanon during times of intense strife for fear that I would be kidnapped and held for ransom. Sami knew that when a Lebanese was kidnapped, the purpose was sometimes for money but other times for revenge. To humiliate a family, the kidnappers would cut off body parts of the one kidnapped and mail them back to the family.

Because of Sami's fearless witness, he knew he had some enemies—in fact, quite a few. Sami told me years later that being kidnapped was his greatest fear during the war. Every morning Sami left home aware that he might never see Joy again.

In all this adversity Sami was single-minded for the gospel, a trait that reminded me of my father. Both men have one message, and one message only: Jesus Christ and Him crucified (1 Cor. 1:23).

Sami told me once how he had come face-to-face with his deepest fear one day when he was on his way up to the mountains surrounding Beirut for a Bible study.

"Franklin," Sami said, "I suddenly noticed a motorcycle approaching me. The rider pointed a gun at me and signaled for me to follow. I became uneasy when we left the main road and I was taken to an unmarked building in an isolated area.

"Within minutes, I found myself locked inside a dark and dingy room. My hands shook as a horrible fright welled up inside. I was startled when a different group of gunmen burst through the doorway and quickly strip-searched me. The only thing that crossed my mind was that they would find the New Testament in my coat pocket. But when they turned to leave, I was shocked to find it still there.

"After they left, I tightly held God's Word in my hands, but I was too afraid to read. The words just blurred in my eyes, and my mind whirled at the thought of what was happening to me. Would pieces of my body be sent to Joy, as the terrorists had done with other kidnapped victims? Since I was a Christian, I figured the end was at hand, and my only recourse now was to pray.

"In that cold, silent room I lifted my voice quietly up to the Lord. An overwhelming sense of peace settled my soul.

"When I regained my composure, I opened the Scriptures and began to read the promises of my Savior. I felt the strength of the Lord rest upon me.

"Then I heard footsteps coming down the hall. I was determined to live these last few moments for His glory. When the men entered the room, I knew I was in for the beating of my life.

"A man escorted me into another room for questioning. The interrogators came in, and I was prompted by the Holy Spirit not to cower, but rather to confront them boldly.

"'Who are you?' they asked.

"'I am a servant of the Lord Jesus Christ,' I answered.

"All of the men stopped dead in their tracks. They were not accustomed to this kind of response. For a few brief moments they just glared at me! I had a deep awareness from God that they would not lay a hand on me.

"They asked me why I didn't wear a clerical collar.

"'I do not want to be any different from my people. I want to be identified with their suffering and hardship.'

"The guards motioned for me to go with them down a long hallway and presented me to their commanding officer. He looked at me contemptuously and started to interrogate me.

"'I will only answer questions about the Lord Jesus Christ, my church, and my family,' I said with conviction. 'I have nothing else to say. I am not a political figure; I represent the King of kings and Lord of lords, and you have no authority over me,' I said confidently.

"The officer was visibly shaken, and his hands trembled as he left the room. I had faith in the Lord's protection, but still I wondered what would happen next. As I stood there contemplating the result of my actions, the door creaked open and the commanding officer appeared before me.

"'You are free to go,' he said quietly.

"'No, not until I see the men who captured me.'

"The officer was stunned and speechless. He finally said, 'Why would you make such a demand?'

"'I'm not going to leave here until I confront the men who wrongfully kidnapped me!' I was thinking of what the apostle Paul did in Phillipi. ("I eagerly expect and hope that I will in no way be ashamed, but will have sufficient courage so that now as always Christ will be exalted in my body, whether by life or by death" [Phil. 1:20 NIV]).

"The man walked away with a sheepish look and left me alone. I prayed for guidance. When the commander returned, he led me outside into the light. There my captors stood beside my car. I walked up to each of them and extended my hand and gave each of them a gospel tract.

"I turned and got in my car and drove away. I've never felt as free as I did at that moment!"

Sami is one courageous man! I have wondered what I would have done if that had been me and the commander told me I was free to go. I think I would have split as fast as the cartoon character the Road Runner, leaving only a trail of dust behind.

Our donors loved Sami and gave generously to the work in Lebanon. One favorite project was the Karantina Church. I encouraged Sami to buy the church building they were renting, as well as some surrounding property. During the war the property was very affordable. I believed this would make a strong statement to the community that war or no war, Sami's church was there to stay. If the various factions in the war had their territory staked out, why shouldn't Sami and his church stake out their territory, build their base of operations, and fly high the banner of Christ?

As always, Sami responded well to the challenge. He and the faithful members of the Karantina Alliance Church expanded their outreach in the city. They opened a coffee shop, clothing factory, distribution center (it now employs a large number of refugees), and medical clinic that cares for thousands of poor people each year. An even more daring move was the establishment of a Bible school in this Muslim-dominated area of the world.

I was in my office when Sami called. "You must come, my brother. You need to see this for yourself."

It was late June of 1982. The Israelis had invaded southern Lebanon on June 6; their goal was to find and destroy the strongholds of PLO terrorists who had been attacking civilians in northern Israel for years. Sami saw a tremendous opportunity to share the gospel.

"Tens of thousands of refugees are streaming from southern Lebanon into Beirut, away from the advancing Israeli army," Sami said on the phone. "You've got to come, Franklin."

I agreed to make the trip. The problem was, how was I going to get to Beirut? The airport was shut down, and I couldn't make it there through Damascus. I told Sami I would somehow get there as quickly as I could.

A few days before, some people I knew at Operation Mobilization (OM) had told me about their work in northern Israel and in southern Lebanon. They had asked me to pay a visit. Perhaps Samaritan's Purse could provide financial help for their ministry.

I called the OM people in Israel and told them my dilemma. I wanted to get into Beirut, but I wasn't sure how I was going to do it with the war in full swing.

"Fly to Tel Aviv, and we'll meet you at the airport," said one of the OM representatives. "We know the Israeli commander at Matula, which is at the Israeli-Lebanese border. The Israelis have convoy after convoy of ammunition heading north. I don't think we'll have any problem slipping you into one of the convoys and getting you to Sidon."

"If I can only get to Sidon," I told him, "then I can get my friend from Beirut to meet me."

"By the way," he said, "while you're in Sidon, could you stop to see our relief work in the Palestinian refugee camps? Our workers are discouraged. Having you come by would lift their spirits."

I assured him that I would.

I called Sami and asked, "Can you meet me in Sidon the day after tomorrow. It will be late afternoon, about 4 P.M. Can you get there?"

"The Israeli Army is somewhere between Beirut and there, and I might have difficulty," he said and then paused. "But if you can make it, I can make it. Where are we going to meet?"

"I'll meet you at your cousin's pharmacy," I told him. I had been there once before; his cousin lived right in the heart of Sidon. "Okay," he said. He hung up, and I was on my way.

The next day I flew from the U.S. to Tel Aviv, landing at about 7 A.M. I had told Sami I would meet him in the afternoon, but I had no idea if I could make that rendezvous.

To add to my anxiety, the man from OM was two hours late in picking me up. He was a laid-back fellow who wasn't in a hurry.

As we headed toward the OM office in northern Israel, he suggested we stop for lunch.

"Stop for lunch? I don't want to be rude," I said, "but I haven't flown all night and gone to all this expense to waste time stopping for lunch! I have to get to Sidon by 4 P.M. and then to Beirut by dark. I'm not sure the Israelis are going to let me cross through their military positions." He understood and we pressed onward.

When we got to the Israeli-Lebanese border, the gate was wide open. Nobody asked for a passport or identification. The Israelis probably thought that no one in his right mind would want to drive through this area anyway. We pulled behind an Israeli convoy and followed it. By this point in the war, the active conflict had already moved north of Sidon to the outskirts of Beirut. Most of southern Lebanon was under Israeli control.

We made it to Sidon by 3:30—I couldn't believe it! As we pulled in front of the pharmacy, there stood Sami with his trademark smile. He came toward me, his arms outstretched for a hug. "My brother, how in the world did you get here?"

I explained about the help from Operation Mobilization. When I asked how his trip had been, he grinned. I had known Sami long enough to recognize that his smile meant he had had an exciting day avoiding PLO artillery shells and Israel's bombing runs. "Just another normal day in Lebanon. Now you go with me to Beirut before dark," he said.

Our situation in Lebanon was dangerous to say the least, but I believe when we are in the Lord's will and following Christ, we are His responsibility, and He will look after us. Until He has accomplished His purpose through us, nothing can touch us without His permission—we're "bullet-proof," so to speak.

Before we left Sidon, I wanted to keep my promise to see the OM work. Sami was eager to go with me. We spent an hour with the OM team, and I left a check from Samaritan's Purse to show our support.

It was now late afternoon. Sami insisted, "Brother, we must go. I want to cross the Israeli lines before evening light is gone. If we drive up on their positions in the dark, they may shoot first and ask questions later."

We left in Sami's car. Miles before we reached Beirut, we began to hear the distant boom of artillery shells and exploding bombs. The PLO was making a final stand in the central part of the city, and the Israelis were trying to blast them out without destroying the whole town; they were using a technique the Allies used later in the Gulf War—precision bombing.

We reached the outskirts of Beirut just before dark; however, the Israeli Army detoured us east on a back road that led up the side of a mountain overlooking the city. This road supposedly would be safer because it was farther away from the PLO snipers.

We drove on without interference until we reached the town of B'abda, the site of the presidential palace. As we entered B'abda, we realized that the Israelis' heavy cannons were positioned on a parallel road above us. As we made our way below, the Israeli Army opened fire with their big guns on the Palestinian positions beneath us. The sound was awesome—no rock concert could ever compare! We not only heard the sound, we felt it. The earth shook. It reminded me of a violent summer thunderstorm with one nearby crack and lightning strike after another. The Israelis were pounding the PLO positions.

When the cannon fire started, Sami instantly stomped on the accelerator. The traffic was heavy, but Sami roared down the road, zigzagging in and out, passing as many cars as he could.

"Slow down!" I yelled, grabbing the door handle to brace myself. "You're going to kill us!"

Sami ignored my pleas. He had lived in a war zone too long; he knew what was coming. Sure enough, within seconds the PLO responded to the Israelis with a heavy rocket attack, trying to knock out the Israeli guns. Some of the rockets fell short and landed on a village. Others dropped on the road where we were driving. If Sami hadn't driven like a half-crazed New York cabbie,

I think we would have been hit. Several rockets exploded just behind our car, digging craters and flinging dirt and rocks into the air.

We reached the Damascus Highway at Hazmiyeh, a critical junction near the front line. Just as we drove into the intersection, PLO snipers opened up. The bullets whizzed around us, hitting the pavement with a "splat" sound, then ricocheting away with a whine. Sami kept the pedal to the floor, swerving the car back and forth to make us a more difficult target. He didn't slow down until we entered a series of narrow city streets, which finally hid us from the crosshairs of the snipers' scopes.

It wasn't until later that I realized how dangerous this trip had been. At the time, I wasn't afraid of getting hit. I was more worried about dying in a car accident! Although it was a life-and-death situation, this kind of chase is exciting while it's happening. Through the whole ride, I had a sense of peace that I was on a mission for the Lord and He would take care of me. Later, I got the shakes!

After what seemed like eternity, we reached Sami's home in a "quieter" part of town on the other side of Beirut and away from the fighting.

That night, as I tried to sleep with the sounds of the artillery still booming in the distance, it occurred to me that I might have been the first civilian in over thirty-five years to travel by automobile from Tel Aviv's Ben Gurion Airport to Beirut in one day! I thanked the Lord for His protection.

For the next several days, I accompanied Sami around Beirut. The whole city was in chaos. Sami's immediate concern was the families of his church. Time and time again, he risked his life—and mine too—as we delivered food to their homes under a rain of bullets.

At 3:15 Sunday morning, a barrage of cannon fire woke us up. We learned later the Israelis had launched their heaviest attack on West Beirut. They were advancing from the south to take control of the airport and the refugee camps to the north.

The PLO countered by pointing its guns toward civilian areas of East Beirut. This was a frantic attempt to create panic in the rest of the city. The PLO knew it was losing. Rockets and artillery shells landed all over the area. Fortunately, none of them hit Sami's house, but they came close.

I was supposed to preach at Karantina Church that morning, but Sami said, "I have canceled the service, my brother. It's too dangerous. You cannot preach today."

I could see he was getting ready to leave the house, so I asked where he was going.

"I'm going to buy food and take it to the people who can't get out."

"I want to go with you."

"No, no. Impossible."

"Sami, I'm going with you."

"I will not permit this, my brother. It is too dangerous."

"Well, Sami, if God can protect you, don't you think He can protect me?"

He stared at me and shook his head. "All right," he finally said, and then he gave me that Sami Dagher grin, which I interpreted to mean we were going to have an interesting day.

As we left his home we went through a village on the outskirts of Beirut. "Look, look my brother." Sami laughed as we screeched to a stop in front of a bakery that was open, "The Lebanese will never miss a chance to make money. Let's buy some fresh bread."

We filled the trunk with as many loaves as we could cram in. A few blocks away, he saw the butcher shop was open. Again we stopped, and he bought ten kilos of beef, which filled up the backseat of the car.

Beirut normally had some of the worst traffic congestion in the world, so it was strange this morning to see all the streets empty. Without warning a shell hit the road a hundred yards in front of us with a tremendous *BOOM*. Asphalt and shrapnel flew everywhere. Sami didn't even slow the car down.

We went from home to home. Most of the people, with fear written all over their faces, were hiding in basements. When we made our way inside the shelters, the heavy, smoke-filled air often choked us. Sami never hesitated. Flashlight in hand, we walked through the hallways and into the basements, calling out names of his flock.

"Sami! Sami!" Their voices would answer with joyful excitement.

"My brother, see their joy," he said to me. "For seven years they have lived with agony and death all around them."

I helped Sami carry in small plastic bags that contained a loaf of bread and about a half kilo of beef. When he handed over the bag, the people cried and embraced us.

Before we left, Sami always prayed and read a verse or two of comfort from the Bible.

In the middle of the day we drove to the church building to check on a family that lived there. It was reassuring to see and talk with them and know they were well. When we got ready to leave, I went out to turn the car around. Just then PLO artillery shells struck the building next to us. The sound was so loud that for a few seconds I thought the church had been hit.

Sami, who was locking the door of the church, turned to me and yelled, "Come!"

He didn't need to yell—I was already running for cover. I dove down a little corridor and knelt under some steps with Sami a split second before another shell hit. Concrete and steel crashed to the ground. I was sure the next shell would land where we hid.

This wasn't just an adventure anymore. Fear clutched at my gut as I thought of what it would feel like to be buried under tons of concrete and steel. We waited several minutes and nothing happened. But in those brief moments, I grasped a little more clearly the mental suffering under which these people had lived for years.

As we crouched under those steps, Sami looked at me with that famous grin and a twinkle in his eye and asked, "Brother, do you think you are in God's will?"

With those shells dropping almost in our laps, I wondered for a moment—but only for a moment. No question: I was right where God wanted me to be—with Sami Dagher and his church.

This is what Samaritan's Purse was meant to do, I thought. *Help people like Sami Dagher. His ministry demonstrates true Christian compassion at work.*

Cracked Curtains of Iron and Bamboo

Christian compassion shaped the lifework of my grand-parents and parents, no matter what the cost. My father took one of his riskiest ventures in the name of the Lord when, in the late seventies, he accepted an invitation to preach in Hungary. This would be his first opportunity to minister in a country behind the Iron Curtain.

The invitation came through the efforts of Dr. Alexander Haraszti, a Hungarian immigrant who had lived in the United States for twenty years.

When Daddy accepted the invitation, he immediately began catching flack from the Christian community. People accused him of hobnobbing with the Communists. Others said he was compromising.

"It's an opportunity to preach the gospel," Daddy said simply. "Even if some of my friends don't understand, I'm going to go and preach the gospel of Jesus Christ every chance I get—especially behind the Iron Curtain."

That trip opened the door to other Eastern-bloc nations.

In October 1978 he ministered in Poland for ten days. At Poznan he preached a sermon for the first time in his ministry in a Roman Catholic church. He prayed during the service there that the Holy Spirit would unite the hearts of Roman Catholics and Protestants in worship together.

At Katowice sixty-five hundred people jammed into the cathedral where he was scheduled to preach. Many in the crowd were young people.

Still the critics railed. "Billy Graham is compromising. Billy Graham is selling out."

"The Communists are using you for propaganda," someone told Daddy.

"Fine," Daddy answered. "And I'm using them to get the gospel out."

When I heard Daddy criticized for going to these Communist countries, it made me mad. I knew he had accepted the challenge to preach in Eastern-bloc countries because he believed with all of his heart that God's Word is stronger and more powerful than any Communist propaganda and dogma.

It wasn't long before my father was asked to speak in Russia, the invitation again arranged by Alexander Haraszti.

Dr. Haraszti seemed to be a master at winning the Communists' favor by using their own terminology. I love the story of how he convinced the Soviet ambassador to the United States, Anatoly Dobrynin, to allow Daddy to preach in Russia.

"Why don't you invite Billy Graham to speak in Russia?" Dr. Haraszti asked the ambassador.

"Dr. Haraszti, why should we allow him to come to Russia?"

"So Dr. Graham can thank Lenin for converting the Orthodox church."

Mr. Dobrynin took off his glasses. He stared at Dr. Haraszti. "Explain yourself," he said.

"Very well," Dr. Haraszti answered. "The Orthodox church during the time of the czars was proud, rich, and didn't seem to need God. When Lenin took their property, he stripped the church of its power. Then the church turned to God. Consequently, Dr. Graham would like to thank Lenin for converting the Orthodox church."

As Dobrynin looked Dr. Haraszti over, a faint smile appeared on his face. "You know," he said, "we never looked at it that way."

We had a lot of discussion in our family about Daddy's going to Russia. During that phase of the Cold War, many westerners thought everyone in Communist countries was ruthless, atheistic, and evil. In fact, a kind of hysteria filled people's emotions about Communists, especially the Russians.

Some folks thought if Daddy went to Russia, Communist officials might trump up some charge against him and throw him in prison. One person even suggested, "One of those Communists could slip poison into his food."

Even Mama expressed concern, not so much for Daddy's safety, because she knew he was in God's hands, but because she was concerned that he was working too hard by taking too many speaking engagements.

I was afraid for Daddy too. Yet at the same time, I understood his reasons for wanting to go. In my heart I believed as he did—that the gospel of Jesus Christ is more powerful than any weapon or propaganda the Communists could use.

So Daddy went to Russia in a hailstorm of criticism. He had told the Russian officials ahead of time that he would be available to preach anytime, anywhere. But they only allowed him to preach inside church buildings.

All of the churches he visited were very small, but each one was packed full of people, with crowds circling the building outside as well. Of course, it didn't matter to Daddy whether many people or just a few came.

"Only the KGB come to your meetings," one critic said, inaccurately. "They keep the people who want to hear you away."

"The KGB needs Christ too," Daddy said. "In fact, I can't think of a crowd I would rather preach to."

He would use any opportunity to present Christ to his listeners. Moreover, in the crowds were hundreds of believers and hundreds of tape recorders; his message was copied and distributed by the thousands from one end of the Iron Curtain to the other.

Daddy never spoke against Communism in his sermons, which of course gave his critics back home more "ammunition."

"I preach Christ and Him crucified," he said, quoting the apostle Paul, "and I leave the rest to God."

Yet in private he spoke with Soviet officials about allowing more religious freedom. And I believe he did the right thing. He knew it wouldn't help if he spoke publicly against their political system.

Prior to Daddy's first visit to Moscow in 1982, the world began to hear about the Siberian Seven. In June 1978, these seven Pentecostal Christians fled to the American embassy, seeking political asylum. Since that time, they had lived in a ten-foot-by-ten-foot room in the embassy basement.

The Siberian Seven knew that if they left the American embassy, the Communist government would severely punish them by imprisoning them in one of the famed gulags, or they might even execute them.

Eventually, one of the seven, Lida Vaschenko, went on a fast, which the media called a hunger strike. She vowed not to eat until the Soviets released her family and allowed them to emigrate.

Concerned about their dilemma, Daddy spoke with Soviet Ambassador Dobrynin on behalf of the Seven before going to Russia. The United States had already declared its willingness to accept them as immigrants. However, if the Communists released them, the Soviets would lose face in the eyes the world. The situation had come to a classic Mexican standoff. Both sides were looking for a way to resolve a tense international situation.

While Daddy was in Moscow, he was determined to pay a pastoral visit to the Siberian Pentecostals in the embassy even though both the American ambassador and the Soviet government were opposed to such a visit. The foreign press in Moscow was hoping Daddy would publicly condemn the Soviet government for the treatment of the Siberian Seven. But my father knew this was not the way to solve the problem.

Daddy met with a very high official in the Soviet government, who arranged for him to meet with Boris Ponomarev, a politburo member in charge of foreign affairs. He knew that the situation would only change if high-level Soviet officials were persuaded to act.

"May I make a suggestion?" Daddy asked one of the high officials. "I think I may have a solution to your dilemma concerning the Siberian Seven."

"Please do, Dr. Graham. I would like to hear your comments."

"Have you considered the possibility of allowing the Siberian Seven to go back to their homes in Siberia without fear of reprisal? This would show the world that you are acting in good faith. Wait a few months. Let this crisis pass. Then allow them to apply for emigration status through the normal channels. This way all sides can resolve this issue without losing face."

The official stared at my father in silence. Finally he said, "Dr. Graham, thank you." His puzzled expression seemed to indicate, *Why didn't we think of that?*

Lida Vaschenko ended her fast. And several months later, all seven returned to Siberia, without punishment. Eventually, the Soviets allowed the seven to emigrate to Israel. From there, they went to the United States.

Later one of the government officials told my father in private that his suggestions were instrumental in resolving this crisis. As far as I know, Daddy has never made any public statement about his intervention on the Seven's behalf. But God had used him. And that's what counted.

Daddy just kept accepting invitations. And in 1982, again through the efforts of Dr. Haraszti, he went to the German Democratic Republic (East Germany) and Czechoslovakia. Communist officials carefully controlled Daddy's schedule during that trip, but they never hindered his preaching nor tried to tell him what to say.

In 1984, Daddy asked me to go with him on another of his trips to Russia. I literally jumped at the chance, for the simple reason that Daddy wanted me to go. It would also be the first time in years he and I could spend extended time together as father and son.

I decided I would do whatever I could to help him. I'd carry his briefcase if he wanted me to. I'd make sure he had his early morning coffee, collect his laundry, field telephone calls, and intervene with visitors who insisted on seeing him. But most of all, I wanted to be with my father. I might have been thirty-two years old, but I relished the chance to travel with him and be there if he needed me.

As I think of it now, I believe that trip to Russia was probably the beginning of our adult relationship.

When Dr. Haraszti arranged the trip, he told me how pleased he was that I was going.

"To the Russians, it is extremely important to have you along," he said. "You will honor them greatly by your presence. Your father has so many invitations to meet with people, he can't possibly accept them all. If he sends one of his associates, they won't accept him. But they will accept his son."

During the official functions on that trip, I sat at my father's right, the place of honor according to Russian protocol. On several occasions I acted as his representative and met people on his behalf.

Whenever we went to formal luncheons and dinner meetings, I sensed the tension in the room. Like Daddy, I knew these officials were trying to use him for propaganda purposes. Sure enough, at each meeting the Soviet leaders stood up and made long speeches defending Communism, the Russian position in the world, and the conflict in Afghanistan, while damning Reagan, Star Wars, and America in general.

We had to sit and listen to all those harangues. Sometimes the speeches lasted for what seemed to be hours. At times, though, Daddy and I sensed that some government and party dignitaries didn't believe their own speeches. It seemed like they were merely giving us the official party line for those listening via the hidden microphones in every room.

When it was finally Daddy's turn to speak, he never responded to any of the anti-American charges. In fact, he didn't speak about anything political. Instead, Daddy simply talked from his heart about his relationship with God.

He would tell how he had grown up on a farm, and as a boy how he would watch the sun rise over the fields and ask himself, "Is there a God?" Then he would tell about how he had concluded that there was, and he always quoted John 3:16: "For God so loved the world that He gave His only begotten Son, that whoever believes in Him should not perish but have everlasting life."

No matter what the place or occasion, Daddy kept his message on spiritual issues. Sometimes he told how he had found Christ and that he knew his own sins were forgiven.

Each time Daddy spoke I could see the Communists' rigid masks falling from their faces. Without fail, by the time Daddy finished the leaders had melted. They seldom said anything in response—but I could see the difference in their expressions.

As Daddy was leaving these functions, the officials lined up to give him warm handshakes and enthusiastic words.

"Thank you for coming, Dr. Graham," one after another would say. "Thank you, Dr. Graham, for what you said."

Finally, in Leningrad, one Communist official did ask Daddy, "Dr. Graham, how can we have in our hearts this same peace that you have?"

Daddy made clear to him what salvation was all about. He told the man plainly what it took for him or anyone else to come to faith in Christ. It was an incredible moment.

Day after day, I was impressed with the way Daddy always directed his messages as well as his responses to questions back to Christ. He wouldn't allow himself to get sucked into any political issues or controversies about nuclear weapons, disarmament, or the like. We attended these meetings two and three times a day. And as I heard Daddy's answers to questions over and over, something was being drilled into me.

After several days of this, I prayed, "Lord, give me that ability. In every interview I do from now on, allow me to do the same. I want to be able to take any reporter's question and turn it around to focus on Christ."

To me, that was what truly mattered. Political issues would come and go. It was the gospel, the power of God for the salvation of everyone who believes, that would endure. That's what I wanted to talk about.

I was amazed by how eloquently Daddy spoke, and yet he kept his words and concepts simple. Every time he preached in the churches he gave an invitation to accept Christ, and people always responded. How many Communist officials came to Christ I don't know, but I am sure there were many.

One special milestone was when we were in Estonia at the Oleviste Baptist Church speaking before the largest Baptist crowd Daddy faced in the Soviet Union. I had given greetings and read the Scripture for my father, and said an opening prayer before my father's address. Daddy, through his interpreter, told forty-five hundred people there that night, "This is an historic moment for me, because it's the first time that my son and I have participated together in a service." It was a moment I'll never forget.

It was also an exhausting two and a half weeks. I saw what a mental workout and physical challenge it was for Daddy. But I never saw him waver.

Daddy was one of the few from the West in those days to go and preach the gospel in the heart of the Communist world. President Gerald Ford said of Daddy's involvement: "There's no doubt that Billy Graham, on his many visits to Eastern Europe and the Soviet Union, has lighted the flame."[1]

President George Bush was quoted: "One of the Lord's great ambassadors, the Reverend Billy Graham, went to Eastern Europe and the Soviet Union. And upon returning, spoke of a movement there toward more religious freedom. And perhaps he saw it before many of us because it takes a man of God to sense the early movement of the hand of God."[2]

The following year, 1985, I accompanied my father to Romania. At the time, that country was widely recognized as the most repressed of all Communist nations in Europe, with the exception of Albania. Romanian President Nicolae Ceausescu was one of the old, Stalin-type dictators, and he ruled Romania with an iron hand.

At the same time, though, Ceausescu refused to come completely under Russian control. For example, he wouldn't allow Russian troops to be stationed on Romanian soil.

So the U.S. government began wooing Ceausescu. They gave Romania most-favored-trade status with the United States, and of course, Ceausescu didn't want to lose that.

With those kinds of considerations at stake, Ceausescu allowed Billy Graham to come to Romania to preach.

Daddy had already proven in Czechoslovakia and Russia that he wasn't going to speak about politics. He had come only as a religious leader and as an ambassador for Jesus Christ. And that's exactly what he did in Romania.

Daddy spoke for the most part in Orthodox and Baptist churches. In every city, the churches were jammed full. In some cases, as many as thirty thousand people stood outside trying to get in.

At one event, a Romanian pastor smiled at me and whispered that Ceausescu could never get a crowd that big. In order to attract large audiences for him, the government had to close all the factories and declare a holiday!

But the large crowds were frightening the Communist leaders. On several occasions, riots almost broke out, and the police didn't know what to do.

In Timisoara, Daddy was scheduled to speak in an Orthodox church. There had been no advertising for the event, but somehow the people found out about it. When we arrived, one hundred thousand to one hundred and fifty thousand Romanians surrounded the building and filled the large plaza in front. Police formed rings to hold the people back.

As Daddy stepped out of the car, however, a voice cried out, "Bill-ee!" Immediately, others took up the cry. Within seconds, all the people were chanting, "Bill-ee! Bill-ee! Bill-ee!"

Daddy rolled up his Bible in his right hand and held it above his head. He kept waving his hand and smiling at the crowds, without ever saying a word.

That scene said it all. It was a moment of triumph for the gospel of Christ as he held the Word of God above his head.

As I watched that amazing scene, I thought, *He doesn't have to speak. He's simply holding up the Bible—and they all know the Word of God is more powerful than anything the Communists have to offer.*

The people stepped back as the police cleared a path for us to walk into the church. The whole crowd tried to surge forward still chanting "Bill-ee, Bill-ee, Bill-ee." Daddy walked straight ahead with the Bible in his hand.

As I looked at the police, I saw the terror in their faces. Maybe they were afraid the people would turn on them. Maybe they feared they would lose their jobs.

All I know is, the crowd's enthusiasm didn't diminish.

"Bill-ee! Bill-ee! Bill-ee! Bill-ee!"

The chanting continued long after we had gone inside.

A few years later, revolution came to Romania. Many people have given partial credit for that monumental event to my father's trip there. I believe they may be right.

"It was the beginning of a *religious* revolution," one person told us.

During that trip, my father's actions had another important effect on me. As I witnessed his ministry in that country, I felt God impressing on my heart that He wanted me to preach. I felt *a growing, inner stirring* to preach the good news of Christ. But it was a stirring I wouldn't act on until years later.

Throughout our trip to Romania, I heard my father preach three or four times a day. I watched as people came pouring forward. And I was thrilled to see it all happen.

Being with Daddy on that trip had a huge impact on me as a son. It was both challenging and encouraging to see God's hand at work in my father in that way. And without question, it changed the direction of my life.

In 1988 I made another trip, this one made special by my mother. She had gone back to China with her brother and sisters in 1980 to see the place where she had been born and raised, to see where her parents had served as missionaries for twenty-five years. This time she wanted Daddy to see her old home place, and they wanted me to go with them.

I was honored. What an opportunity! I wanted to see where my mother had been born, as well as see China for myself.

The most impressive part of all was going to my mother's birthplace, now called Huaiyin, a conglomerate of many cities in the north Kiangsu province, three hundred miles north of Shanghai. Huaiyin straddles the Grand Canal, which is the oldest man-made, hand-dug waterway in the world and stretches over six hundred miles.

We rode in an official motorcade, and it took all day for us to get there. That afternoon, about thirty or forty miles outside of Huaiyin, we noticed people standing along the road as we passed each village. As we got closer, the people started clapping, and they continued until the motorcade passed.

Daddy probably thought the people were clapping for him. Yet he looked puzzled too. He wondered how they knew he was coming.

As we got closer to the city, the crowds grew larger. When we finally reached the compound of the old Huaiyin General Hospital, thousands of people were standing outside. And they all were clapping, but not for Billy Graham.

They had heard that Dr. Nelson Bell's daughter, Ruth, was returning.

The mission station had been opened in 1887 by Absolom Sydenstricker, the father of Nobel-Prize-winning novelist Pearl S. Buck.

The Presbyterian hospital had provided continuous ministry for more than fifty years, until it was closed by the Communists following their takeover in 1949. During those years, nearly every family within a few hundred miles had some kind of contact with the hospital. Whenever anyone became seriously ill, he or she ended up there.

My grandfather and other missionaries had planted thousands of spiritual seeds during those years. When the Japanese forced him out in the early 1940s, he lamented over the few converts to the gospel. Seldom did a day pass when he didn't think about his Chinese coworkers and wonder how they fared.

In those days, it was estimated that there were less than eight hundred thousand Christians in all of China.

Incredibly, during the thirty-year period that China was without missionaries, the number of believers multiplied into the tens of millions. The spiritual seeds, sown so faithfully by the missionaries, had exploded into a bountiful harvest.

Our meetings with the Chinese leaders were similar to those in Russia, only the Chinese were not as dogmatic as the Russians. They didn't go for posturing and constantly spewing out the official line. When we sat down to talk with China's government officials, we had interesting conversations.

On the other hand, the Chinese seemed to be much stricter against religious gatherings than the Russians had been. Daddy spoke at several churches, and in each case the churches were small by our standards.

Yet the Chinese Christians seemed a bit braver to me in the face of Communism than the Russian believers. In fact, the Christians we met there were openly defiant, and we had to be extremely careful about some of the meetings we had with them so that our involvement would not be interpreted as a political statement. And just as he had done in the Eastern-bloc countries, Daddy preached only about Christ and avoided politics.

The entire trip was extraordinary. And I'll always be grateful to my parents for letting me go with them.

Now, as I think of how the church in Huaiyin mushroomed so incredibly in just thirty years, I get even more excited about the work I do at Samaritan's Purse. If one missionary hospital could have that kind of influence for Christ, then there's no measure to what God can do through missionary medicine worldwide.

Whenever people ask me, "Is mission work effective?" I answer, "You bet it is!" I've seen firsthand the fruit of seeds planted years ago, by missionaries like my grandparents.

It was encouraging to be able to look backward in China and see the results of the labors of missionaries like my grandparents and others. Yet at the same time, we were also looking forward, trying to find ways to train Christians in the Bible in America.

One of those ways was through The Cove. Officially, this is known as The Billy Graham Training Center.

As far back as my early college days, Daddy had spoken about finding ways for laymen to be trained in God's word to be effective evangelists in areas where they lived and worked. At one time he had toyed with the idea of opening a Bible center. But there were a number of those around, and besides, that wasn't quite what he had in mind.

I remember the time when a prominent black activist had just come to the faith. He was in danger of being exploited by Christians to give his testimony for Christ. My parents had rejoiced over what God had done for this influential man. But in their opinion, he was too young in the faith to handle that kind of exposure.

"He needs to mature first," Mama said. "He needs to spend time studying and learning."

"But where could he go?" Daddy asked.

"Maybe we need to build a place for people just like him," Mama answered.

That's when they began to talk seriously about a short-term training center. They had a vision to build some type of retreat center near Asheville, a quiet, picturesque mountain town. It would be a place where folks would do nothing but study the Bible.

So, in 1978, with the help of my Uncle Melvin (Daddy's younger brother) Daddy found a tract of land near Asheville called Porter's Cove. It was a beautiful piece of land, near the southern end of the Blue Ridge Parkway, which seemed ideally suited for building such a center.

But Daddy kept quiet about buying it. BGEA board members reasoned that if the property owners knew Billy Graham was the potential buyer, they might jack up the price. So a foundation in Texas bought the property for the BGEA. All told, about fifteen hundred acres were purchased.

But the method used in purchasing that piece of land nearly caused a scandal. In fact, it's the only incident that has come near to harming Daddy's reputation in all the years of his ministry.

Somehow the story about how the BGEA acquired the land leaked out. And the *Charlotte Observer* came after Daddy full force.

For weeks articles appeared in the paper, implying Daddy had used money from some kind of secret fund. Their tone suggested that the foundation had inappropriately bought the land and that Daddy had purchased it to build a showplace to attract Christian tourists. The truth was, he had only wanted a training center, a place for people to study the Bible.

Daddy lost heart over that incident. It was the first time I'd ever seen my father look crushed. He didn't lash back at his critics, but he did try to set the record straight. Still, it hurt him to know that people might think he would do something underhanded.

Finally, Daddy decided to give the property away to stop the attacks. I understood his reasoning, but told him I thought he was making a mistake. He gave the land to Columbia Bible College

(CBC). CBC had a Christian high school, called Ben Lippen, and a summer conference ground near Asheville. Their main building had burned down, and they were in need of help.

During that time, Daddy had other big projects going. One of them was the planning of a conference for itinerant evangelists from around the world. It was to be held in Amsterdam. "The BGEA doesn't have funds to develop this property with our conference coming up," Daddy reasoned. "We'll give it to CBC and let them develop it for ministry." He gave permission to CBC to use his name to raise money for construction. Once CBC had the property, they put up a big sign just off Interstate 40 that read: *Future Home of the Billy Graham Training Center.*

Every time I drove by, I thought, *I wish Daddy hadn't given that property away. His name is being used, and he's got no control over it.*

Over the next five years, CBC was not able to raise sufficient funds to fully develop the property.

In 1988, Jerry Miller, who served as the property's director for CBC, came to see me one day. He asked me to consider approaching the BGEA board to seek funding for The Cove. Jerry wasn't asking for himself. He was concerned that the project be built right since it carried Daddy's name.

"We won't be able to build this center unless your father gets behind us and helps raise money," Jerry said. "CBC just doesn't have the resources."

I was very skeptical. I knew for a fact that the BGEA board wasn't interested in giving another dime to the project.

"Listen, Jerry," I said, "you know that Daddy not only gave CBC this property, but he raised money for the chapel to boot. In my opinion, the only way this training center can ever be done right is if CBC gives the property back to Billy Graham. That way he can build the training center he's had a vision for all along."

Jerry just stared at me. Then he nodded his head. "Franklin, you're right."

"Well, how can we get the property back?"

"I don't know. Give me a few days to look into it."

The moment Jerry left, I called Daddy.

"If CBC gave the property back, would you take it?" I asked. "Would you be willing to build the training center?"

Daddy was quiet. I knew he was thinking through all the implications.

"Yes, Franklin," he said, "I would like to have it back. I think we made a mistake by giving it away."

Jerry talked to the CBC board and later asked me to write an official letter, which Daddy signed, asking for the property to be returned to the BGEA on the basis that CBC didn't have the money to develop it. This had been one of the conditions the BGEA had given them originally.

When CBC's board received the letter and discussed it, they voted to return the property.

After the transaction was finished, Daddy asked if I would chair the oversight committee of the board that would build The Cove. Until then, there hadn't been any long-range plan for the BGEA. Some of the older members of the BGEA didn't like to think about what would happen to the organization when Daddy could no longer preach. Because The Cove would be one of the future ministries of the BGEA, I felt a particular thrill at being asked to take leadership of that committee. If we built The Cove according to my parents' original vision, it would be there to train men and women in the Word of God to be soul winners, evangelists, and church laymen for generations to come. Long after Daddy would leave this earth, there would be a training center that bore his name.

As one person said, The Cove could easily become "the place where the memory of Billy Graham's ministry will be most faithfully presented and his vision most imaginatively embodied." But building The Cove became a controversial project, just as I had expected. I knew some people would oppose it simply because it was a new idea. And others would disapprove of it because it would be located in Asheville instead of Minneapolis, the longtime headquarters of the BGEA.

Daddy occasionally waffled about the project. I think it was because he wanted harmony among all, but Mama and Daddy wanted to see the project go forward. They had put a lot of prayer into it.

We completed the first phase of The Cove in 1990. It included a beautiful Bible training center tastefully designed and decorated to blend in with the rugged mountains of western North Carolina. Two lodges, the Shepherd's Inn and Pilgrim's Inn, were also built on the property. There are no distractions from feasting on the only textbook used—the Word of God. I feel there's no other place like it in the world. We have had people attend conferences from all fifty states and Canada as well as from Asia, Africa, and Europe. God put this burden on the hearts of my parents and has blessed it. There are miles of walking trails where you can get alone with God and pray. Daddy has insisted on having the finest Bible teachers in the world. They come from England, Africa, Canada, and all across the United States.

There is no finer director than Jerry Miller, who left CBC to assemble the most gracious and efficient Christian staff.

Mama and Daddy go to the meetings often just to listen to the speakers and have fellowship with those who attend.

The success of The Cove speaks for itself. I believe The Cove will be a legacy of my parents that God will use to His glory for many generations. *

---

* If you are interested in more information about The Cove, please write me here at Samaritan's Purse, P.O. Box 3000, Boone, North Carolina 28607.

No More Hitler

Now and then I get strange phone calls, but this one was really bizarre.

"Franklin," my secretary said on the intercom, "there's a woman on the phone who wants to talk with you. She says she represents some contra general in Nicaragua. Will you take the call?"

In the mid-eighties our government was in the middle of a red-hot controversy over the United States' involvement in Nicaragua.

My curiosity got the best of me. "Sure, I'll speak to her," I replied.

The woman on the other end of the line introduced herself. She was obviously an American—either that, or she was great at faking a midwestern accent.

"Mr. Graham, I represent General Henry of the contra forces," she said. "I'm calling you because they are in desperate need of doctors. The general has heard that you can send doctors to help people for short periods of time, and that you can provide medicine. Is that correct?"

"Yes, it is," I said. "However—"

"Could the general call you? He can explain exactly what he has in mind."

"Sure, he can give me a call," I said, secretly hoping I'd never hear from him. It sounded like a can of worms. I didn't think I wanted to get involved.

Three days later, my secretary buzzed my office again.

"There's a call from a Captain Henry in Honduras. He says he is with the Nicaraguan Resistance Forces. Will you talk to him?"

Captain? I thought. *Is this the same man the lady spoke with me about on the phone a few days ago?*

"Sure, put him through," I said.

I wondered what I had gotten myself into.

"Good afternoon, Mr. Graham. This is Dr. Henry," the voice said in perfect English.

What in the world is he—a doctor, captain, or general? Maybe he had reduced his rank in case someone was tapping his line. I was growing skeptical.

"What can I do for you?" I asked.

"Mr. Graham, we have heard of the fine work you have done in Guatemala and in other places. I'm responsible for all the medical work within the contra army. And we desperately need physicians. Could you send some doctors to us here at our army hospital in Honduras—near a place called Aguacate?"

Hmm, I thought, *this isn't good.* Oliver North had just been in the headlines, testifying before Congress. I didn't need this kind of involvement. I might find myself sucked into a situation where I'd be in trouble with the State Department.

My mind went to work, trying to find a polite way to tell this man no.

So I said, "Sir, we're glad to help people who are in need. But I'm not sure you want my help. You see, all our doctors are Protestant, evangelical, born-again Christian physicians. I'm sure you don't want us."

"Oh, that presents no problem," he answered. "We'll be happy to have Christian doctors." That didn't discourage him at all. I thought, *What else can I say to cause him to lose interest in us?*

"Sir, you don't understand. Wherever these doctors go, they want the freedom to share their faith in Jesus Christ—"

"I can think of no difficulty—"

"Sir, I'm still not sure you understand. These doctors not only bring their medical skills, but they talk to their patients about Christ. They hold worship services, preach, and urge people to turn to Christ. Wouldn't that be a problem?"

"Oh, no problem whatsoever."

By then I realized nothing was going to discourage him. Yet I wasn't about to commit a corps of doctors to the contras based on a phone call and a few assuring words.

"I'll tell you what," I said. "I can't ask our Christian doctors to go anywhere, especially to a war zone, unless I first go myself to survey the situation and assess the need. That's been a long-standing policy of mine."

"Yes, that makes sense," the general (or whatever he was) said with enthusiasm. "You must come, by all means. We shall be delighted to have you at any time." That wasn't exactly what I wanted to hear.

"But—" I stammered, "I just don't see any way I could clear my calendar. I can't get down there for another few months." My only hope was to stall him.

"We believe you are the people who can help us," he said. "Our men are dying, but we'll wait."

We exchanged a few more words before saying good-bye.

"I shall be calling you again," he told me. "And thank you, sir."

In effect, I had just committed myself to visit Honduras—if this fellow pursued the matter. I could only hope he would get discouraged and forget about asking for our help. But even as the days rolled by, his words lingered in my mind.

One month later, Dr. Henry called again. I was surprised. I thought he had forgotten all about us. Obviously this guy was persistent.

"Mr. Graham, I still have you on my calendar. I just want to confirm the day—are you still coming?"

I've given my word, I thought. *I can't get out of it.*

I reluctantly confirmed a date for my visit.

I began praying for guidance. This was one of toughest situations I'd ever been in. I knew that by going down there, I would be risking my life.

I knew something of the situation. For years Nicaragua had been ruled by a hated dictator, Somoza Debayie. Then, in 1979, aided by pressure from the U.S. and the Organization of American States, a general uprising from citizens (calling themselves Sandinistas) drove the dictator and his family and the hated national guard from power. Inside the Sandinista movement was a small but well organized Marxist corps that grabbed control of the movement after the revolution, executing those within the movement that opposed them.

Unfortunately, the Sandinistas tried to turn the country into a Marxist state modeled after Cuba. And when the nationals who had helped the Sandinistas get to power realized what was happening, they left. Some went into hiding in remote areas to begin a counterrevolution. They became known as the contras. At first they had no support from anyone. After President Reagan took office, he gave credibility to their cause and began to support them both publicly and covertly.

I had heard both sides of the issue, but I didn't know what to believe. One thing was sure—I had been glad not to be involved. Now I was hooked. I had to go.

As I began praying over the situation, I remembered the biblical story of Gideon and his fleece.

Gideon wasn't sure if God wanted him to lead Israel's armies. So, one night, he laid some wool on the ground. He prayed that if it was God's will for him to lead Israel, the wool would be wet from dew the next morning—but the ground around it would be dry.

In the morning, it was just as Gideon had asked. The wool was wet and the ground was dry.

But Gideon still doubted. He prayed again, this time saying, "God, tomorrow, if the fleece is dry and the ground around it is wet, then I'll know for sure it's Your will that I lead Israel's armies."

The next morning, only the wool was dry. The ground was covered with dew.

I decided that this contra dilemma required a fleece. My piece of wool would be very simple: If God wanted Samaritan's Purse to become involved with this "general," we would have to use the opportunity to evangelize the contra army. But how to do that I had no idea. I prayed and asked God to send a Hispanic evangelist. After all, if we were going to send doctors to Nicaragua, we had to be able to rely on someone to clearly communicate the gospel of Jesus Christ in Spanish. This was the reason we would go at all.

In November 1988, I finally scheduled my trip to Nicaragua. No way was I going to go alone, so I recruited several others, including Dr. Melvin Cheatham, a neurosurgeon and member of the World Medical Mission board of directors. (Later he authored a wonderful book, *Come Walk with Me,* about his ministry through World Medical Mission at Kenya's Tenwek Hospital.) I wanted Mel to size up the potential for a medical ministry. I also called Roger Flessing, a longtime friend who now has his own video production company. I wanted Roger to record the trip on video so we could show potential physicians what the conditions were like. I also contacted Norman Mydske, the director of Latin American Ministries for my father. He was not only fluent in Spanish but knew the evangelical leadership in all of the Latin American countries. I needed Norm's counsel in helping to size up the potential spiritual ministry and whether or not we should get involved.

We arranged for the woman who had originally called me on behalf of General Henry to meet us at the Miami airport. From there we all would fly together to Tegucigalpa, the capital of Honduras, where she would introduce us to the "general."

The woman looked to be in her late forties and had bright red hair. She was obviously very "in" to the guerrilla thing: Around her neck hung a striking necklace made of machine gun bullets.

I was already apprehensive about the trip, so the sight of this militant-looking woman with bullets around her neck was unnerving.

When we landed in Honduras, Henry met us at the airport. As we shook hands, I thought he looked somewhat like a short Fidel Castro, only with a trimmed beard and mustache. He wore army fatigues, a T-shirt, and an olive drab army cap.

He greeted us warmly and kept repeating, "Thank you for coming. Thank you for coming . . ."

Henry was accompanied by a man who introduced himself but whose name I didn't catch—he just smiled a lot. The man wore a guayabara shirt typical to Latin America and sharply creased, light-colored slacks. Compared to the general and the other soldiers in their moldy fatigues, he looked somewhat out of place. *Who is he, and what is he doing here?* I wondered. I decided not to ask—at least yet.

We all climbed into a four-wheel-drive vehicle, left the capital city, and headed for the hospital, which was in an area in the eastern part of Honduras. It was close to the Nicaraguan border, near a supposedly secret CIA landing strip controlled by the Honduran army that everyone seemed to know about. American-flown helicopters brought wounded contras there from across the border. CIA flights landed frequently, bringing in supplies. As we drove along the bumpy road, I felt a little uneasy. Everything about the trip was so clandestine. I wasn't liking the looks of this.

I started a conversation with Henry. I was surprised that he spoke freely and openly about himself. He was a fascinating person and told one story after another about his experiences. After a couple of hours, I knew quite a bit about his life, his family, and the contra army.

"Here," he said, smiling. "Look at this." From one of his fatigue pockets he pulled a picture of himself at the White House, posed next to President Reagan. I was impressed.

We had traveled for perhaps four hours when the general indicated to his driver that we should stop for something to eat. The driver pulled up to one of the little general stores found along roadsides all over Central America. I guessed this was not going to be a five-star dining experience. The place was not much more than a broken-down shack with a few signs nailed up in front, advertising Coca-Cola and other products in Spanish.

From the outside, it looked dirty—a classic greasy spoon. We went inside and sat at one of three tables. The place wasn't just dirty, it was filthy.

Henry helped us order, and the food turned out to be roasted chicken—at least that's what I think it was. When the waiter arrived with the plates, I mumbled a blessing, asked no questions, and dug in.

Sitting across the table from me was the man with the guayabara shirt. He had said nothing to this point other than an occasional yes or no. I decided to find out who he was.

"What's your name?" I asked.

"My name is Ruben Guerrero."

"Are you Honduran?"

He shook his head.

"Nicaraguan? Are you from Managua?"

"No," he said, smiling. "I'm from Dallas, Texas."

"Dallas? You have to be kidding."

"No, that's where I'm from."

"Really? What do you do in Dallas?"

"I'm a Southern Baptist Hispanic evangelist."

I couldn't believe it!

"What are you doing out here?"

"I'm preaching to the contras."

I stared at him in amazement. Then Ruben began to unfold his story. "A few years ago I was pastoring a small, Hispanic church in Longview, Texas. I felt discouraged in my ministry. I prayed that God would use me someplace in the world where I was needed— somewhere no one else wanted to go.

"So, my brother, I'm down here. And I tell you, we have had great meetings. I have personally seen many soldiers come to faith in Christ."

Ruben still lived in Texas, but he traveled to Honduran jungles to spend a month at a time with the contras. Then he returned to

Texas for a few weeks to be with his family and try to raise support for his ministry.

"Let me get this straight," I said. "You're a Southern Baptist evangelist?" I had to verify the details. I remembered the "fleece" I had laid before the Lord weeks earlier.

"That's right," Ruben said.

"You don't know how right it is," I said, grinning. "Ruben, listen. These people are asking me to send doctors down here, and I'm willing to send them if we can. But if I do, would you be willing to go into the hospital to preach?"

"My brother, there is nothing I would rather do!"

Long before we reached the contra hospital at Aguacate, God had answered my fleece with what I felt was a firm "yes" that we should be involved. And the fleece now had a name—"Brother Ruben."

The vast majority of the contra soldiers we met at the hospital were just kids—boys and girls barely in their teens. Many of them had seen their mothers and fathers killed by the Sandinistas. They had fled to the jungles for safety, teamed up with others like themselves, managed to get a few guns, and had begun to fight for a way of life they believed in. They wanted to be free.

They all had been wounded. Some had legs blown off, eyes shot out, or bullets pass through bones, maiming them for life. They were all treated together in the most primitive conditions. It was a tough situation. Yet I never heard one of them complain.

After meeting Dr. Henry and Ruben and seeing the desperate medical needs of the contras, I returned to Boone determined to get Samaritan's Purse involved in some way.

I called Lowell and Dick Furman, first thing. I told them everything I had seen and about Brother Ruben. Mel Cheatham called them as well and went into detail about the types of procedures he thought needed to be performed, the quality of the medicine and equipment, and postoperative care. I asked the Furmans if they would be willing to put together a team and go to the jungles of Central America as soon as possible to help these poor people.

Lowell and Dick agreed and took a team several weeks later. During that time the hospital had a backlog of surgical cases. The Furmans literally worked night and day. This hospital had never seen anybody like them. Ruben preached on the wards going from bed to bed, sharing the gospel with each patient. Scores of soldiers made decisions for Christ.

A few months after Lowell and Dick returned, Henry came all the way to Boone for a visit.

"Thank you for sending the doctors," Henry said. "They have been a great help."

Then Henry looked at me with an endearing expression he often wore. "You know, Mr. Graham, our men and women face death every day. Would you help us start a chaplains' corps for our army? As our soldiers go to the field, they don't know how to die."

A couple of years earlier, my father had published a book entitled, *Facing Death and the Life After.* Henry saw it on my desk.

"Please," he asked, "may I have this? I have to have this book."

I gave it to him and asked, "Would you like to meet the author?" I called Daddy and told him about Henry, and he and Mama invited him to Montreat for a visit and a cup of tea. On the way down, we discussed what we envisioned the chaplains' corps would be.

Samaritan's Purse had several other big projects in the works at that time, but to me this was to take priority.

After Henry returned to Honduras, he called to confirm a date when I could come down with Ruben and some of my team to initiate the chaplains' program. I had some major concerns.

First of all, much of Central America comes out of the traditional Roman Catholic church. Even though we have many friends in the Catholic church, I was a Protestant, born-again evangelical. The chaplains would be trained with that theological background.

I was concerned that this might create an unforeseen problem with Henry and the contra leadership.

"I assure you, that's not a problem with us," Henry said.

The conversation sounded awfully familiar.

"Okay," I said. "We'll do it. But I'll have to get back in touch with you."

I needed some time to think this one through. Samaritan's Purse is a relief agency, not a Bible school or seminary. How would we pull this off? Was this just a different spin on the "God room" principle?

I sent one of our staff members down to check out a potential training facility located at contra headquarters in a place called Yamales. He came back ecstatic. I don't think I had ever seen him so excited about a project. He assured me it would work. I called Ruben. "Your friends in Nicaragua want us to train a chaplains' corps," I told him. "Will you help us do that?"

"Yes, Franklin. I'd love to be part of that."

"Great, but we'll need others too."

We put together a simple curriculum, and I contacted Raul Ries, pastor of Calvary Chapel of Golden Springs, located in southern California. He agreed to go with Ruben to Yamales and help train the contra chaplains.

The contras had an interesting way of choosing their chaplain candidates. The leaders would go through each company and point at a person, often at random, saying, "Okay, you be chaplain." By the time we got there they had picked a group of 140 jungle fighters to train as chaplains.

As the men and women stood at attention before our staff, I thought to myself, *What in the world are we going to do?* These were tough guerrilla fighters who knew very little—if anything—about Jesus Christ and His claims.

We had our work cut out when we realized that we would first have to convert these newly appointed chaplains. At every teaching session, we presented an evangelistic message, followed by an invitation to every person to come to Christ. Each time a handful of soldiers, with tears streaming down their faces, came forward. These young, tough warriors were committing their lives to Christ in front of their battle-hardened friends.

After six months, every one of the men and women had made a decision for Christ. And they all wanted to be baptized, so a pit was dug in the ground and filled with water. One by one they came, stepped into the muddy water, and were baptized by Ruben.

Every contra had a nickname so if he or she were ever caught by the Sandinistas, real names wouldn't be disclosed. One man in the chaplains' corps was called Hitler. He had been an executioner in the contra army. Apparently his cohorts had chosen his name well, because at one time Hitler had been very proficient in his responsibilities.

Hitler was one of our promising young chaplains, and after he came to Christ, he excelled in every area and soon became the head chaplain! One of his assignments was to give the announcements following each lecture.

One day as Ruben was finishing up he said, "Now Hitler will come and give us our announcements."

Hitler stood up before his friends. In Spanish he said to Ruben, "My name no Hitler."

"That's fine," Ruben said. But we didn't give his change of name much thought.

The next day, Ruben announced again: "Hitler's going to—"

"No—no more Hitler. No, no. That no longer my name."

"Well," said Ruben, "we've been calling you Hitler for the past several months. If you're no longer Hitler, then what is your name?"

"Lazarus," he said with a smile. "Call me Lazarus. For I have been raised from the dead."

Everyone applauded as Ruben put his arms around Lazarus and hugged him tight. There were tears in everyone's eyes.

I couldn't help but think of the words of the apostle Paul: The gospel is the power of God for the salvation of everyone who believes (Rom. 1:16). The gospel has the power to change a Hitler into a Lazarus.

A Scripture passage comes to mind: "Therefore, if anyone is in Christ, he is a new creation; old things have passed away; behold, all things have become new" (2 Cor. 5:17).

At the graduation ceremony, Samaritan's Purse provided every chaplain a cap with a logo, a gold cross for their uniform, a case of Bibles, and a backpack in which to carry his or her spiritual ammunition, the Word of God.

At last the contras had an official chaplains' corps.

Later, we supplied more than fifteen thousand Spanish Bibles for the chaplains to distribute to the soldiers. They in turn gave every contra soldier a personal copy.

When the war ended and the troops were disbanded, these ex-soldiers walked back into Nicaragua carrying their Bibles, not their weapons. Many from the chaplains' corps went back to their villages and started churches of their own.

Some—including Lazarus—wanted to pursue higher education, so we contacted the Central American Mission Seminary in Managua. The foreign missionaries had left during the civil war, but the Nicaraguan teaching staff had stayed. Unfortunately, they were without students.

"If we pay your faculty for one or two years," we offered, "would you take these former contras as your students?"

The teachers agreed without hesitation.

It was an exciting time for us. We were helping the former contra chaplains get a seminary education, and at the same time we enabled the seminary to reopen.

Nicaraguans like Lazarus had spent years living and fighting in the jungle. Now they were ready to apply their fierce discipline to studying the Bible.

Lazarus was in the seminary's first graduating class. Within months of completing his education, he built and pastored one of the larger new churches in Managua.

Definitely—"No more Hitler!"

Operation Desert Save

In August 1990, President George Bush appeared on national television and made a bold declaration: The United States was drawing a "line in the sand" to prevent further Iraqi aggression after their invasion of Kuwait.

That was just for starters. Soon Americans began to hear about "Operation Desert Shield." U.S. troops would be sent to the Saudi Peninsula to shield Saudi Arabia from Saddam Hussein's Iraqi army. But would our troops be enough? Would Saddam back off? Or would there be war? There was a lot of speculation about sanctions and whether or not they would force Saddam to withdraw from Kuwait.

For weeks I pondered that question, as did millions of other Americans. I felt a particular concern over the situation because I had worked a lot in the Middle East and knew it well. I was concerned especially that the United States wanted to protect Saudi Arabia, possibly one of the most closed, wicked countries in the world—a nation where there is absolutely no religious freedom outside of Islam; a nation that hates and despises Christians and Jews; a nation where women are treated as men's personal property at every level of society. I knew that many American lives could be lost for a nation whose government would imprison one of its own citizens for merely changing to another religion from Islam.

In September 1990, a month after the President's television appearance, I made my third trip to the Middle East that year. I wanted to personally assess the situation following Hussein's invasion of Kuwait. What I saw convinced me that Samaritan's Purse could surely do something.

When Saddam's troops invaded Kuwait, the foreigners in that tiny country had to flee immediately, leaving everything behind. Tens of thousands were also rushing out of Iraq. With the talk of war, nobody wanted to stay. The only escape route left was into Jordan—the small country situated between Iraq and Israel.

Many of the refugees had been workers in the oil fields of Kuwait and Iraq. As they fled, many were accosted by Iraqi soldiers who robbed and on occasion raped and beat them. In addition to all of that, on their way to Jordan, the refugees had to pass through hundreds of miles of desert.

Once these frightened people arrived, Jordanian soldiers and police redirected them to huge holding camps for processing. They were kept in these primitive camps until they could be repatriated to their home countries, which included Pakistan, Sri Lanka, Bangladesh, India, and the Philippines.

I had taken one of our board members with me, Skip Heitzig, pastor of Calvary Chapel in Albuquerque, New Mexico. I wanted his advice and spiritual support. I had confidence that Skip would support our efforts and that his church would be a tremendous resource, not only for finances but with personnel and volunteers. A close friend, Dennis Agajanian, also accompanied us. Both of these men are tough as nails, and I knew that if we ran into any trouble they wouldn't cut and run. A Christian friend of mine in Jordan got some vehicles, and we drove across the desert to the Iraqi border.

When our team arrived to witness the situation, the temperature was easily one hundred degrees Fahrenheit. I stared out at the massive sea of refugees and felt the heat of the desert sun. My heart was moved.

Many of the people were simple laborers, but others were businessmen from India or Indonesia. Some were Filipino women who had been flight attendants for Kuwaiti Airlines, many still with their uniforms on. Social class didn't matter; all were forced to live and sleep in the most primitive circumstances on the desert sand. They had no place to wash and no bathrooms. Worse, they had no fresh food or cold water. In most cases, all they had to eat was a little stale bread.

Immediately, Samaritan's Purse took action. We ordered the shipping of food and supplies, including powdered milk, vitamins, and bottled water from Amman, Jordan's capital city. We secured blankets too. At night the temperature in the desert could drop to the mid-forties.

The Jordanian authorities gave us permission to distribute the supplies, and we arranged for our contacts to buy twenty tons of fresh fruit and vegetables for the camps twice a week. Churches in Jordan were recruited to help do the distribution for us.

Samaritan's Purse provided a copy of the *JESUS* film, and the Jordanian Christians showed it at night in the camp. Interestingly, the International Red Cross objected to our spiritual activities and reported us to the Jordanian authorities. To my surprise, the authorities welcomed what we were doing and let us remain.

The little hospital at Mafraq became extremely valuable to this entire operation. The staff there provided much of the logistical support that we needed by supplying us with volunteers, interpreters, and drivers. We couldn't have accomplished our goals without their help.

The hospital was strategically located, right on the main road heading to Jordan from Iraq, the path of the refugees. Many times I thought, *God sure didn't put that little hospital there for nothing.*

The code name for our project (at this time) was "Operation Desert Save."

It was upsetting enough that our country was preparing to shed American blood to preserve the Saudis' oil. Yet what bothered me most was that despite our giving of American lives for *their* country, we weren't allowed to acknowledge our faith publicly in Saudi Arabia, much less to live it openly.

As unbelievable as this may seem, when our military went to Saudi Arabia, not even the chaplains were allowed to wear crosses in public! And, to my understanding, that was by direct order of the American commander General Norman Schwarzkopf, for whom I have the highest respect. No doubt he was deeply concerned that we not offend the Saudis since they were, in effect, our hosts. The general had a tough job, and I'm sure he didn't want any more problems to contend with.

Still, I wondered, *What kind of war are we getting into? We are good enough to give our lives for the Saudis, but not good enough to live out our faith in their presence?* This troubled me.

Because of its harsh religious laws, Saudi Arabia has always been one of the hardest countries to get the Christian message into. Certainly many of our troops were believers, and there were many chaplains as well. What could we do? I began to wonder, *How can we use this strategic moment in history to penetrate this nation with the good news that God loves the Saudis and that Jesus Christ died for them? How can we make an impact for God's kingdom?*

About that time I was scheduled to speak to a large Calvary Chapel men's conference hosted by Raul Ries in Palm Springs, California. It was during my flight there that an idea came to me.

A few weeks earlier I had read a "Dear Abby" newspaper column in which she urged her readers to mail letters of encouragement to U.S. troops. She had suggested they write to:

ANY SERVICE MEMBER
OPERATION DESERT STORM
APO NEW YORK

The military would forward the letters to the troops.

Abby's idea had been right in line with the public's support of the impending war. People quickly responded with literally tons of letters. Soon the military had so much mail, they had to use jumbo 747 jets just to carry it.

That's when the thought struck me: *Saudi censors will never be able to censor all this mail. It's coming in such volume, they can't possibly open every letter and package.* Suddenly, I knew what to do. That evening at the men's conference, I unfolded my plan.

"Think about this," I said to the crowd of six thousand men. "Much of the Middle East has been closed to the gospel for centuries. Saudi Arabia is Islam's geographic center.

"Right now there are over two hundred thousand American and Canadian service personnel stationed in the Persian Gulf. And I think we need to do all we can to use their presence to share with the people of that region the faith that our nation was built on.

"I have lived in the Middle East. I have a great love for the Arab people and for those of the Islamic faith. After all, they are of the seed of Abraham. But I see an opportunity that we may never have again, and that is to be a witness for Jesus Christ."

I had been told by American service personnel that the Saudis were giving literature to our military officials to distribute to our troops in order to help them be more "culturally sensitive." In fact, this literature was the equivalent of an Islamic tract to convert men and women to Islam. Our Christian soldiers wanted tracts of their own that explained the Christian faith to give in return. I thought, *Why not?*

I challenged the men crowded into the arena: "Here's what I want you to do. I want each of you to write letters to our troops. Encourage them and let them know you are praying that God will protect them. Then enclose a tract in Arabic that clearly explains the Christian faith. Subtly drop the thought that while they are in Saudi Arabia, they may have an opportunity to share it with someone. Samaritan's Purse will provide the tracts.

"How many of you would be willing to write ten letters a day for ten days for a total of one hundred letters?"

It looked like every man present raised his hand. Now I had only one problem: I didn't have any tracts! I figured I could get them somewhere, but where?

I remembered a man I had met while taking part in a meeting in Dayton, Ohio, a few months earlier. He approached me one night and handed me his business card with a tract, saying, "If you ever need my help, I'll be glad to provide you tracts in any language."

One of the first things I did when I returned from the men's conference was to put a call in to the "tract man." I got right down to business: "I need two hundred thousand tracts in Arabic to send to Saudi Arabia. Can you help?"

"We've got several to choose from," he said. He told me about the various versions. "Which one do you want?"

"I don't know. Fax them to me, and I'll choose one."

When I received his fax, I laughed. Needless to say, all of them were printed in Arabic! I couldn't read Arabic, and neither could anyone else in our office.

But I knew someone who could. I faxed them to a friend in the Middle East with a note, "Tell me which one of these is best."

When I received his quick response, I placed an order for two hundred thousand copies—one for each member of our troops in the Persian Gulf.

A couple of weeks later, a truck pulled up to our office in Boone, and we started unloading dozens of heavy boxes. It sure seemed to be a lot more than I had imagined. I asked the guys in the office to count them. One box multiplied rapidly to forty. It didn't take long to realize that a horrible mistake had been made; instead of two hundred thousand, we had nearly a million. We told the truck driver he had delivered many more than we had ordered.

He looked at me and said, "I'm just the delivery man—sign here," as he handed me the shipping statement.

After the truck pulled away, I called the supplier to explain the situation. He laughed. "Well, I guess if you can get rid of a couple hundred thousand, you can probably get rid of a million just as easy. God bless you."

I have to admit, his response made me laugh too. "It'll be a challenge, but I guess you're right," I said. "We'll see what we can do."

Soon we began contacting churches and telling them our plan. "Let's nuke them with tracts," I said. "Every time a soldier opens a letter, a tract will fall out."

I suggested all kinds of things to do, although I don't know if anyone followed my suggestions: "Have young women use colored stationery and perfume it so it appears to be a love letter. A soldier may just groan when he finds out it's a tract. But even if he throws it onto the sand, the wind will blow it where it will. Let's cover the desert floor in tracts. Saturate them!"

It was an exciting time at Samaritan's Purse. Our phones stayed busy as we heard from churches requesting five or ten thousand tracts. Then one asked for thirty thousand. We even had one church ask for one hundred thousand!

"We're going to do it," I told the staff. "We're going to reach our Saudi friends with the gospel!"

We sent one hundred thousand letters of encouragement to the soldiers from Samaritan's Purse alone—each with a tract inside.

In the "Dear Abby" article, she had encouraged her readers to write on the outer envelope as a return address, "Operation Dear Abby," so the recipients would associate the letter with her.

I thought, *What a great idea.* So, I decided to help Abby with her campaign by suggesting that all of our letters be sent with the return address marked "Operation Dear Abby." After all, it was her idea—she should be the one to get the credit.

Countless tracts were flowing into Saudi Arabia. I had another idea: The plan was working so well, why stop now? We could send New Testaments too!

Just before Christmas of 1990, we decided to send a Christmas package to our troops. It included a specially prepared music cassette tape arranged by my good friend, Tommy Coomes, executive director of Maranatha! Music. He gave us thousands of cassettes. We also included another letter of encouragement and a New Testament in Arabic.

We mailed over thirty thousand of those holiday packages in the name of Samaritan's Purse. Included in each was a little card that read:

> *Dear Fellow American:*
> *Now that you are in the Persian Gulf, you may find that you have some spare time. Don't waste it! Instead, why not try learning to read a little Arabic?*
> *Enclosed is a copy of the New Testament in the Arabic language. You may want to get a Saudi friend to help you read it.*
> *We're very proud of you, and we pray that God will protect you and bring you safely home to your loved ones.*

I never dreamed a copy of one of these Arabic New Testaments would get the attention of General Schwarzkopf.

I was stunned when I received a phone call from Riyadh, the capital of Saudi Arabia. "This is Colonel Hogan [not his real name]. I'm calling from Saudi Arabia," the voice said. "General Schwarzkopf has asked me to speak with you."

I figured the phone call spelled trouble.

"There's a lot of concern about what you're doing by sending these New Testaments," he said. "Don't you realize you're putting a lot of American men and women in harm's way?"

"Sir, with all due respect, I'm not putting anybody in harm's way," I answered. "Saddam Hussein is putting a lot of men and women in harm's way. Our government is putting a lot of men and women in harm's way. I didn't start the problems over there."

"But you understand the Saudis' concern about religious pollution in their country," the colonel said. "After all, we're here to protect the Saudis, and they are an Islamic nation, not Christian."

I noticed he didn't say we were there to fight a war—but rather to protect the Saudis. (At that time the military movement was called Operation Desert Shield—to shield the Saudis from Saddam. Only later, when the coalition forces invaded Kuwait and Iraq to drive out Saddam Hussein, did it become Operation Desert Storm.)

"We, as chaplains, are not here to evangelize," Colonel Hogan continued. "We're here to provide for the spiritual needs of our men and women in uniform. Our responsibility is to them only. Period. Is that understood, Mr. Graham?"

"Colonel, I appreciate that. Everyone in this country is backing and supporting our men and women in uniform. We're proud of you. But I'm going to be honest with you, sir. The religious unfairness has upset me and a lot of others in America. Our men and women are being asked to put their lives on the line—possibly to spill their blood to protect the oil there. And you, a chaplain, can't even wear your cross in public! The Saudis want our blood, but not what we believe in."

"But, Mr. Graham, you have to understand their perspective..."

"Sir, the Cross of Jesus Christ is what made America great. America was built upon the Christian faith of our ancestors. It ticks me off that the Saudis are pressuring our military to restrict our religious expression. It doesn't sit well with the American people either."

After I finished, a hush fell over the line.

"I understand what you're trying to do," Colonel Hogan finally replied. "I'm an evangelical too. But I'm under orders . . ."

"So am I, sir—orders from the King of kings and Lord of lords—to go into all the world and preach the gospel and make disciples of every nation."

Colonel Hogan paused again. "I understand," he said. "I guess you might as well know some of the results of your work." He began sharing stories of the spiritual activity among our soldiers: baptisms out in the desert—in foxholes, of all places.

As our conversation began to conclude, I determined that if Colonel Hogan flat-out asked me to stop sending tracts and Bibles, I would. When your country is at war and the military asks for your cooperation, in my mind you do it.

To my surprise, though, he never asked. "It was good talking to you, Franklin," he said. "I hope maybe we can meet someday." Then he hung up.

Not once during that hour-long conversation did he ask me to stop sending literature.

Our efforts must have had quite a powerful effect. When General Schwarzkopf wrote his autobiography, *It Doesn't Take a Hero,* ours was the only spiritual work he mentioned.

In one chapter Schwarzkopf talked about the religion of the Saudis. Upon the General's arrival at the Riyadh military headquarters, he had met Lieutenant General Prince Khalid Bin Sultan al-Saud, commander of the kingdom's air-defense forces and the man King Fahd had appointed as Schwarzkopf's counterpart. The chapter speaks of the Saudis' fanaticism and unwillingness to allow anyone freedom of religion. Schwarzkopf writes:

> *The touchiest issues almost always involved religion. Within days of my arrival, Khalid called with his hair on fire: "You have brought a rabbi into this country who is saying that for the first time in history, the ram's horn will be blown on Islamic soil!" Jews blow the ram's horn as part of their observance of the new year, the holiday of Rosh Hashanah. I very much doubted that a U.S. Army chaplain would say anything that inflammatory, but I sent my staff chaplain scrambling. We eventually discovered that the rabbi in question was neither*

*connected to Central Command nor present in the
Middle East—he was an Army chaplain in the United
States who'd been quoted in an Israeli newspaper.
Someone had clipped the story and sent it to the king.*

*The Saudi concern about religious pollution seemed
overblown to me but understandable, and on a few
occasions I agreed they really did have a gripe. There was
a fundamentalist Christian group in North Carolina
called Samaritan's Purse that had the bright idea of
sending unsolicited copies of the New Testament in Arabic
to our troops. A little note with each book read: "Enclosed
is a copy of the New Testament . . ."*

*One day Khalid handed me a copy. "What is this all
about?" he asked mildly. This time he didn't need to
protest—he knew how dismayed I'd be.*[1]

Though I felt like I had gotten off the hook with Colonel
Hogan, trouble seemed to dog us on this project. One afternoon
someone from the U.S. Postal Inspector's office contacted us: "I'm
calling to inform you that you have broken the law," the man said.

My heart began to pound—boom, boom, boom. *What have
I done now?* I thought.

"What are you talking about?" I finally managed to say.

"Sir, you have been sending Bibles and religious material to
Saudi Arabia. We have had strict instructions that religious material,
alcohol, and pornographic literature cannot be sent to Saudi
Arabia."

Hmm, I thought, *the Bible, whiskey, and pornography all
lumped together.* I got angry.

"You say I've broken the law," I answered. "Tell me—is it
against the law to send the Bible through the mail?"

"Yes, it is."

"It *is?*"

"Well—it's against Saudi law."

"Whew, man, you had me scared for a minute. I don't live in Saudi Arabia—I live in the United States of America. I didn't know the Saudis had taken over."

"Well, ah, you see, Mr. Graham, you have to understand that we're in a wartime situation . . ."

He ranted for a while, trying to tell me we couldn't send Bibles or religious material through the mail if Saudi Arabia was its destination.

"Sir, this is still America," I repeated.

"Well, you'll be hearing from us."

After we hung up, I thought, *Man, I'm in trouble now.* But I wasn't afraid. In fact, I felt pretty good about everything we'd done. Apparently we had upset some folks, and that implied that our "Operation Desert Save" was having an effect.

Some time later, the man from the postal inspector's office called again. "Mr. Graham, did you send out envelopes with 'Operation Dear Abby' on them?" The post office had traced the letters to us.

"I certainly did," I said. Then I told him about reading the "Dear Abby" column. "I'm just doing what the columnist urged us to do."

"But why did you stamp 'Operation Dear Abby' on your envelopes? Why didn't you put 'Samaritan's Purse' on them?"

"Well, it was Dear Abby who suggested we write," I said.

"Don't you realize you have made her very upset?"

"Me? I had no intention of upsetting her," I said.

"I see," he said. "My question for you, Mr. Graham, is this: Are you going to continue doing this in her name?"

"If it's upsetting her, then, no, of course not."

"Well, it has upset her—a lot."

I think she was afraid of some possible terrorist attack or something. "Sir, you can let her know we won't be using her name any longer," I told him.

That was the end of our conversation—and the end of our involvement with "Operation Dear Abby." But we did continue to send tracts and Bibles out from Samaritan's Purse.

Operation Desert Save generated many wonderful letters from the field. Following are excerpts from a few.

A sergeant in the 82nd Airborne Division wrote:

> *Your gift arrived and found me in a sandbag-fortified foxhole in the Arabian desert. As soon as I received your package, I dug right into it. It was only the second time I've received mail since being deployed to the war front. I had to pull out my flashlight to read because the sun had gone down.*
>
> *The following morning, I borrowed a Sony Walkman from one of my soldiers to enable me to listen to the tape you sent. It was fantastic.*

The sergeant added that the music touched him so deeply, "Tears of joy began to flow. I pulled my cap down over my eyes so that my tears of unspeakable joy would not be confused as stress symptoms by my men."

He thanked us for the Arabic New Testament and promised to pass it on.

Another letter came from a soldier who wrote, "I gave the Bible to a person in my platoon who knew a Saudi Arabian who wanted a Holy Bible."

Another soldier wrote, "The Saudis give us tracts trying to indoctrinate us with Islam. Thank you for giving us something we can give back to them to explain our faith in Jesus Christ."

Of all the responses we received, I was touched most deeply by a letter from an A-10 pilot. After the war was over he wrote, "Just two weeks earlier I had been trying to kill those guys. Then

I found myself in an army hospital talking with an Iraqi POW. I gave him the Arabic New Testament."

We received many other letters from enlisted soldiers and noncommissioned officers thanking us for the tracts and New Testaments.

Not long after the Gulf War ended, I received a call from Colonel Hogan. "Mr. Graham, do you remember that we talked from Riyadh a few months ago?"

"Yes, sir, I sure do."

"While I was there, General Schwarzkopf ordered me to confiscate all the Bibles and tracts you'd sent and mail them back to you."

My heart sank.

"I'm sorry to hear that," I said.

"We confiscated about a hundred."

"Well, that's too bad," I said—but inside I was rejoicing! We had mailed out thousands of Bibles and tracts, and they had confiscated only a hundred.

"Listen, Franklin, I met a young man over there," Colonel Hogan added, "a foreign construction worker. He's a believer who has organized a distribution system for the tracts and New Testaments. He's based his methods on the KGB model—organizing a number of small groups in which no one knows another person's last name. That way, if anyone is caught and tortured, he won't be able to give away the whole network.

"A few of his distributors are Saudi citizens. But most are foreigners who work for Saudi companies. Secretly, they're getting Bibles into the hands of Saudis."

Fascinating, I thought. *But why is he telling me this?*

"Oh, by the way, Franklin—all those Testaments we confiscated to send back to you? Well, with the war and all, somehow we, uh, lost them."

Was he telling me this construction worker had them? "I'm sorry to hear that," I said. I wanted to stay neutral until I knew where the conversation was going.

"Do you have any more?"

"Yes, sir, do we ever. Several pallets. Why?"

"Well, if you get them to me, I'll see they get to where they need to go." I couldn't believe what I was hearing.

I said, "Thank you, sir, great talking with you."

We were thankful to God that the door had stayed open so long. And we believed He had answered our prayers: Hearts in Saudi Arabia were being opened to Him, and lives were being changed by the gospel.

I really do appreciate the sensitive position that General Schwarzkopf was in. He's a great man—a brilliant general—a real hero. I can understand why he took exception to what we were doing. He was a man under authority. But so was I.

CHAPTER 19

"God Doesn't Love the Kurds!"

The Gulf War had ended, and Iraq was on its knees.

Immediately, I felt compelled to help my believing brothers and sisters in that devastated country. They were discouraged and needed to know that Christians in the West cared for them—that the war hadn't been fought against the Iraqi people, but against Saddam Hussein.

I knew just where to go to try to bring help to the Iraqis. I called Sami Dagher in Beirut.

"Why don't we take food and medicine to the churches in Baghdad?" I suggested to Sami. "We can distribute it to the poor and use the opportunity to preach Christ. We may never have another opening like this one.

"You speak the language, Sami. And being Lebanese, you'll have no trouble getting across the Iraqi border. Can you put together a team from your church to go into Iraq?"

Sami was ecstatic at the idea. "I'm ready, my brother, at any time," he replied.

We provided Sami with enough money to buy a convoy of food and medicine—about ten or eleven tractor-trailer loads. Then he put together a team to take the convoy through Syria into Jordan and finally into Iraq.

The team members ran into an obstacle almost immediately when they were delayed by soldiers at the Syrian border. The Syrians hate the Iraqis, and the border guards didn't want Sami's convoy to pass through with the aid. Sami had to negotiate for two tense weeks before managing to get the trucks across the border.

Once inside Iraq, the team had no problems. Iraq's minister of the interior gave Sami complete freedom to distribute food, clothing, and Bibles. He also gave the team permission to work with the Kurds in the north and the Shiites in the south.

Once Sami began assisting the churches in Iraq, he discovered some church buildings that had been accidently damaged by American bombing. Samaritan's Purse quietly helped Sami repair those structures.

Then came the next step of our ministry in Iraq. In early 1991, Sami called me to say he was sending five young, single men from the Karantina church to Iraq as missionaries.

"Franklin," he said, "it's my prayer these young men will never come back to Lebanon."

I was a little shocked. "What do you mean, Sami?"

He laughed. "I pray they will fall in love with Iraqi women and then stay in Iraq and start churches."

Sami picked five young single men he had personally trained in the study of God's Word. Each one knew how to preach. They had come from an army of young men I think of as Sami's "young lions." They're both tough and faithful in their purpose and commitment to Christ.

After the war for the liberation of Kuwait ended, most American troops were shipped home. Some military units were immediately sent back to the Middle East, however, this time to Turkey and northern Iraq. They were needed to protect the Kurds from Saddam Hussein.

Saddam's enemies within Iraq had seen his defeat in the Gulf War as an opportunity to move against him. For years, the Kurds in northern Iraq had fought Saddam to try to win their own independent state. And now they decided to launch an all-out attack against the Iraqi army.

But Saddam, with lightning speed, moved his Republican Guard to the north and began driving the Kurdish rebels back toward Turkey. As a result, hundreds of thousands of Kurdish refugees had to flee for their lives into the mountains.

Our ministry team heard unbelievable reports about the atrocities taking place there. Iraqi soldiers were tying Kurdish children to their tanks so the Kurds wouldn't shoot at them. Pregnant women were being bayoneted. And entire villages full of women and children were being massacred.

As I watched the televised reports, I was moved by the Kurds' struggle for freedom. I felt that Samaritan's Purse had to do something.

Yet, as I had learned from Bob Pierce years before, I knew I had to see the situation for myself. I called a couple of my board members and asked them what they thought about Samaritan's Purse helping the Kurds. "Franklin, by all means, let's do it," they told me with enthusiasm.

I had heard of the Kurds years before, when I worked at Mafraq. They lived in an extremely remote part of the world. It was a strategic opportunity to bring healing and Christ's love to a nearly "forgotten" people in a time of crisis.

In April 1991, I decided to lead a small team to Ankara, Turkey. From there we would go into eastern Turkey, where many of the Kurds were fleeing.

Our supporters had sent us money to help the Kurds, but we didn't have the manpower to provide the work. So we contacted Operation Mobilization (OM) in England, whose workers in Turkey spoke both Turkish and Kurdish. They didn't have the money to do the kind of relief work needed, but they had the manpower. OM was a perfect fit with our ministry.

Our two teams met in Ankara, where we planned the trip. We decided we would fly into Diyarbakir, a city in central Turkey. From there we would drive to our final destination.

That's when we learned that the Turkish airline service was on strike. We were stuck in Ankara. The only option was to charter a plane. We could locate only one, a small, ancient-looking, single-engine Cessna. The cost was exorbitant, but we felt we had no choice.

We flew out on a cold winter day. The old plane creaked and groaned while climbing. When we reached eleven thousand feet, the plane began to ice up. Most modern airplanes have deicing devices, but this one didn't. Soon we hit heavy snow, too, and it, along with the ice, began to accumulate on the wings.

The old plane's windshield was so loose that snow began drifting into the cockpit. In just a few minutes, a thin film of white had covered my legs. I looked out the window and saw snow-capped mountains poking through the clouds below us. I thought, *This is getting dangerous.*

When we flew into a heavy layer of clouds, the plane started losing altitude. Our pilot seemed confused. I looked over at him and suddenly realized he didn't know much about flying an airplane on instruments. He obviously wasn't instrument-rated. He was doing his best to maintain his composure, but I could read the fear in his eyes.

"Can I fly the plane?" I asked. "I'm a pilot."

"Oh, please, please!" he answered, as if he had just been saved from a death sentence.

I took over the controls. The pilot had the maps, so I asked him to locate our position. But he was too disoriented and couldn't do it. Finally I helped him find out where we were.

By this time the ice had really built up on the plane and was adding some dangerous weight. If it continued to collect this way, I knew we wouldn't get very far. We would have to go down, and that meant landing in the mountain range.

The plane's heater was not working, so the inside temperature was well below freezing. Our breath made icy little clouds.

I turned and yelled back, "Hey, guys, this is a good time to pray! The situation isn't good."

To make matters worse, the alternator failed. Now we had no electrical power. We would have to rely on the plane's batteries to operate the radio.

I told the pilot to turn off all the electrical equipment to save the batteries. We would need them to power the navigation equipment to make an instrument approach into Diyarbakir.

I looked at the pilot's hands. They were shaking uncontrollably. We were still at least one hour away from our destination.

We finally made it over the mountain range, and I dropped the plane to a lower altitude. After a while the ice stopped building up. We all sighed and thanked God.

When we landed at Diyarbakir, I was determined never to fly in that plane again. Even if this meant driving all the way back to Ankara, I didn't care. Once had been enough. I had my feet planted firmly on soil, and they were going to stay there for a while.

Julyan Lidstone and a team from OM met us at the airport with two vans. I liked this guy. He was a go-getter. Julyan was a Brit who had lived with his family for a number of years in Turkey. I knew after meeting him that we were in for one interesting trip.

Julyan told us that it would take six hours to drive to where the Kurdish refugees were hiding up in the mountains of eastern Turkey.

As we got closer to the Iraqi border, we encountered Turkish military checkpoints every five to ten miles. The soldiers looked mean and sullen as our vans approached. I couldn't help but think that their ancestors massacred Armenians by the millions at the turn of the century because of their Christian faith. We were fortunate that there was a lot of U.S. military traffic on the road, because they waved us right through.

At the end of six hours, we reached a deep valley that would lead us to our destination. The valley was named Isikveren, which means "the valley of light." At this point I thought, *It reminds me more of "the valley of death." Why didn't they name it more appropriately?* The roads were no longer paved, and the better ones were nothing more than snow-covered gravel. I looked around at the mountainous countryside. It seemed utterly desolate and wild.

We stopped several times to ask for directions. Not one of the people we spoke to smiled. They just stared at us with dull eyes.

I noticed that virtually everyone was carrying a gun. It looked like the old West. The mood of the people and the desolate landscape were making me feel extremely uncomfortable.

All the Turkish villages we came to looked like armed camps. Barbed wire had been strung completely around them, with gun emplacements here and there. High-intensity lights lit up the village perimeters after dark. Maybe that's why they called it "the valley of light."

"If you had any doubts that this is a war zone," Julyan said, "now you know differently."

He pointed to fortified buildings with Turkish soldiers surrounding them. "The Turks own the towns but not the countryside," he added. "The Kurds own the countryside. That's how the war goes."

Eastern Turkey has a very large Kurdish population, and the Kurds in that region had been waging guerrilla warfare against the Turkish government for years—the same as in Iraq.

Now the Turks found themselves caught in a catch-22 with their enemy. As a result of the international attention drawn to the Gulf War, the Kurds, under attack from Saddam, had attracted worldwide sympathy. And the Turks had been forced to allow the U.S. military and international relief organizations to help the Kurdish refugees from Iraq.

Needless to say, the Turks weren't too pleased that millions of Kurds were pouring into their country and receiving help.

It was late afternoon when our small caravan finally arrived at the end of the valley.

"We can't drive any farther," Julyan explained. "This is all one-way traffic. It goes up in the morning and comes down in the afternoon. We're too late to drive up."

"Does that mean we have to walk the rest of the way?" I asked.

"It's only five miles at most," he said encouragingly.

We climbed out of the vans and started the long trudge upward. It was tough going. We had no water or provisions of any kind. And the farther up the mountain we climbed, the colder it got. The bitter wind penetrated our clothing and pricked like needles. It was miserable, but we kept on hiking.

Finally we came to a plateau near the top of the mountain and spotted our destination—the hospital at Isikveren. We walked in and immediately saw that this "hospital" was little more than a first-aid station run by several Irish relief workers.

We decided to walk a little farther up the mountain, to the next ridge. I wasn't prepared for what I saw there. Huddled in the snow were about one hundred thousand people, trying to keep warm with flimsy pieces of plastic wrapped around them. These were the Kurdish refugees. They were frightened and shaking from the cold.

Turkish troops had been positioned in the area to keep the Kurds from moving further across the border into Turkey. The soldiers weren't letting the Kurds move down the mountain, where they could be warmer and drier.

We knew immediately that if something wasn't done quickly, these people were going to die. Already many had starved to death. Yet the Turkish soldiers showed no sympathy. Their hearts were as cold as the weather!

U.S. fighter planes regularly flew overhead on observation runs. I suppose they were trying to reassure the Kurds of their presence. But probably more than anything, they were sending a message to the Turks: "We're watching you—so you'd better keep your fingers off your rifle triggers."

That day at Isikveren, we were stunned—heartbroken—by the hardships of the Kurds. Everywhere we looked, someone was trying to scratch a hole in the frozen ground for a grave.

I watched as one young man dug a shallow grave with his hands. Next to him on the ground lay a tiny bundle—obviously an infant. I had to look away. I couldn't help but think about my own kids back home, warm and safe at our farmhouse in western North Carolina. I wondered how I would have felt if I had been in his shoes?

At one point, a tractor pulling a farm wagon wound its way toward the Kurds. As soon as the starving people saw the wagon, they all screamed and ran toward it.

The vehicle moved along the ridge, and someone inside the wagon began throwing out loaves of stale and moldy bread. The refugees elbowed and fought each other desperately to grab the precious food.

The scene reminded me of how farmers back home fed field animals in winter. My heart ached.

Just before dark, we heard helicopters. When we looked up we saw American choppers circling overhead. They were landing along the ridge, and U.S. troops were jumping out.

A Kurdish man turned to me and said in English, "This is a day that will go down in Kurdish history."

"Why is that?" I asked.

"Because this is the day the Americans came to save the Kurdish people."

A thought struck me: *What a time to preach the gospel to these people! America is number one with them right now. They're eager to listen to anything we have to say!*

"Julyan," I said, "you've been praying for years to have this opportunity, and now you've got it. You need to get a bigger team in here. Samaritan's Purse will help you. We'll send doctors and nurses. Now is the time to get started!"

A group of Kurdish men had gathered around us. Quickly, a member of the OM team opened his Bible and began reading Scripture to the surrounding Kurds.

I wondered how they would respond. Would they become angry or want to debate? Yet, as I watched them, I saw that they were genuinely interested.

Except for one Kurdish man who became angry. He shouted in English, "God doesn't love the Kurds!" He gestured toward the thousands of people huddled in the snow behind us.

"Oh, yes—God does love the Kurds," the missionary replied.

"No, He doesn't love the Kurds!" screamed the angry man.

"But He does! Listen." He read from John 3:16: "For God so loved the world that He gave His only begotten Son, that whoever believes in Him should not perish but have everlasting life."

The crowd was getting larger now. I backed up a couple of steps, afraid that a serious confrontation was about to start.

"What's your name?" the missionary asked the angry man. When he replied, the missionary read John 3:16 again—this time inserting the Kurd's name in place of the words "the world."

"You are part of the world—and this means you," the missionary said. "It means God loves you. God loves all the Kurds."

The man seemed a little startled. "Read it again."

The missionary read the passage once more—again inserting the man's name.

The Kurd's anger had begun to melt. He stared at the missionary in surprise.

"Yes, me," he said. "That is right. God loves me."

The whole crowd listened as the evangelist continued to speak. In simple words, he presented the gospel to them.

It was an incredible beginning to our work with the Kurds.

Later that afternoon, our team started back down the mountain. Sean Campbell, director of Samaritan's Purse-Canada, suddenly pointed to a woman carrying a sick child. The Turkish soldiers weren't letting her pass through to take her child to the hospital. They insisted the child was already dead.

The woman cried and pleaded with them to let her go through.

Just then, an American Ranger—a member of the Army's elite fighting unit—walked up. In one hand he carried his M16 assault rifle. With the other arm he scooped up the sick child and walked right past the Turkish soldiers, as if to say, "I dare you to try to stop me."

The Turks backed up as the Ranger took the child into the hospital.

I was proud of this young man and proud to be an American.

For several months, we supported a team of Christian workers associated with OM. Dr. Don Mullen, an outstanding cardiac surgeon, was one of the first people to drop everything and head for the Turkish/Iraqi border. He coordinated the medical teams that worked there for two or three weeks at a time.

The OM team focused on evangelism as they assisted in the field hospitals. They performed every kind of duty imaginable—nursing, washing patients, helping sick children, digging latrines, and, when necessary, digging graves.

Traditionally, Kurds are Muslims who hate Christians. But the gospel's influence changed many hearts. Now the Kurds saw Muslims killing each other while Christians were helping to ease their suffering in the name of Jesus Christ.

Then, as quickly as the door had opened, it suddenly shut and we were no longer welcome. The politics had changed. But we thanked God that He had allowed us to take full advantage of our time there to bring emergency assistance and the gospel to the Kurds. A tragic situation had provided an opportunity for God's Word to penetrate into areas it had never gone before.

And many Kurds learned that God really does love the Kurdish people.

Benchmarks

In life we all have events that become benchmarks that we either date time to or measure things by. One of those benchmark years for me was 1992. While it was a difficult year in my life, it was also a time of tremendous personal spiritual growth.

All of my life, rumors, untruths, and allegations have floated around about me or my family. I learned early to ignore them, to develop a thick skin and go on. But this year was different.

The boards of directors of Samaritan's Purse and our medical arm, World Medical Mission, had a serious disagreement with the Evangelical Council for Financial Accountability (ECFA) over the interpretation of a few of their seven standards for membership.

Samaritan's Purse and World Medical Mission had been members of this voluntary association of religious organizations since 1981. Both of our organizations had met everyone of their standards—then and every year since.

In both the Christian and secular worlds, Billy Graham has one of the most respected names on earth. I am proud to be his son and carry his name, a responsibility I take seriously.

I had been a member of the BGEA board of directors since 1979 and currently serve as a vice chairman of the board. I also chair The Cove committee, which oversees the Billy Graham Training Center in Asheville. In addition, I have served on the finance, budget, and audit review committees appointed by the board. This has given me extremely valuable experience.

When I became president of Samaritan's Purse, I worked closely with our board of directors to build the organization by mirroring the BGEA, copying their policies and procedures, establishing a strong independent board and all the appropriate committees to ensure proper accountability. Samaritan's Purse has never had a financial or management crisis. It has grown year after year.

After becoming president in 1979, the first recommendation I had made to the Samaritan's Purse board was to have an outside audit done by a certified public accounting firm and make it available each year to the public. The government doesn't require this of nonprofit organizations, but it's a standard I have always insisted on. I personally feel that if an organization is supported by public donations, it has a responsibility to report how the funds have been used to ensure public trust. I have watched my father all these years and seen the integrity of his ministry. I wanted nothing less than the highest standards and the same integrity for our ministry.

Unfortunately, during this time certain media outlets saw an opportunity to blow this disagreement with ECFA out of proportion—trying to make it look as though there was some type of scandal in the making, which there was not.

Television crews came to the office and even my home, wanting statements and talking to my neighbors. School kids said ugly things about me to my children. Some days they came home in tears. Jane Austin comforted them the best she could. It hurt us to see them in pain. They were too young to understand and frankly, at forty, I was having a hard time understanding myself.

During this time my workload doubled. In February Dr. John Wesley White, my close friend and associate evangelist with the BGEA, suffered a massive heart attack minutes before he was to speak at Peoples Church in Toronto.

I was in India, preaching. Dennis Agajanian was with me when I received a call from my office saying that John was in critical condition. His crusade director, Grover Maughon, had called asking if I would come home and take his crusade schedule starting the next week in Eugene, Oregon. Dennis and I boarded a plane and returned to the United States.

I believe Satan uses discouragement to work against Christians, and believe me, I was one discouraged preacher. I did not feel prepared or adequate for this task. As John's life hung in the balance, I felt torn in many different directions. How can I do the work at Samaritan's Purse and this too? Should I tell John's team no? But I didn't want to let John down. He had stood beside me, and I didn't want to disappoint him. But I had no enthusiasm or energy to carry on.

I remember getting on my knees one night during a crusade and pouring out my heart to God. I felt broken inside. "Lord, You blessed me with the leadership of Samaritan's Purse. I've tried to be faithful to You all these years. If I have sinned, forgive me. You have given me life. You can do with me as You see fit, I am Yours. But I promise You this, as long as You give me breath, I will not quit preaching the gospel. Give me the strength to deliver Your word for the spiritual battle that will rage in the arena tonight. And Lord be with John. If it be Your will, give him a complete and full recovery."

That night when I finished preaching and gave the invitation, a large crowd streamed down the aisles responding to Christ. It was as if the Lord was saying, "Be faithful to Me, I will take care of the rest and will give you strength for the task." I thought of Isaiah 59:19: "When the enemy shall come in like a flood, the Spirit of the Lord shall lift up a standard against him" (KJV).

Over the next several months John began to slowly recover. At each crusade during this time, the team placed a call to John. We all gathered around the speaker phone, and from his recovery bed John would read a passage of Scripture and lead us in prayer for the evening's meeting.

In late June of 1992, George Hoffman, the Samaritan's Purse director in London, came to visit. He asked me about the events of the past several months and listened intently. When I finished, he said rather sternly, "Franklin, for the last few months you have allowed this disagreement with ECFA to distract you from the ministry that God has called you to. Get back to work!"

At first his "Dutch uncle" approach made me uncomfortable, but as his words sank in, I realized he was speaking the truth. I had allowed this issue to divert me.

"Franklin," George continued as he sat up on the edge of his chair, "let people judge you for the work you are doing. They'll see the truth for themselves. Don't worry about the critics. Just get back to the task at hand, helping the poor in Jesus' name."

I was thankful for friends like this who sensed my heart and did what they could to lift my spirits and spur me onward.

George's enthusiasm was infectious. I saw the sparkle in his eyes, and I became excited again about all that Samaritan's Purse was involved in around the world.

That wasn't all George had to say, though. Looking back, I know that the Lord sent George to Boone that day to challenge me anew.

"By the way," he said, "I've just come back from the battlefronts of Bosnia. They need a hospital, Franklin. Do you have any medical supplies down at the warehouse that we could send?"

I thought for a moment and then remembered: "George, we have an entire hospital!"

"What do you mean?" George was intrigued.

"There's a civil defense hospital packed in crates. We bought it a few years ago from U.S. surplus. It has X-ray machines, operating equipment, tables, beds, sheets, and other supplies—the works. Want to see it?"

"You bet I do," he said, bounding from his chair toward the door.

As we headed toward the warehouse, I felt a spring in my step and a lighthearted joy come over me. It grew as I watched the astonished look on George's face when he gazed at the stacks of metal shelves holding medical equipment ready for use in the war-ravaged country.

"Franklin, this is absolutely perfect. More than I could have ever imagined." This English statesman was like a kid at Christmas. "Just think what all this will do for the people in Bosnia and Croatia."

The thrill of it all seemed to spread like fire. Within a couple of days the equipment was loaded and ready to ship. By now my adrenaline was pumping. Just seeing all of the volunteers who came to help pack was energizing. I realized how much it meant to them to be able to reach out and help those in dire need.

The response from the community for this project was so overwhelming that we decided to hold a news conference. Because of the recent exposure we had received due to our misunderstanding with ECFA, all the network affiliates sent camera crews and reporters to cover the story of how Samaritan's Purse was involved in helping to alleviate some of the suffering caused by the war in Bosnia. Several local papers covered the story, too, and positive articles about the ministry appeared in newspapers throughout the state.

The biggest surprise, though, came when I was contacted by *GQ (Gentlemen's Quarterly),* a men's international fashion magazine. They expressed interest in wanting to do a feature article. What did I know about fashion? I wear jeans and cowboy boots! But the editors sent a writer to Boone to interview me and later interviewed my parents. The *GQ* article prompted some interest from the major television networks, which in turn triggered several feature stories in national publications.

Dr. Ross Rhoads, vice chairman of our board of directors, called one day. He and his dear wife, Carol, have been pillars of support to me and Samaritan's Purse over the years. As Ross often did, he was calling to pass along information that he felt would encourage me. He told me about a young man he thought would be willing to help.

"His name is Mark DeMoss," Ross explained.

The DeMoss name was certainly no stranger to me. I was familiar with the DeMoss Foundation that Mark's late father had founded. His mother, Nancy, leads the foundation that supports Christian work all over the world.

"But what does Mark do?" I asked Ross, wondering how he could lend a helping hand.

"Mark has his own public relations firm in Atlanta. He has been a friend for years, and I think he can help you. Will you talk to him?"

"Absolutely," I said.

Mark came to Boone and looked at both sides of the disagreement and said, "I think I can help."

Another man the Lord sent my way was Richard Capin, a man of tremendous integrity, and interestingly enough, one of the founding board members and former chairman of ECFA who had just retired from their board. Mr. Capin had helped author ECFA's seven standards. He is also a CPA and cofounder of Capin & Crouse, one of the most respected auditing firms in the country (and one used by many Christian organizations). Mr. Capin was concerned about the rumors and misinformation that were being circulated. He offered his help. I thought, *Who better to review our position in this disagreement?*

I welcomed him to Boone and opened all of our books and records for his careful review. He spent hours talking to our auditors, going through our files, and checking out each of ECFA's concerns and questions.

When he finished, he closed the books and came into my office and took a seat. "Franklin," he began in a very compelling way, "get back to the work God has called you to. Let me handle the communication with ECFA."

And he did. He wrote a letter and told them: "I have conducted an extensive investigation into the accounting, budgeting, and governance processes of these organizations and have thoroughly reviewed the audit services with their auditor. I am extremely impressed by the level of involvement of the Boards of both organizations and the controls that they exert."

Boy, was this sweet music to my ears! To have a man like this come alongside, offer his professional assistance, and extend his hand of fellowship, encouraged me greatly.

Others like Bill Bright, founder of Campus Crusade, called to lend their support. "Franklin, I believe in you," he said. "Let me know if I can ever help you."

These phone calls of support meant the world to me. One by one, others encouraged me and offered their help.

By year end with the help of Mark DeMoss, Richard Capin, and others, this disagreement was worked out satisfactorily with Samaritan's Purse having not changed any of its positions. Unfortunately, when misunderstandings occur, rumors seem to always surface. But we thank God for His guidance and direction. We learned a lot through this process and believe that ECFA did as well. This was a difficult year for me—a defining year. But it turned out okay.

There are those who question the role of volunteer accountability groups such as ECFA, particularly in light of the recent scandal with the Foundation for New Era Philanthropy that rocked the world of nonprofit organizations. Some three hundred nonprofits, including more than one hundred ECFA member organizations, stand to lose over one hundred million dollars of donors' money that was placed in escrow with New Era, which promised to match these funds with funds from a pool of anonymous wealthy donors whom they allegedly represented.

In what has been reported as one of the biggest Ponzi schemes in history, New Era filed for bankruptcy in May of 1995, jeopardizing the future of many respected organizations and ministries. Some will no doubt go under.

The Philadelphia Inquirer on June 4, 1995, headlined their editorial: "A lot of watchdogs snoozed and eagle eyes blinked to allow New Era to weave its incredible schemes."

Samaritan's Purse was approached about becoming involved. I thank the Lord that He gave us the wisdom to say no.

Will ECFA discipline these one hundred organizations? I don't know. I sincerely hope not. There were a lot of good organizations that were hurt by this deception. We should strengthen and encourage one another.

As the apostle Paul exhorted the church in Ephesus: "Be kind to one another, tenderhearted, forgiving one another, even as God in Christ forgave you" (Eph. 4:32).

My benchmark year of 1992 finally ended—what a relief! It had been tough and draining, but the Lord had used the trials and stress to achieve some wonderful things for Samaritan's Purse and me.

Through Mark DeMoss's efforts, there had been opportunities to appear on CNN's *Larry King Live,* ABC's *Good Morning America,* and numerous other programs. Each time, I was able to share with national audiences about the work of Samaritan's Purse around the world. But best of all, as I had learned while observing my father years earlier in Eastern Europe, I was able to point each interview toward Christ. As Jesus said, "And I, if I be lifted up from the earth, will draw all men unto Me" (John 12:32 KJV).

Lifting up Jesus—that's what really counts, regardless of the circumstances.

Dennis—A Friend through Thick and Thin

It's often said that a person can count his true friends, those he can trust with absolutely no reservation, on one hand. Through thick or thin, heck or high water, they'll be by your side— rock solid. When I think about that kind of friendship, Dennis Agajanian comes to mind.

In the mid-seventies, Daddy asked me to help him with one of his crusades in Lubbock, Texas. That's where I first met Dennis and his twin brother, Danny. Both are tall, broad shouldered, rugged individuals who stand head and shoulders above the crowd. They have a distinctive western style with their black cowboy hats, western belt buckles, and size-thirteen, double-E cowboy boots.

The Agajanians are extremely talented and can play almost any musical instruments. On top of that, they are gifted songwriters. Daddy has used them a lot in his crusades and at precrusade events, like high school assemblies and on college campuses. They do everything they can to drum up interest and attract people to the meetings.

The first time I heard them, they were performing a mix of gospel, bluegrass, and their own style of Christian rock-and-roll at an outdoor concert on a university campus, with thousands of students cheering them on.

I hit it off with Dennis the instant we met on the campus of Texas Tech. Dennis is a Californian, but I felt as though he had come from the deep South. I soon discovered that Dennis loved four-wheel-drive trucks, motorcycles, guns, and more important, the Lord Jesus Christ. That makes him my kind of guy. He's tough as a nail and not afraid to go anywhere or do anything. But he's also got a tender heart for the Lord and a real burden to see lost men and women come to faith in Jesus Christ.

A year after the Lubbock crusade, Mama invited Dennis to play in chapel at Montreat-Anderson College. Then she took him to Pack Square, which is the heart of downtown Asheville, sixteen miles from Montreat. Not only is Dennis a fabulous musician, he's a pretty good street preacher. Like the apostle Paul, he's "not ashamed of the gospel."

Leave it to Mama to find just the spot for Dennis to perform, right in front of a porno shop. (Actually, that was the only parking place she could find.)

Dennis saw an opportunity. Before Mama knew what was going on, he sat on the hood of her car and played to the people going in and out of the porn shop.

Mama and a few others stood off at a distance and egged him on. He didn't flinch as he got right in the porn shop customers' faces with little sound bites: "You're going to hell. You need Jesus." No question—Dennis has a way of getting people's attention!

"Get out of here!" screamed the shop owner as he cursed him.

Dennis continued to sing and preach.

The store owner called the police.

Within minutes, a policeman appeared and threatened Dennis with arrest if he didn't stop immediately. But he did a double take when he saw my mother standing next to Dennis grinning like the cat that had just swallowed the canary. He wasn't about to arrest Mrs. Billy Graham, so he said, "Mrs. Graham, you can't do this. Do you have a permit?"

"Permit?" Mama asked. "This is a free country."

"But, Mrs. Graham," the policeman continued, "this is against the law. Please, Mrs. Graham," he pleaded.

"Okay," she said reluctantly. Of course she was loving every minute of this. Mama doesn't run from conflict. She had Dennis for the afternoon and wanted to keep him busy.

Mama packed Dennis up and headed to the sheriff's department to get the permit. But while she was there, she saw another opportunity.

"Can Dennis play for the prisoners?"

"Mrs. Graham, of course he can play," the sheriff said, glad to resolve the problem so easily.

Mama and Dennis spent the afternoon in jail, moving from cell to cell, Dennis singing and preaching.

I remember Bob Pierce once described my mother the same way he did Sami Dagher: "Franklin, your Mama's got guts for Jesus. That's why I love Ruth." If he had ever met Dennis Agajanian, Bob would have said the same thing about him.

Dennis is a lot of fun to travel with. He has a heart for missions and has traveled with me all over the world. We went together to Beirut during the war, and Dennis played at Sami Dagher's church and in orphanages throughout the city. He puts as much energy into playing for one hundred kids with artillery shells exploding nearby as he does playing for seventy thousand men at a Promise Keepers event. Dennis always gives 100 percent.

One memory that stands out in my mind is the trip Dennis and I took to Ethiopia during the tremendous famine in the early eighties. Samaritan's Purse was involved in helping provide food and medicine to the believers. The government was run by a brutal Marxist dictator. Hundreds of pastors had been killed and others imprisoned with no one to care for them. Samaritan's Purse had secretly fed them. Those churches allowed to remain open were closely watched and monitored by the secret police.

I learned that it had been ten years since the pastors in that country had gathered for a time of spiritual renewal. I thought it would be an encouragement to do something special for them.

Samaritan's Purse sponsored a four-day conference on the compound of the Sudan Interior Mission (SIM) headquarters in the capital city of Addis Ababa. We paid for the pastors' transportation and lodging and brought Greg Laurie from Harvest Christian Fellowship, Roy Gustafson from the BGEA, and others to lead the conference. Dennis provided the music and won the hearts of every man there.

The pastors were ecstatic about Dennis. They had never seen anyone handle a guitar like he did. Johnny Cash once said of Dennis, "He's the fastest flat-picking guitarist in the world."

Dennis played his heart out, and the Ethiopian pastors loved it. Some of the pastors played guitars also. After the meetings, they surrounded Dennis to learn all they could from him. He stayed with them into the wee hours of the morning giving them tips and teaching them new songs.

One afternoon Dennis went out on the street with his camera just like a typical tourist. The secret police were stationed directly behind the mission compound and were keeping a close eye on the conference from their military communications tower. They spotted Dennis just as he was framing a picture with the tower right smack in the middle. Just as he snapped the shutter, he was pounced on by a dozen plain-clothes secret police. They grabbed him and threw him up against the wall, calling him a spy. This big tough cowboy who eats nails for breakfast melted like butter.

I was standing at a distance, not wanting to be too closely identified with him! I hollered out, "Hey, Dennis, maybe God's going to give you a prison ministry, and you can sing like Paul and Silas. It's gonna take an earthquake, for sure, to get you out!"

Dennis didn't crack a smile—he wasn't amused.

I decided I needed to find someone to go to his aid and called on some missionaries who explained the situation to the police. After thirty minutes of discussion, the police agreed to let Dennis go if he would turn over his roll of film. Dennis was glad to accommodate their request.

As only Dennis could do, he fumbled around as he opened the camera case and managed to switch the roll. He handed the police an empty one—they never knew.

In 1982 Dennis invited me to participate in the Colorado 500. It's a charity motorcycle event held annually in Basalt, just north of Aspen, Colorado.

The purpose of the ride is to raise money for scholarships for some of the poor school districts in the western part of the state. The man behind it, Wally Dallenbach Sr., was once a top Indianapolis race-car driver and currently works for the Champion Automotive Racing Team (CART).

Wally started the Colorado 500 by inviting a few of his racing buddies, such as Al Unser and his son, Al Junior, Bobby Unser, Parnelli Jones, Dan Gurney, Tom Sneeva, and others. The charity ride has remained a by-invitation-only event since the beginning. My invitation to ride came through Dennis's influence. He knew I would get a real kick out of riding my Honda over the Rockies. Today, this event attracts hundreds of riders from all over the world.

The ride lasts a grueling four days and crosses some of the roughest terrain in the world. It's fun, but serious business. There are places we ride where if your motorcycle slips off the trail, you could fall a thousand feet.

I remember a few years ago when Dennis arranged for Pete Robinson to be invited to the Colorado 500. Pete had been my closest childhood friend. His parents were missionaries to Korea. Pete was one of these guys who could do anything and was afraid of nothing. It didn't matter how bad things got, he always had a smile on his face. The worse it got, the bigger the grin.

That year on the ride, Pete and I got stuck on the side of a cliff at about thirteen thousand feet in an early autumn blizzard.

The storm hit unexpectedly, and our motorcycles were quickly buried in a drift. We couldn't see more than a foot in front of us, and the wind had to be blowing seventy miles an hour. We were cold and exhausted from trying to push through the snow. As dusk set in, I began to wonder if we would make it off the mountain before nightfall. But I wasn't scared—I had Pete! When I looked at him he said, "Aw shaw, we'll get out of here." And we did. Pete didn't let obstacles get the best of him. He was a fighter.

The next year Pete received a call from his doctor while he was on the Colorado 500 ride. He was informed that recent medical tests revealed lymphoma cancer. His doctor told him to return to Duke University Medical Center in North Carolina. Dennis and I rode to the top of Ima Jean Pass and spent time there praying for Pete. He was not only my friend, but a friend Dennis loved as well.

The news Pete received from his doctor a few days later was not good, but even then he wasn't discouraged. He hopped a plane at the end of the week and returned to Colorado in time for the award banquet. Pete had no idea that he would be presented with the Perseverance Award that night. As he rose to accept it, everyone rose to their feet in a rousing ovation for a man they had all grown to love and admire. Pete's Christian testimony was as vibrant that night as the wide grin on his face.

Pete passed away in February of 1991 at the age of forty-three. Dennis and I lost a trusted friend and buddy we could always count on. The Lord used Pete's life to speak to many of the guys involved in the Colorado 500. Still to this day, riders come up to me and talk about Pete Robinson. He definitely made an impact!

Like me, Dennis is always looking for new angles to help bring people to Christ. He knew the Colorado 500 would be a great opportunity to share the gospel with some men who would never show up at a crusade or a Sunday morning church service.

Wally Dallenbach and his wife, Peppy, have given me an opportunity each year to share the gospel with the participants.

Since this is the most prestigious off-road motorcycle ride any-where, it is a great opportunity to tell these men about God's Son.

There have been occasions where people have been seriously hurt—or died from heart attacks. Dennis and I have been asked to bring comfort to family members and, in one case, lead a memorial service.

Over the years we have made many friends. A number have become great supporters of the ministry of Samaritan's Purse.

It's interesting how God uses people from all walks of life to accomplish His will and purpose. Dennis is one of those people whom God used to encourage me through the years. And Dennis has not only introduced me to guys in the Colorado 500, but also to many pastors of my generation, including Greg Laurie of Harvest Christian Fellowship in Riverside, California, and Skip Heitzig of Calvary Chapel in Albuquerque, New Mexico. These two men pastor megachurches and now serve on the board of directors of Samaritan's Purse.

I'm honored to call Dennis Agajanian, this giant of a man with a heart as big as the outdoors, my friend.

A Little House of Peace in a Sea of Shame

I can't be just a spectator. I have to be a participant.

I suppose that's what makes Samaritan's Purse a little bit unique. I don't believe in sitting behind my desk eight hours a day; I believe in *leading* Samaritan's Purse—and to lead means to go with my team into the field. Until I can smell it, touch it, and feel it, I can't comprehend the complete scope of the need.

Like everyone else, I watched the war erupt in the Balkans (the former Yugoslav republics). But I couldn't fully understand what was happening until Peter Kuzmic took me to that part of the world in 1992. Peter is a well-known evangelical leader in Croatia and president of the famous Evangelical Theological Seminary in Osijek. He wanted to show me firsthand the suffering that was taking place in that land.

We began to give support to the refugees who had fled the cruel fighting in Bosnia and Croatia. Our efforts began with trying to meet the most urgent needs facing the refugees that winter. At the top of the list were blankets and sleeping bags. The winters in that region are bitterly cold, especially in the mountains. When people have had to flee their homes, leaving everything behind, suddenly the very simple basics become the most important: shelter and food.

We teamed up immediately with the evangelical Christians and began distributing aid through their churches. Wherever we go, I always believe in working through the local church. When all is said and done, the church will then get the credit and earn the right to preach Christ. People will remember that in their hour of need, when they were homeless and sick, it was the church that came to their rescue.

In war zones, food distribution must be organized in such a way that individuals can receive their food parcels with precision timing in order to narrow their risk of being exposed to enemy fire. Often when we bring a convoy of food into an area and set up a distribution center, local officials fear artillery attack. Enemy soldiers target the center of town, or wherever the convoys stop, and shell it. Their goal often is to kill as many civilians as possible.

Our goal is to be so organized that it takes only a minimum amount of time to complete the distribution program. The recipients are prepared as well. They don't stand around and talk to their neighbors. They hoist the boxes up on their shoulders or into a wheelbarrow and run for their lives.

Food distribution is not an easy task. It was Jan van Barneveld, director of Samaritan's Purse-Holland, along with some of his friends, who came up with the idea of taking food in bulk, breaking it down and prepackaging food staples in thirty-pound boxes containing flour, salt, sugar, macaroni, rice, cooking oil, high protein biscuits, and a tin of meat.

One such effort was done in the southern city of Mostar, the capital of Hercegovina (one of the regions of Bosnia), which like Sarajevo was split along ethnic lines. The situation in this ancient medieval city was in many ways worse than Sarajevo, which had gained a lot of international attention. Very little publicity was given to Mostar.

Mostar had been world famous for its architecture, dating back many centuries. Now the once beautiful city was being shelled daily, and the death toll was overwhelming.

While in Mostar we met a Pentecostal preacher who pastored a small church. We learned that he was trying to minister to Muslim refugees who had fled the fighting in nearby neighborhoods and were living in empty school buildings on the outskirts of town. Often his cupboard was bare. This pastor humbly asked for our help. I assured him that we would dispatch a convoy of food from Holland so that he could accomplish this task.

Once the convoy was well on its way to Mostar, I decided to join the team for the final leg of the journey so that I could see this pastor and the work he was doing. To get there we had to fly to Zagreb, the capital of Croatia, and connect with a locally based plane that took us to the Dalmatian coast city of Split. From there we were met by members of the Bosnian army, who escorted us across the Croatian border and into Bosnia.

Once we cleared the border area, I realized we were totally on our own—leaving behind all law and order with absolutely no one to come to the rescue if we got into trouble.

Mostar sits at the bottom of a deep valley. We took a road that winds over a high mountain pass, then makes a quick corkscrew downward toward the valley floor.

When we reached the pass, we stopped and asked soldiers along the side of the road if any shells had fallen in the past hour or so. We thought that if things had been relatively quiet, we could proceed. If not, we would wait.

The soldiers assured us that all was quiet for the moment, so we drove on as fast as we could in hopes that we would avoid the snipers along the route.

We made it without incident and drove to the city government offices to notify the minister of social care, Ilija Zulejevic, of our distribution program for the area.

The pastor went with me. He'd been under a lot of pressure from Bosnian/Croatian officials to cease his food distribution to Muslims, but he hadn't given in. He thought if the government saw he had international support for his relief activities, they would allow him to continue without fear of reprisal.

After a long forty-five-minute wait, the minister finally appeared. I couldn't help but notice that his clothes hung loosely from his body. I assumed the war had taken its toll on him physically. I was anxious to share with him what we hoped to accomplish in his city and the help we had brought with us for his people.

The minister graciously greeted us, and as we began to get acquainted shells started exploding in the distance.

Though the meeting had just gotten underway, my objective suddenly was to state our business and head for safer territory. The minister didn't even flinch. He apparently had become used to the shelling and it didn't seem to phase him.

I tried to keep my comments brief. I explained to him who we were and why we had come. He seemed to be pleased we were there, however for a much different reason. It quickly became obvious he had something else on his mind—certainly not our food distribution.

He asked me, "Mr. Graham, may I show you a videotape?"

Another shell exploded—boom! My heart pounded. But the minister didn't budge.

This guy's nuts, I thought. *I didn't come to Mostar to watch a video.*

"I wish I had time," I tried to explain politely. "Maybe on another visit?"

We talked a few more minutes. The shells kept pounding. The minister was insistent, "Mr. Graham, I would like to show you a videotape."

"It is getting late, and we must go," I said.

"But if you don't have time to see the tape, would you mind if I explain to you what's on it?"

I concluded that he was either going to show me the tape or tell me about it, so I let him talk.

"By all means, sir, tell me about the video."

"You see, Mr. Graham, we captured some enemy soldiers and found this videotape in their possession. They had taped themselves raping a nine-year-old girl. Would you like to see the tape?"

"No, sir," I said, thinking, *I'd like to be able to sleep tonight.*

"Mr. Graham, why do men do these things?"

I knew the answer: The heart of man is wicked, the Bible tells us. But with those shells crashing down, I didn't think there was time to explain.

The minister was not finished. He went on, "They brought the girl's father into the room and told him to rape his own daughter. He refused. So they put a gun into his mouth and blew his brains out the back of his head in front of his daughter.

"Then they brought her older brother into the room. They told him to rape his sister. The boy saw his dead father and probably thought the only way to save his life was to obey them. So he did. Afterward, they blew out his brains. Then they laughed. Mr. Graham, it's all right here on this videotape."

The minister paused and stared at me. "What I don't understand is that after the soldiers killed the girl's father and brother, why did they have to saw off her legs, causing her to bleed to death?"

Now my blood was boiling. The minister finally had my undivided attention. The shelling outside became secondary. I thought, *If I had been in that room, with my hands on a gun, I would have brought justice down.* My heart was flooded with hatred for those men I had never seen. How could they do such an evil thing? No punishment could be too severe.

Now I knew I couldn't resist answering his question. Talk about an open door.

As I pondered what to say, I had to remind myself that Jesus Christ had died on the cross for those soldiers who committed such horrible crimes. And just as He had forgiven me, God was willing to forgive those sadistic soldiers—if they would confess their sin, repent, and ask Christ into their hearts by faith. When Jesus shed His blood at Calvary, He did it for the entire world. The Bible says, "For all have sinned, and come short of the glory of God" (Rom. 3:23 KJV).

I looked at the minister and said, "Sir, the Holy Bible says that the human heart is desperately wicked and needs to be changed. The only way our hearts can be changed is by coming into alignment with almighty God. And the only way that can be done is through His Son, Jesus Christ."

The minister listened intently as I explained the way of salvation to him. What a marvelous opportunity the Lord had given to me that day.

When I finally left his office, I was still shaken. I turned to the director of projects for Samaritan's Purse, Kenney Isaacs, and said, "We're not going to come to this part of the world and hear about these kinds of things and *not do something about them*. We know that scores of girls have been raped and have no place to go. Many have been separated from their families or their husbands have been murdered.

"Kenney, we have seen on all the major networks how soldiers in this part of the world are targeting women for rape. I read that one reason they do this is to demoralize their husbands, fathers, and brothers who are in the Bosnian army. We can't help that poor girl the minister told us about. But we can help those who are still alive, afraid, and lonely.

"We need a home for these girls. And we need it over here, in this country. Let's find those girls, Kenney. Let's rent a house and start taking care of them."

Kenney fully agreed. But he responded with a lot of practical questions.

"Where am I going to find the girls, Franklin?" he asked. "And where am I going to rent the house? What's my budget? How long are we going to do this ministry?"

"Kenney, I don't have the answers. You find the house, and rent it. I'll go home and tell our supporters about it. We'll see if they're willing to give funds to help these girls."

"But who's going to run the house here?"

"I don't know that either. But I know God has somebody in mind."

I headed back to the states. Kenney stayed behind to look for housing. Not only did we need the finances for this project, we also needed a very special couple that could oversee this project for us in Croatia. I knew that these girls, if we could find them, would need special care and lots of love and understanding. They would have scars and wounds that only God Himself could heal.

As I mulled all of this over, the Lord brought to mind a couple named John and Esther Fitzstevens. They were American missionaries in Vietnam with the Christian and Missionary Alliance. In fact, Esther had been born and raised in North Vietnam before World War II. Her parents were pioneers there in the evangelical church in the 1920s and '30s.

After John and Esther married, they returned to missionary service in Vietnam. When they were forced to flee Vietnam at the end of the Indo-China War, they had started working with refugees in Hong Kong. Then Vietnam opened up again, and they went back from time to time to work with the church there.

The more I thought about John and Esther for the girls' home in Croatia, the better I liked the idea. *They know what war and suffering are all about. They would be the perfect couple for this task. They would be patient and loving.* But would they be available—would they even be interested?

When I finally got back to my office from Croatia, lo and behold, who were there but John and Esther Fitzstevens—all the way from Southeast Asia. My mind spun. "What are you doing here?" I asked.

"We finally did it, Franklin," they said, "we have just retired." My heart sank a little. I knew they had been contemplating retirement, but I couldn't quite imagine John and Esther leaving the Lord's work for rocking chairs!

John and Esther are a unique, gifted couple. Esther is one of the most vibrant individuals I've ever known. She is an outgoing Christian who reaches out to everybody around her with a contagious sparkle in her eyes and infectious smile. She doesn't need to speak another language to communicate with those of another dialect: She breaks down barriers—by speaking heart-to-heart. Esther is at her best when she has her arms wrapped around those who are hurting, weeping with them. Yet she exudes joy when others are experiencing unspeakable happiness.

John, on the other hand, is quiet, laid back, stately, and every inch a Christian gentleman. He is one of the most distinguished men I know, with his steady thinking and head of silver hair.

So, here the Fitzstevens were, sitting in my office. Their presence was like God's confirmation—they belonged in Croatia.

To my surprise, the reason they had come to Boone was to talk about what role they could have with Samaritan's Purse.

"We're not quite ready to call it quits," they told me. "We feel that God still has something for us to do, and we've been praying for His guidance."

I felt a peace come over me. I looked at this faithful couple and thanked the Lord for answering our prayer—and theirs.

I shared with them our plan for the girls in Croatia. It was like a light switch went on. They told me it sounded like something they'd really like to do and promised to pray about it and get back with me. Just a few hours later they told me they were ready to go.

In the meantime, Kenney had called me from Zagreb. "Franklin, you won't believe it. I've found a beautiful house just outside of the city—it has gardens and fruit trees. It's in a quiet neighborhood, and the house can handle up to fifteen girls at a time.

"Not only that, but I met a female medical doctor pretty high up in the Croatian government. She said she can lead us to the Bosnian girls coming into Croatia looking for refuge and safety. This doctor told me that the Croatian government would welcome our attempt to help these girls and would be willing to refer them to our home for women."

"Kenney, all the pieces are falling into place. John and Esther Fitzstevens have agreed to run the house for us," I told him.

Kenney was riding high when we hung up. So was I!

Within a few short weeks, we had the house rented, cleaned, and ready for John and Esther to arrive. For the next year and a half, the Fitzstevens were parents to over sixty pregnant girls, many victims of rape, others who were left widowed by the war.

Often Esther sat up late at night with the girls in her arms. These young women sobbed as they told stories that made Esther sick to her stomach. Esther comforted them as only she could, and John was the strong father figure that many of them had never had before. The girls received lots of tender loving care, but more important, they heard about Jesus. Many of these young mothers came to know Him as their Savior. We treasure the testimonies we heard. Here are a few.

Jasminca* had spent ten horror-filled days in one of the worst concentration camps in the country. She reported that soldiers would come in at night and turn on a flashlight. If the light fell on a woman, the soldiers would rape her; if it fell on a man, they would shoot him. The light fell on Jasminca many times, but she survived the camp, then fled to Zagreb and to our Home.

Vasvija* was expecting twins when rebel Muslims came into her home and shot her husband. His mother walked in and saw her son dead—she had a heart attack and died. Vasvija had fled on foot and after many days found her way to our home.

Arijana* was guarded and withdrawn. She was the one girl we felt we weren't reaching. Her father recently wrote to us and said, "When my daughter became pregnant, I thought there was no hope for her—that her life had ended. But then she went to your Home. As a result of the love she experienced there, she's a new person."

Daniella* has been living at another shelter since she left our home some months ago. When she leaves there, where will she go? Her parents rejected her because she had been raped [That is common practice in the Muslim culture], but she found love and the Lord in our home. A Muslim girl had encouraged her in those early days to let us pray for her,

*Names have been changed for protection.

saying, "Your burden will be lifted like when they prayed for me, when my heart was so heavy too."

As I write this, the war in Bosnia continues, and Samaritan's Purse remains heavily involved there.

For example, we've been helping suffering Muslims in an area known as Orasje, which borders the Sava River in North Bosnia. Orasje is another city that is shelled every day. To get there you have to ford the river on a small, homemade ferry. The bridge was blown up.

Despite the dangers and hardships involved, a Muslim relief group in Orasje operated a soup kitchen. We supplied them with food so they could provide hot meals for widows and orphans in the city. Occasionally we also distributed food to the whole community. The wonderful Muslim man in charge of the relief operation in Orasje once told me, "You Christians are the only ones who help us."

"You mean that there are no Muslim relief groups from the Middle East—from Saudi Arabia or Iran—helping you with funds?" I asked.

"No—you Christians are the only ones."

Whenever I'm in Orasje, I go by the mosque to say hello to the local imam (pronounced "e-man," a Muslim priest). I like to shake his hand and show him courtesy. It's important to build bridges of friendship. He always seems so appreciative that I would stop by for a visit. On one occasion I was there with an ABC film crew. The beautiful mosque had been hit in an artillery attack, its roof blown away. The imam, needless to say, was heartbroken.

The next time I went by to see him, I learned that he had been wounded in the leg by a piece of shrapnel and was in a hospital in Turkey for treatment.

Several months later, I returned to the mosque and was pleased to see the imam back. We greeted each other warmly. He told me that while he was in Turkey, the hospital staff repeatedly asked him, "Which Muslim countries help you?"

"None of them," he answered. "In the town where I live, only the Christians help us."

"You can't say that here!" the people warned him. "Don't dare speak of that." (Turkey is a Muslim country.)

"But it's true," he protested. "Christians from America have come, and they help us."

"We don't care. Just don't say that around here!"

As the imam shared his story, I realized our simple acts of kindness, done in the name of Christ, have had an impact. I remembered Jesus' words:

> *For I was hungry and you gave Me food; I was thirsty and you gave Me drink; I was a stranger and you took Me in; I was naked and you clothed Me; I was sick and you visited Me; I was in prison and you came to Me. . . . Assuredly, I say to you, inasmuch as you did it to one of the least of these My brethren, you did it to Me. (Matt. 25:35–36, 40)*

No Devils Left in Hell

I first visited Rwanda in May of 1994. One of *Time* magazine's cover stories in April of that year read: "There are no devils left in hell. They are all in Rwanda."

When I saw Rwanda with my own eyes for the first time, I understood why this quote from a missionary had appeared on the cover of *Time*. If any place on earth could resemble hell, Rwanda was it.

April 6, 1994. The news reports flashed across television screens worldwide: The President of Rwanda, Juvenal Habyarimana, a Hutu, had been killed in a mysterious plane crash near Kigali, the capital city. The Hutu majority blamed the Tutsi minority, and almost immediately, reprisals began. Men, women, and children were slaughtered in the streets by roving gangs wielding machetes and butcher knives.

The UN peacekeeping forces fled, leaving behind a stranded international community to get out on its own. There were immediate calls for western intervention to prevent the Hutus from exterminating the Tutsis. Most of the world chose to look the other way.

To the north, along the Ugandan border, the Tutsis had a small guerrilla army they had been secretly training in the jungles. That small, ragtag army was the only hope the Tutsis had for survival.

When the media reported that people were being butchered all over the country, I could not just stand by and do nothing. I figured if Satan was going to loose his demons, then we Christians needed to be right in the middle of the battle. In my opinion, the church needed to respond by caring for the hurting and dying in the name of Jesus.

As thousands of refugees were pouring into neighboring Tanzania, I called our team together. "Folks, we've got to do something. We've sent teams to Somalia, Sudan, and other parts of Africa in times of crises—why not do the same for Rwanda? Let's set up a clinic in Tanzania for these people."

Whenever we send staff into volatile areas of the world such as this, I am naturally concerned for their safety. I think to myself, *Franklin, one of your team members can get killed over there. Are you prepared to handle that kind of loss?*

As I thought about all of the implications in Rwanda, I was reminded of the dedication of our team. I knew the answer to my question was yes. Why? Because our people are committed to the work God has given us to do, and we all sense His prodding to help the suffering of this world. But everyone needs to understand that going to the field with Samaritan's Purse involves risk. And we face not just war, but exposure to every possible disease.

The ditches and gutters that litter this world are ugly places, filled with human tragedy. They are arenas clouded by dark spiritual warfare—evil powers that seem to lurk at every turn. We have to slip into spiritual armor as we serve the King of kings and Lord of lords.

Everyone who is a part of our team—including our volunteers—understands this principle. We are just one heartbeat away from death. We all need to be prepared to go to heaven when that time comes. I am proud of the team God has given us at Samaritan's Purse.

Not long before the war in Rwanda erupted, Samaritan's Purse had opened an office in Nairobi, Kenya's capital. Knowing that war and famine would be on the increase in Africa, we wanted to build a beachhead, well stocked with supplies and medicines, from where we could move at a moment's notice. When the war broke out in Rwanda, we were ready.

I knew we could make a difference in the lives of those refugees—people who had lost their homes and loved ones. They had suffered horribly. They needed to be comforted and bandaged.

Secular organizations such as Doctors Without Borders, the International Red Cross, and other international relief groups had responded. I respect these humanitarian organizations, and they do outstanding work. But their goal is to deal with the physical needs only. Ours is to offer both physical and spiritual assistance.

I don't ever want to miss the opportunity to share God's love, especially with those who have been exposed to such violence. And we Christians need to continue to be on the forefront of this kind of medical ministry. The church of Jesus Christ brought modern medicine to Africa in the last century. We should continue leading the way. As the Lord said, "He has sent me to heal the brokenhearted, to proclaim liberty to the captives, and the opening of the prison to those who are bound" (Isa. 61:1).

By May more than a million Tutsis had fled into Tanzania. The world watched in horror as pictures were broadcast of thousands of bodies floating down the rivers. Countless people died along the roads while fleeing to safety.

We sent an advance team to scout out the land. Dr. Michael VanRooyen from Chicago volunteered to go along with Jim Harrelson from our home office. They entered Tanzania and dropped out of sight for about ten days. I began to get a little worried.

"Jim Harrelson is calling, Franklin," my secretary announced. Was I ever glad for that interruption. What a relief to finally hear his voice.

"It's a no-go," Jim said. "They're not going to let us in." He was referring to the UN.

I couldn't believe it. "What do you mean, they're not going to let us in? They're turning down our help?"

"Yep!" Jim replied. "It's very political, Franklin. They're just not going to let Samaritan's Purse work with the Rwandan refugees in Tanzania."

To think that they would put their political agendas before the welfare of the refugees made me angry.

I tracked down Kenney Isaacs, our "can do" project director for Samaritan's Purse.

"Get over there right away, Kenney. Our guys have hit a brick wall. Let's not take no for an answer."

Kenney caught a flight that very night. Again, we had to wait in silence as another long week passed without hearing from Africa.

I had to leave for Russia to check on another project. I kept calling my office, asking, "Have we heard from Kenney?"

What a welcome relief it was to pick up the phone in a Moscow hotel room and hear Kenney's voice on the other end of the line. I was dismayed, to say the least, when Kenney's news wasn't any better than Jim's.

"Here's the scoop, Franklin. The UN reps will not give us permission to work here." He proceeded to fill me in on the details of his many conversations with a rather no-nonsense woman from the Bronx who was serving as the UN director in coordinating their relief efforts. She seemed absolutely determined to keep all evangelical groups out.

"We've worked with the UN in Bosnia, Somalia, and the Sudan. You know who we are," Kenney insisted as he continued pleading with her.

"Yes," the woman said, "but all the needs here are covered."

"What do you mean, covered? They're not covered."

"They certainly are," she said matter-of-factly.

"More than a million people crossed into Tanzania last week. You mean you've got enough medical staff to care for one million people?" He pushed his point, knowing good and well there weren't adequate relief workers on site.

"It's covered, I tell you." It was clear that she meant "No matter what you want or say, we're not letting you in."

Kenney wasn't about to give up. "We're here to help," he insisted, as he pointed to a refugee camp nearby. "You've got thirty thousand people in that camp alone. Don't you need some help there?"

"An organization from Europe has that responsibility," she said.

"They've got only one nurse!" Kenney exclaimed. "They've got one nurse for thirty thousand people, and you say it's covered?"

"Yes," she shot back dogmatically.

"We've got a team of twenty-five doctors, nurses, and logistical staff right now in Nairobi standing by ready to come and—"

"I've told you, Mr. Isaacs, it's covered. You can't go up there."

Kenney presented a multitude of alternatives, but the UN slammed the door right in his face. He sounded about as discouraged as I had ever heard him.

As Kenney talked on, my blood simmered. Bureaucrats get under my skin—especially when peoples' lives are hanging in the balance. One of the great human tragedies of our century is lives lost during crises because of political red tape.

As my mind searched for a way around the apparent road block, I questioned Kenney. "You're going to let that woman stop you?" I challenged.

"You've never met anybody like this lady in your life, Franklin. She's the most stubborn individual I've ever seen."

I knew Kenney was exhausted, but this woman really had him defeated.

I remembered the account recorded in Acts 16 when the apostle Paul wanted to go to Asia, but the hand of the Lord prevented him. I asked myself, *Is the Lord preventing us from going to Tanzania for a reason?* There just didn't seem to be any other explanation as to why the UN was deliberately keeping us out. Not ready to give in, I thought of another idea.

"Kenney, we might be going about this the wrong way. Maybe we should march right into Rwanda itself and avoid the Tanzanian border altogether." My suggestion didn't seem to strike well—at first.

"They're killing each other over there! Franklin, have you forgotten there's a war going on? It's just not safe."

"Kenney," I tried to calm him, "there have to be some safe areas—they're not fighting in every town. Of course we don't want to go right into the heart of the war. Remember, people are scattering—we need to find those places of refuge inside Rwanda. Why not go in behind the Rwandan Patriotic Front (RPF)—the rebel army lines?"

I don't think my idea thrilled Kenney at the moment, but his hesitancy to answer told me he thought it was worth a try.

"Hadn't thought about going that route," he said with some uncertainty. "The only thing is, nobody seems to know much about the RPF. They're kind of a mysterious bunch. Even the State Department is a bit in the dark."

"Well, why don't we go find out for ourselves?" I waited for his comeback.

When Kenney broke the long silence, he said, "How in the world am I going to do that?"

"Go to Uganda, drive down to the Rwanda border. Poke around a little—ask the Uganda military if you can cross the border."

I knew Kenney's mind was whirling as he considered the consequences. "Do you know anybody in Uganda?" he asked.

"No," I said. "Just go there. You'll find someone who can help." I knew if anybody could pull it off, Kenney could.

As the international phone line crackled in my ear, I heard Kenney mutter—but all that really mattered were the words I clearly understood: "Okay! I'll call you when I get back."

When I hung up the phone, I was a little apprehensive, but I sensed in my heart that God had a purpose and a plan for us to reach out in some way to the Rwandan people. I prayed that God would keep His hand of protection on Kenney and give him wisdom and direction as he entered a little corner of hell on earth.

A few days later, the voice of a more encouraged Kenney Isaacs came across the line, this time from Uganda. His mood had obviously brightened. I could even hear excitement in his voice.

"Franklin, I think it's going to work after all. I have made contact with the rebel army. Can you get here immediately?"

I had already started my trip home from Russia, but I changed course and boarded a plane for Nairobi.

Within a few days, Samaritan's Purse had a team of fifteen doctors and nurses along with a three-month supply of medicines. With help from Africa Inland Mission (AIM), Mission Aviation Fellowship (MAF), and Jungle Aviation and Radio Service (JAARS—a division of Wycliffe Bible Translators), we loaded up three airplanes and flew from Nairobi to a little dirt airstrip near Mbara, Uganda. Kenney was there with two large trucks waiting for us. His pacing back and forth told me he was anxious to start the journey into Rwanda.

Since the hour was late, we spent a restless night in an Ugandan hotel in Kibali. Early the next morning as the sun was piercing the clouded sky, we climbed into the trucks and started toward the border. We were sure of our destination—Rwanda—but we had no guarantee that we could enter the country.

As we approached the Uganda-Rwanda border station an hour later, we saw several Ugandan soldiers propped up against the railings, lazily blowing their tobacco smoke into the air.

"Can we cross?" I asked, not sure they would understand.

"Yes," said one. Another shrugged with disinterest.

"Do you want to see our passports?"

"No," came the reply from the stone-faced guard.

"Will we have any problem coming back into Uganda?"

"No, no problems."

I never anticipated such an easy crossing!

He shoved a large ledger into my hands. "Sign here." He pointed with a nicotine-stained finger to the bottom line. We all put our passports back in our pockets and moved into Rwanda with no problem.

In Uganda we had been traveling on a well-maintained asphalt highway, but that road nearly disappeared as it stretched across the border. It was apparent that the terrain of the land had changed

291

drastically—the road was little more than a trail that the jungle vegetation was rapidly reclaiming. As we bumped over the enormous potholes, I commended Kenney for setting us up with some sturdy four-wheel-drive vehicles.

We drove only a quarter mile before reaching the Rwanda border checkpoint. A rebel soldier, holding a Russian AK 47 assault rifle, was standing in front of what once had been a guard station. The building had been nearly destroyed. Through the shattered windows we could see large pieces of concrete dangling from the ceiling. As we emerged from the trucks, the soldier stopped us abruptly.

"We've brought doctors, nurses, and supplies to help the Rwandan people," I said, hoping we wouldn't be detained long. "Who do we need to talk to?"

"Do you have a business card?" the guard asked in halting English.

A business card? I thought. I stared at him, wondering if I had misunderstood. "We've got our passports." I held mine up.

"No. Not that. A business card," he replied gruffly. Funny, of all the documents we had, none of us seemed to have a business card, of all things. I looked at Kenney as we both fumbled through our jackets.

Sean Campbell, our Canadian director, came to the rescue by producing a dog-eared card that he pulled from his wallet. The guard seemed satisfied as he carefully studied it, then laid it aside. "You must now go see Christine," he said.

"Where do we find her?" we asked.

"Over in the banana grove in that hut," he pointed ahead.

We pulled our vehicles off the road, parked, and walked through the thick grove in search of Christine. We entered her "office" and sat down, wondering when, or if, Christine would appear. The room was sparsely furnished, just some chairs and a rickety old table.

Thirty minutes must have passed before we saw Christine. She was obviously a Tutsi—they are among the tallest people in that part of Africa. Christine was a striking woman who looked to be at least six feet, two inches.

After we greeted one another, she invited us to sit. We explained who we were and told her what we wanted to do. As we spoke, she carefully wrote down everything we said, as her table squeaked and wobbled.

"We have doctors, nurses, and medical supplies. We have seen on television what has been happening in your country, and we've come prepared to help," I said. "Is this possible?"

As she continued writing, she asked, "Where are your doctors and nurses?"

"Right there," I pointed through the window.

"Where are your medicines?"

"In the trucks," I said. "We can have a clinic up and running in just a few hours."

She rose from her chair and motioned for us to follow as she headed for the convoy.

She peered into one truck, examining the supplies and writing on her pad before moving on to another truck, feverishly making more notes, seldom looking our way.

"You will need to see Dr. Camille," was her final evaluation. "He is to be found at Byumba." (Byumba was the guerrilla army's mountain capital.)

Realizing we had not yet succeeded in obtaining the permission we needed, I asked, "How do we get to Byumba?"

"The roads are mined. You'll have to have a guide," she answered.

"Where do we find a guide?"

She paused for a moment in deliberation and then said, "I will guide you."

That suited us just fine.

Things don't move too fast in Africa. And that day was no exception. After waiting an hour or so while Christine prepared for the trip, we were more than ready when she reappeared, ready to go.

As we drove through the Rwanda countryside, we did not see a living thing. Our vehicles raced past village after village: no chickens, no goats, no people. The houses stood empty, fields of crops seemed as though they were ready for harvest—but daily life had been brutally interrupted. It was eerie, as though everyone had left on a trip and would return any moment. The air reeked from the stench of bodies decomposing right where they had fallen in death.

The UN estimated that close to a million and a half people had died during the three-month genocide. During World War II, Adolph Hitler could not kill that fast.

I wondered what we would find when we did catch up with the thousands of victims who had survived this bloody tribal war.

We drove on, mile after mile, with no sign of life as far as the eye could see. *And to think that the UN had turned us away from helping the Rwanda refugees fleeing into nearby Tanzania a few weeks earlier.* I shook my head in wonder. *Politics! How can people play their little political games when lives are at stake?*

Conflict and obstacles don't deter me. But having to almost force our way into a place like Rwanda to help suffering people—that was a new wrinkle.

By the time we arrived in Byumba, Dr. Camille had left. The rebel army's communications were poor; they didn't have sophisticated equipment like two-way radios or cellular phones. Their walkie-talkie was a runner on foot, and he was immediately dispatched to find Dr. Camille. Again we waited—for several hours. I don't know if Christine became impatient herself, but she said with authority, "Come. I know Dr. Camille would want you to see this."

We got back into our vehicles, just glad to be moving again, and headed down the mountain toward the front lines to a place called Rutare, about fifteen miles north of the capital city.

The Hutu government forces controlled Kigali, and the slaughter of Tutsis still raged. Those who could escape were fleeing to this mountain area.

As we approached Rutare we began to notice a huge mass of people—at least sixty thousand—huddled along a barren ridge not more than a few hundred yards wide and two or three miles long. (Within ten days the number would swell to one hundred thousand.) Most of them were without adequate shelter, some existing in small grass huts in which four or five people lived.

From the road we were traveling, we could hear the gunfire in the distance and see the smoke suspended in the skies over Kigali.

As we slowly eased up the side of the mountain it suddenly occurred to me why it appeared as though the Lord had hindered us from working in Tanzania. The absence of relief agencies here was evident. There was just a sea of humanity desperately trying to survive. As I looked into the faces of the multitudes, I realized, *This is where God wanted us all along.* No politics to contend with—just the reality of hopelessness. The door was wide open.

We weren't able to see Dr. Camille until the next day, but when he finally arrived, he drilled us about our intentions. When he was convinced that we had no motives other than to help the Rwandan people, he gave us permission to set up camp. The fact that we were born-again evangelical Christians didn't bother him at all. We couldn't roll up our sleeves fast enough.

The rebel army had a small clinic at Rutare—no doctors and very little medicine—and only one nurse practitioner. We set up our field clinic on their property and began seeing patients that very day. Our staff encountered every medical problem imaginable—malnourished children (many with gunshot and machete wounds), malaria, cholera, dysentery, and a host of other tropical diseases.

As the days rolled by, we discovered how cautious the guerrilla army was about what groups they were letting into their country to provide assistance. They were skeptical of most. We felt fortunate that we had passed their inspection, and when they saw what we were doing and sensed our commitment, they did everything they could to accommodate us. Samaritan's Purse rotated teams and personnel back and forth across the border with no problem.

It wasn't long before we were told about hundreds of children whose parents had been butchered. As the Tutsis were fleeing Kigali and surrounding areas, they would come upon small children sitting beside the decaying corpses of their parents. Time was critical during their escape. The escaping Tutsis couldn't stop long enough to find out if there were other adult relatives still living who could care for the children. So they simply swept the kids up in their arms and carried them away from the advancing Hutu soldiers, then let them loose in the mountains. There they were roaming the hills, some said, "like packs of wild animals," with no one to care for them.

Kenney Isaacs was horrified when he learned of this. He called me one day after I had returned home.

"The rebel army asked us if we could feed these children. What am I supposed to do?" Kenney sounded desperate.

"Feed them," I said. I think Kenney was taken back by my quick response.

"Where am I going to get the funds?" he shot back.

"Take it from the clinic budget."

"But we only have enough money to operate the clinic for three or four months," Kenney said.

"Fine. Maybe we'll just continue operation for one or two months instead—but feed those kids!" I insisted. "If God wants us to stay in that clinic, He'll provide."

Normally, Samaritan's Purse leaves child care to other agencies—it's just not what we are equipped to do. But this time there were no other agencies. All I could do was think about a little girl we had encountered at rebel headquarters a week or two earlier.

That first day in Byumba, while we waited to meet Dr. Camille, she caught our eye. It was a peculiar sight. She was sitting in the back of a pickup truck, gripping a small, blood-stained blanket close to her chest. There she was, all alone, rocking back and forth on the hot metal bed of that old truck. Her eyes were glazed as she sang softly to herself the same tune, swaying to her own rhythm.

Sean Campbell and I both have young daughters about the same age. We couldn't help but think of them. We approached the soldier who stood nearby and inquired about her.

"Who is she?" I asked.

"Don't know," he replied.

"Where did she come from?" Sean asked.

"I don't know," the soldier said, obviously agitated by our persistence. He was smoking a cigarette and didn't appear interested in dialogue.

We stood there and watched her. After a few minutes, we asked him again, "Do you have any idea who she is?"

"She's just like all the others—an orphan. Her parents have been killed," he continued. "Somebody picked her up and brought her right here. She'll be taken to Rutare."

"How old do you think she is?" I asked.

"Who knows?" as he blew his smoke into the heavy air.

"What is she singing?"

"Sounds like something in French." The soldier took another drag and looked away.

"Do you speak French?" I asked the soldier.

He nodded.

"Do you know what she is singing?"

The soldier slowly bent down while he cradled his automatic weapon in both arms. He leaned close to the child, straining to make out her words. She didn't even seem to notice him, just stared straight ahead, oblivious to anyone around. She kept rocking back and forth in the scorching African sun.

He struggled to identify the words: "Jesus . . . loves . . . her . . ." He paused. "No . . . me. Something like that."

"Is she singing 'Jesus loves me this I know, for the Bible tells me so'?" I asked.

He looked up at us in surprise. "Yeah, that's it."

Sean and I looked at each other, then stared back at the sweet little child.

I know the lump in my throat had to be as big as the one Sean was trying to choke down.

She continued rocking, singing softly: "Jesus loves me, this I know, for the Bible tells me so."

Everything this little girl had ever known was gone—her mother and father, her home. How she must have longed to feel her mother's loving arms around her. All she had was that blanket and the faith that her parents must have taught her, that no matter what, Jesus loved her.

I don't know what ever happened to that little girl. She faded into the miserable background with thousands of others just like her.

So, the day that Kenney called to find out if we could feed those children, I decided right then that with the Lord's help, we would do everything we could for the many hundreds of kids just like that little girl sitting in the bed of the truck.

At the time, we didn't know how we could possibly feed the nine hundred children the government had spoken to Kenney about, but as we exercised the "God room" principle, over and over again we saw God provide in miraculous ways.

At the outset, I would never have imagined that our efforts would eventually lead us to opening an orphanage in Kigali, which now houses 350 children. The Lord even enabled us to open the Samaritan Academy where 750 kids receive a Christ-centered education in the midst of a war-torn land.

I often dream about what God can do—like what He did in Rwanda—if we allow Him to work in His time, in His way. And because I am a pilot, I do a lot of my dreaming at an altitude of 25,000 feet.

I have been flying now for over twenty years. My parents paid for me to learn how to fly when I was a kid in college. I'm thankful to them for the training, because it has been a tremendous help to me in my ministry.

In the early days, one disadvantage to Samaritan's Purse being located in a rural area was that it would take three hours to catch a plane from the nearest airport. For the sake of my family, I wanted to live in a rural area—but it was killing me having to spend all that time on the road. Driving to the airport two or three times a week was taking a fast toll.

In 1980, we hired a man who had formerly been a pilot with Mission Aviation Fellowship in Africa. One day he said, "Franklin, you really could use an airplane living in a remote place like this."

"Yeah, right!" I said. "Where would we ever get an airplane?"

I didn't give it much thought until a few months later when he approached me again. He had befriended a small-town business-man who owned a single-engine Cessna airplane. The man agreed to let us use his plane if we would supply our own fuel. It opened up a whole new world. Suddenly, I could fly to places like Atlanta, St. Louis, or Washington, D.C., and attend a meeting and be back with Jane Austin and the kids by nightfall.

When the board of directors saw how much time it saved and how it enabled me to more than double my productivity, they encouraged me to use the plane more. I am currently flying a fifteen-year-old Mitsubishi MU2.

For most of the flights I pilot in North America, I'm on my own. Occasionally I'll have one or two staff members with me, but usually I am by myself—away from the office and phones— away from the tragedy life brings to so many people I meet. Except for the whine of the engines and the crackle of controllers' voices over the radio—I'm alone. I think. I dream.

Looking down on God's majestic earth from that altitude is a spectacular sight. The broad outlines of rivers, mountains, forests, deserts, plains, and oceans that weave in and out is like a magnifi-cent piece of tapestry. The beauty of it all clears my mind and refreshes my spirit. There's time to think about important things—

my relationship to God, my wife, my kids, my parents and family, my ministry . . .

I look forward to what the Lord has in store for Samaritan's Purse. He has blessed and guided in so many different ways. As I look back on what has been accomplished in the last eighteen years, I am thankful for the "God room" principle that left a burning impression on my heart. Without it, we would have only accomplished things within our own small realm.

So, it only seems natural to cast a gaze toward the horizon. As I pull back the curtain and try to catch a glimpse of what God might have in store, I can't help but envision a C130 Hercules transport aircraft that could carry a Disaster Response Team, made up of Christian professionals, to any part of the world in a time of crisis. This type of plane can land on just about any kind of runway in the world.

Perhaps one day the Lord will allow us to equip such an aircraft, with medicines, supplies, water, and a MASH-type hospital unit that could lift off at a moment's notice in response to a Rwanda or Bosnia. Instead of taking weeks or months to get medical personnel on the ground in such critical situations, a C130 could be airborne within forty-eight hours, fully equipped and staffed with doctors and nurses from the United States and Canada.

A project of this magnitude could cost as much as $15 million to set up, and possibly $2 million a year to maintain. But the lives it could save and the avenues it could open to the gospel are vast.

We see humanitarian organizations worldwide like the International Red Cross and others responding to human tragedy. They do a tremendous work, but they are missing the most important ingredient for healing the hurts of this world—the message of God's love.

What a testimony it would be to the name of Jesus Christ for a Christian organization to be on the cutting edge of disaster relief— bringing God's redemptive love to a lost and dying world.

Samaritan's Purse is a small organization with limited assets, but God's resources are immeasurable. A dream—yes; a future reality—I certainly hope so, if "God room" prevails.

When we struggled to find a way into Rwanda in the spring of 1994, I never thought that we would be approached by the newly formed Rwandan government to take over their Central Hospital of Kigali (CHK) and help reopen it. But that's exactly what happened.

Following the end of the war in mid-July, Kenney once again was approached by government officials. "Can you help us?" they asked.

"What do you think, Kenney?" I asked. He had spent a fair amount of time in Rwanda. I valued his input.

"I believe we can do this, Franklin, if we begin by opening one ward at a time."

After consultation with our doctors at home and abroad, I said, "Let's go for it."

Kenney swung into action.

This became a major undertaking. The hospital had been used as an execution ground, and many people had died in that place. The former government, in a hurry to bury bodies, dug a mass grave on the hospital compound. We discovered it when we found that the land surrounding the septic tank was filled with corpses from the slaughter that had taken place. We suspected the mass burial spot contained well over eight thousand bodies.

It took weeks to remove the blood stains from the hospital walls and pick up the body parts that were strewn about. Slowly we began to open one ward and then another. In a short time the building once again became a place of healing and life rather than destruction and death.

It would have been difficult to reopen this medical facility without the help of one of our friends and volunteers, Bill Deans, from Charleston, South Carolina. One of the major problems we encountered was the transport of medical equipment and supplies from the States.

Rwanda is landlocked. Since we didn't have our own transport aircraft, Bill began working on the U.S. Air Force to persuade them to carry medical equipment and supplies that he had obtained through generous donations. By the time he jumped through the bureaucratic hoops at the Department of Defense and the State Department, it took over six weeks to successfully deliver the supplies to Kigali. A lot of valuable time was wasted waiting, but bless Bill's heart—he got the job done with the help of Senators Ernest Hollings and Strom Thurmond of South Carolina, Congressman Charles Taylor of the 11th district of North Carolina, and Barbara Blake, staff writer with the *Asheville Citizens Times*.

What a thrill it was for our staff in Rwanda to watch that Air Force cargo plane land at Kigali's international airport, loaded with items that were long overdue and very much needed. If we had just had our own cargo plane, we could have been up and running much faster and could have possibly seen many more lives saved.

When we take on any project, it is not without a strong spiritual emphasis. We hadn't been in the hospital long before we realized that we needed to meet the spiritual needs of these people. Remember, these victims had witnessed genocide. There was hardly a person alive that hadn't had a family member or more killed.

We began looking for a man who could serve as a hospital chaplain. Thousands of patients were streaming in from outlying refugee camps. We wanted to find a way to communicate that Jesus Christ loved them and had died on the cross for their sins. The new government liked the fact that we had a spiritual focus accompanied by our medical outreach.

Shortly after we opened the first ward, Dr. Jo Lusi, one of our volunteer physicians from Zaire, came to help us. He discovered a man who was an answer to our prayers—Pastor Dennis.

We learned that during the carnage, a band of Hutu men had captured Dennis and put a knife to this throat. He knew his life was about to come to an end, so he called on the name of the Lord and rebuked the Hutus in Jesus' name, saying, "Do not touch me."

Suddenly, for no earthly reason, fear seized the men and they loosed their grip.

"I am a servant of the Lord Jesus Christ!" Dennis said. "You have no authority to lay a hand on me."

They looked in amazement and turned away from him in fear.

Only days later, Dennis and his wife were together when another group of men grabbed her and with machetes raised were ready to chop her to pieces. Dennis rebuked them again in the name of the Lord.

"Franklin, something came over them," Dennis told me. "They began to tremble. One by one they dropped the machetes to their sides and fled. I can tell you right now that God sent His angels that day to protect us. There is no other explanation. That is the reason we are alive today."

Dennis had been struggling with why the Lord had spared his life. He felt guilty that he was alive when so many of his people were dead. When we asked if he would help us in the hospital, he said with tears streaming down his face, "Now I know why God has allowed me to live. He has ordained me to be the chaplain of this hospital. Praise His holy name."

Each day as our doctors care for the physical needs of the patients, Dennis and a group of chaplains he has assembled have gone from bed to bed, talking, praying, handing out Bibles and tracts. Hundreds have come to faith in Jesus Christ.

When God allowed us to go into Rwanda during the war, little could we have imagined the opportunities that would result.

Many times I find myself thinking about that little girl singing "Jesus Loves Me" in the back of that pickup truck. I pray that she continues to cling to the Lord Jesus.

Many years ago, Bob Pierce told me something I've never forgotten: "Buddy, you can't help them all, but you can help a few, and it's the few for which we must someday give an account to God."

As long as I'm able, I look forward to helping "a few" in Jesus' name.

Finally Comfortable Being Graham

There was one thing I was never going to do—no way:
preach at a crusade!

Just being Billy Graham's son creates plenty of comparisons;
I don't need to go looking for more. So why would I ever choose
to preach evangelistically? That would be nuts—there isn't anyone
who could fill my father's shoes—me included!

Speaking in public wasn't the issue. As the chief spokesman
for Samaritan's Purse, I'm constantly in front of groups. But that's
different. In those situations I talk about what I've seen and what
our ministry is doing with God's help around the world. But preach
a sermon and invite people to come forward to confess and repent
of their sins and receive Christ into their hearts by faith? Give me
a break—no thanks!

There was only one "problem." In the late 1980s, I became
increasingly convinced that God was calling me to evangelism.
The thought sent shivers down my spine.

Dr. John Wesley White is a dear friend. He has been an associ-
ate evangelist with the Billy Graham Evangelistic Association
(BGEA) and was the first person who sensed this call in my life.
John has worked with my father for over thirty years and is the
most learned man on his team. John also serves on my board at
Samaritan's Purse in the U.S. and Canada. He is a graduate of Moody
Bible Institute and earned his BA from Wheaton College. He was

consecutively a graduate student in the ecclesiastical and historical departments of Queens University, Belfast, Ireland; Trinity College, Dublin University, Dublin, Ireland; and Oxford University, Oxford, England. He earned his doctorate in philosophy at Oxford.

Years prior to his heart attack, John told me on several occasions, "Franklin, I think you have the gift of evangelism." I just ignored him, but he continued to say, "I don't think you ought to hold back from it."

I told John privately, "Evangelistic preaching is what you do—it's what Daddy does. People will automatically compare me to him. I will never measure up in their eyes. I don't need that hassle in my life!"

John just smiled and shook his head. "No one has asked you to be Billy Graham," John said. "Just be Franklin. You have a style of your own that's unique—it's different from your father's. God has given you the gift of evangelism—you can't ignore that!"

"John, I don't need to be perceived as trying to walk in Daddy's shoes. I can hear it now! People will say, 'He's trying to be like his father.' No thanks. I'm going to keep doing what God's called me to do."

"Well, Franklin, I think that's good, because God is calling you to preach, and I have all the confidence in the world that you will be obedient to that calling," John insisted.

That made me bristle! Don't you just love it when other people share what God has told them to tell *you?* Deep down inside my gut, though, I had the same feeling—God was calling me to preach. I first sensed it when I traveled with my father a few years before to Eastern Europe, but was afraid to act on it yet.

John began asking me if I would start preaching at some of his crusades. I did all I could to put him off. But John wasn't alone in his prodding. Dennis Agajanian on several occasions told me that he thought I should preach. Other close friends of mine, like Greg Laurie, began to encourage me as well. I thought they were all nuts. They obviously did not understand the pressure cooker I had lived in all my life.

I believe in my father's ministry. I have admired him and have appreciated his crystal-clear message, where he simply states over and over, "The Bible says . . ." My heart rejoices when I hear my father giving an invitation for people to come to Christ. I want more than anything in the world for people to know that God loves them and is willing to forgive them for all of their sins and that they can have the hope of heaven and eternal life. But I wanted someone else to be the messenger.

Maybe I was just too wrapped up in trying to make my own way in this world—to avoid riding my father's coattails at all costs. Maybe I had a blind spot for what God was trying to do in my life.

John White cornered me again in 1988. "Franklin, I would love to have you join me at my crusade in Juneau, Alaska, next March. Would you come and preach a few nights?" He really put the pressure on me and made it sound so easy; we would share the pulpit, each speaking three times.

In the back of my mind I thought, *If I do this, Juneau sounds like a good place. It's a long way from home. There's probably not much that happens way up there; the people won't be expecting too much! If I fall flat on my face, who's going to know?*

The event was six months away. It seemed so far off. To get John off my back, I hurriedly agreed, figuring that as time passed John might even forget about it.

No such luck. March came quickly. Before I knew it, I was sitting on a platform in Alaska about to preach my first sermon. John grinned and gave me a pat on the back. The citizens of Juneau applauded politely when I was introduced. I was already experiencing new insight on the biblical command, "Pray without ceasing."

Just before I spoke, I quietly prayed, "Lord, I don't have the strength and power to do this. It has to be You filling me with Your Holy Spirit. This is Your arena and the battle lines are drawn." Earlier that afternoon while reading John 15, I was reminded that He was the vine and I was just a branch. Without Him I could do nothing.

With knees trembling, I stood and preached my first evangelistic message. I have no idea what I preached that night, but the good thing about presenting the gospel is that the results don't depend on the skill of the preacher.

As the apostle Paul said in Romans 1:16: "I am not ashamed of the gospel of Christ, for it is the power of God to salvation for everyone who believes."

There is a supernatural power in the gospel. It has to be the Holy Spirit of God drawing people to Himself. The power is not with any man; it is in the spoken Word of God. I learned from my father to fill my sermons with Scripture. Unfortunately, many preachers fail to see this.

When I gave the invitation that evening, about forty people walked forward to give their hearts and lives to Christ. I don't think I've ever been more surprised in my whole life.

I spoke the other two nights in Juneau, and at each service the response was about the same. The experience shook me up, and I wasn't quite sure what to make of it. *Was God changing the direction of my life?* I didn't know.

John was scheduled to hold another crusade just a month later in Huron, South Dakota. "Why don't we share that crusade too?" he suggested.

I immediately accepted. We saw the Lord work in the hearts of men and women in Huron. That week one of the city's leading attorneys stood to give his life to Jesus Christ.

The rest is history. John challenged me to tithe 10 percent of my time to evangelistic preaching. Since 1989, I have tried to give at least thirty-six nights a year to the proclamation of the gospel.

About this time, there had been some discussion within the BGEA about whether the associate crusade program was still effective and should be continued in the future. I asked my father his thoughts. I shared with him that when we go into smaller cities, these crusades have the same impact on those communities as his crusades have in the larger cities. Churches are united and people work and pray together for the same cause—to see men and women come to faith in Jesus Christ.

"When we hold a crusade in a place like Juneau, Alaska," I told him, "it is a BGEA crusade with John Wesley White, Ralph Bell, or Franklin Graham as the evangelist. We are presenting the gospel in cities you could never go to. Thousands of people come to Christ as a result of this extended ministry of the BGEA each year. Furthermore, you don't have to pay me a salary. The Samaritan's Purse board of directors has given me permission to do this. If there are no associate evangelists and something should happen to you, Daddy, and you had to stop preaching, the BGEA would be out of crusade evangelism. Is this what you want?"

After thoughtful silence, he said, "No, that's the heart of our ministry."

Not only did Daddy believe that the associate program should continue, he assigned some of his top men to help us. This gave us a real shot in the arm.

There were some on my father's team who tried to influence my father to stop my preaching with John and the BGEA, but Daddy wouldn't hear of it.

John became not only my close adviser and friend, but also my teacher. I learned from him and took his advice. More than anything else John was an encourager. Every time I stood up to preach, during my message he would say out loud, "Good point, Franklin," or "That's good." Some people might think that would be distracting, but it was a comfort knowing I had a friend like that with me.

Before long, John and I started receiving invitations from all over the country to do crusades together. I even received invitations to hold crusades by myself.

I love the work of Samaritan's Purse, and I believe crusade evangelism and helping the poor and sick around the world go hand in hand. Think about it: *Isn't that what Jesus did during His earthly ministry?* He fed the hungry and healed the sick, but He did it in such a way that men and women would put their trust and faith in Him as the Son of the living God. That's all I want to do.

Each year our crusades have grown. I am doing more crusades on my own these days. John is there always, supporting me in prayer. Many times he takes meetings during the day with senior citizen groups and others who are not able to attend the evening meetings. He is one of the most gentle and humble servants I know. John has encouraged me just as John Minder encouraged my father as a young preacher in Florida, and the late Lindsay Glegg when Daddy first went to England.

After I became more comfortable with the crusade ministry, I often wondered what it would be like to preach in my father's presence.

I wanted Daddy to see our crusades, but at the same time I didn't want him to hear me preach. I knew I would be a nervous wreck; my stomach would be as tight as a hangman's noose. It's hard enough just doing an evangelistic crusade, but then to have the pressure of Billy Graham sitting behind me—the thought of that was almost too much.

But I was anxious for Daddy to see the format I was developing. I use a number of the same platform elements that he uses—crusade choirs and testimonials—but our music is more contemporary, and the meetings are more informal. I often don't even wear a suit and tie—I think I may preach better in my jeans and boots!

Tommy Coomes and the Maranatha! Praise Band join our crusades and people of all ages appreciate their praise and worship music. Dennis Agajanian and his band are with me every night and are always a smash hit.

I wanted Daddy's opinion and advice. But there was a part of me that was scared to death.

I preached for five years before Daddy came to one of my crusades, in Charleston, West Virginia, in May 1994. Daddy had just come from the West Coast, where the world had watched him preach at the funeral of former President Richard Nixon. He arrived in Charleston directly from California.

When my father stood to greet the crowd, he was given a standing ovation. I tried to convince him to preach that night. "Daddy, believe me, they would rather hear you tonight than me any day."

But he smiled and said, "No, son, I came to hear you."

Afterwards, Daddy put his arm around me, hugged me, and said, "I'm proud of you, son." I guess every son wants to hear those words from his father, no matter how old he is.

A few months later, I was preaching a crusade in Raleigh, North Carolina, at Walnut Creek, a large outdoor amphitheatre that holds about twenty thousand people. My sister Anne and her husband, Danny Lotz, had been instrumental in bringing the crusade to their city.

It was an amazing sight to see the amphitheatre jammed, with the surrounding hillside covered with people of all ages. Tom Bledsoe and Ted Cornell blended the grand old hymns with the best of today's praise music.

The moment the invitation started, people were up on their feet headed toward the front of the platform as the Praise Band sang, "Come Just As You Are." When no others could make their way to the front because of the crowded aisles, I had to ask the rest to stand at their seats to accept Christ.

My mother and father both attended. This was the first time my mother had heard me preach. To be honest, I would never have been standing there if Mama hadn't prayed for me all through the years.

Since then my parents have attended other crusade meetings of mine, most recently in Wilmington, North Carolina, and it is always a joy and privilege to have them. I am not as nervous as I was in the beginning when they showed up. I guess I am *finally comfortable being Graham*—Franklin Graham, that is.

As Daddy looks to the future, the only thing he wants to do is preach. He wants to use his strength to deliver the Gospel to the best of his ability. As his son, I want to support him in every way I possibly can.

Maybe one of these days we will have the opportunity to share the pulpit together. If it happens, it will be a great honor. But in the end it doesn't really matter, because this old boy is going to preach the gospel anyway. God has called me, and I want to be a faithful servant of the King of kings and Lord of lords.

My life this far has been what some people call the "front forty." I'm now living on the "back forty." I have no idea how this field will plow. But one thing you can be sure of, this Graham is gonna keep preaching.

A F T E R W O R D

by Ruth and Billy Graham

Watching Franklin grow up has been an experience. Nothing like being fascinated with your own son's life. A lot of what is contained in this book we had never heard before!

However, under all this rebel reminiscing, this book fails to tell you of the tender side of the little boy growing up . . .

The times after Ned was born when Franklin, then six years old, would go back to his mother's room, cowboy boots clomping, jeans at half-mast, carrying a sloshing glass of milk grasped in two grimy hands, "So," as he said to his mother with happy concern, "you will have plenty of milk."

Or the time, looking outside the upstairs window, we saw him struggling up the steep slope of a mountain, carrying on his back a little Ned whose legs had given out.

Or the time when "the rebel's," older sister, Bunny, was miserably homesick in the (then existing) Stony Brook School for Girls, and he used his own meager allowance to buy candy to take to her.

When Franklin and his buddy, Bill Cristobal, headed for England to pick up the Land Rover to drive to Jordan, Ruth got out her Bible to read John 17 as her prayer for the two boys, and was stopped short at verse nineteen, where she read, "for their sakes, I sanctify myself." If for our sakes the Lord Jesus felt the need to sanctify (dedicate or consecrate) Himself to His Father, how much more did she need to?

She put Franklin and Bill "on hold" and set about getting everything straightened out between herself and God.

How often we parents need to do just that.

We understood how difficult it must have been to have a well-known dad, yet we knew the rebellion was not against us personally. The girls would marry and take other names. The boys were stuck with *Graham*.

The fact that, while we knew that he smoked, he would never smoke around us, revealed this innate respect. Instead, at home, he would smoke in his room, blowing the smoke out the window, unaware the updraft from the valley carried the telltale smell of a cigarette right back to our bedroom window.

And Franklin was surrounded by people who really cared about him just like he was.

In short, Franklin didn't have a chance. He had been given to God before his birth, and God has kept His hand on him without letting up all these years.

Franklin once told a group, "If my mom has white hair, it's because of me!" To which she replied, "Don't take all the credit, son. Age has something to do with it."

And with age has come the ever-growing, ever-deepening awareness of the relevance and the assurance of God's promises. Not once has He failed.

When folks say, "You must be proud of Franklin," we realize that it is not a matter of pride, but of gratitude to God for His faithfulness.

With God, nobody's hopeless.

NOTES

CHAPTER FIVE

1. Wilbur M. Irwin, "Under His Wings," *The Baptist Record*, 15 April 1971.

CHAPTER SIXTEEN

1. Taken from an unreleased interview with former President Gerald Ford.
2. Taken from an unreleased interview with former President George Bush.

CHAPTER EIGHTEEN

1. Schwarzkopf, H. Norman, *General H. Norman Schwarzkopf: The Autobiography: It Doesn't Take a Hero* (New York: Bantam, 1992), 334–36.

William Franklin Graham III serves as president of Samaritan's Purse, a Christian relief and evangelism organization that meets emergency needs around the world. Samaritan's Purse works through local churches, missionaries, and Christian missions to spread the gospel by meeting the physical and spiritual needs of victims of war, famine, disease, and natural disasters. Franklin has traveled the world over locating and aiding individuals desperate for immediate help.

Franklin is also chairman of the board of World Medical Mission, the medical arm of Samaritan's Purse. World Medical Mission was founded in 1977 and helps mission hospitals spread the gospel by providing volunteer medical personnel, equipment, training, and financial assistance.

Ordained as a Christian minister, Franklin is chairman of Samaritan's Purse International in the United Kingdom, Samaritan's Purse-Canada, and Samaritan's Purse-Netherlands. He serves on the board of directors of the Billy Graham Evangelistic Association, Blue Ridge Broadcasting, and is chairman of the board of Mafraq Sanatorium, a medical mission in Jordan.

Franklin is author of the biography *Bob Pierce: This One Thing I Do,* published by Word Books. Dr. Pierce, who founded Samaritan's Purse in 1970, introduced Franklin to this ministry of evangelistic compassion.

A graduate of Montreat-Anderson College and Appalachian State University, Franklin holds honorary doctorate degrees from Toccoa Falls College, Lees McRae College, and National University. He lives with his wife, Jane Austin, and their four children, Will, Roy, Edward, and Cissie, in Boone, North Carolina.

STEPS TO PEACE WITH GOD

1. RECOGNIZE GOD'S PLAN—PEACE AND LIFE

The message you have read in this book stresses that God loves you and wants you to experience His peace and life.

The BIBLE says . . . *"For God loved the world so much that He gave His only Son, so that everyone who believes in Him may not die but have eternal life." John 3:16*

2. REALIZE OUR PROBLEM—SEPARATION

People choose to disobey God and go their own way. This results in separation from God.

The BIBLE says . . . *"Everyone has sinned and is far away from God's saving presence." Romans 3:23*

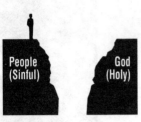

3. RESPOND TO GOD'S REMEDY—CROSS OF CHRIST

God sent His Son to bridge the gap. Christ did this by paying the penalty of our sins when He died on the cross and rose from the grave.

The BIBLE says . . . *"But God has shown us how much He loves us—it was while we were still sinners that Christ died for us!" Romans 5:8*

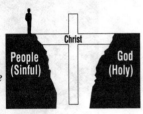

4. RECEIVE GOD'S SON—LORD AND SAVIOR

You cross the bridge into God's family when you ask Christ to come into your life.

The BIBLE says . . . *"Some, however, did receive Him and believed in Him; so He gave them the right to become God's children." John 1:12*

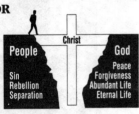

THE INVITATION IS TO:

REPENT (turn from your sins) and by faith RECEIVE Jesus Christ into your heart and life and follow Him in obedience as your Lord and Savior.

PRAYER OF COMMITMENT

"Lord Jesus, I know I am a sinner. I believe You died for my sins. Right now, I turn from my sins and open the door of my heart and life. I receive You as my personal Lord and Savior. Thank You for saving me now. Amen."

If you want further help in the decision you have made, write to:
Billy Graham Evangelistic Association, P.O. Box 779, Minneapolis, MN 55440-0779